School-Based Deliberative Partnership as a Platform for Teacher Professionalization and Curriculum Innovation

Using cutting-edge and frontline research relating to present day problems in educational systems, this volume provides a critical discussion about political alternatives in education to neoliberalism. Based on Engeström's *Cultural Historical Activity Theory* (CHAT), a theory that has potential for new areas of educational research, this book explores a conceptual framework of curriculum innovation in school practice that focuses on processes of mutual meaning-making as boundary crossing between partners from different communities.

Focusing on active professionalization and continuing professional learning of teachers as subjects, agents, extended professionals and curriculum makers in school-based deliberative partnerships with one another and with other educational partners inside and outside school, this volume is divided into eight accessible chapters and covers topics such as political and curricular considerations about educational change, deliberative partnership as a new way for reform, prospects for an innovative curriculum process and putting into action deliberative partnership-based curricular innovation.

This volume is the perfect addition for teachers, teacher educators, researchers and practitioners who are looking to explore beyond the viewpoint that teachers operate in singular communities and the potential and possibility of an alternative framework for teacher learning in the future.

Geraldine Mooney Simmie is a senior lecturer at the School of Education, University of Limerick, Ireland.

Manfred Lang, now retired, was senior researcher of the Leibniz Institute for Science and Mathematics Education (IPN) at the University of Kiel, Germany.

Routledge Research in Teacher Education

The Routledge Research in Teacher Education series presents the latest research on Teacher Education and also provides a forum to discuss the latest practices and challenges in the field.

Professional Development through Mentoring
Novice ESL Teachers' Identity Formation
Juliana Othman and Fatiha Senom

Research on Becoming an English Teacher
Through Lacan's Looking Glass
Tony Brown, Mike Dore and Christopher Hanley

Intercultural Competence in the Work of Teachers
Confronting Ideologies and Practices
Edited by Fred Dervin, Robyn Moloney and Ashley Simpson

Teacher Representations in Dramatic Text and Performance
Portraying the Teacher on Stage
Edited by Melanie Shoffner & Richard St. Peter

School-Based Deliberative Partnership as a Platform for Teacher Professionalization and Curriculum Innovation
Geraldine Mooney Simmie and Manfred Lang

Technology-Enabled Mathematics Education
Optimising Student Engagement
Catherine Attard and Kathryn Holmes

Integrating Technology in English Language Arts Teacher Education
Donna L. Pasternak

Research-Informed Teacher Learning
Critical Perspectives on Theory, Research and Practice
Edited by Lori Beckett

For more information about this series, please visit: https://www.routledge.com/Routledge-Research-in-Teacher-Education/book-series/RRTE

School-Based Deliberative Partnership as a Platform for Teacher Professionalization and Curriculum Innovation

Geraldine Mooney Simmie and Manfred Lang

LONDON AND NEW YORK

First published 2020
by Routledge
2 Park Square, Milton Park, Abingdon, Oxon OX14 4RN

and by Routledge
52 Vanderbilt Avenue, New York, NY 10017

Routledge is an imprint of the Taylor & Francis Group, an informa business

© 2020 Geraldine Mooney Simmie and Manfred Lang

The right of Geraldine Mooney Simmie and Manfred Lang to be identified as authors of this work has been asserted by them in accordance with sections 77 and 78 of the Copyright, Designs and Patents Act 1988.

All rights reserved. No part of this book may be reprinted or reproduced or utilized in any form or by any electronic, mechanical or other means, now known or hereafter invented, including photocopying and recording, or in any information storage or retrieval system, without permission in writing from the publishers.

Trademark notice: Product or corporate names may be trademarks or registered trademarks and are used only for identification and explanation without intent to infringe.

British Library Cataloguing-in-Publication Data
A catalogue record for this book is available from the British Library

Library of Congress Cataloging-in-Publication Data
A catalog record has been requested for this book

ISBN: 978-0-367-26459-8 (hbk)
ISBN: 978-0-429-29340-5 (ebk)

Typeset in Bembo
by Taylor & Francis Books

Contents

	List of illustrations	vi
	Preface	vii
	Acknowledgments	xiv
1	Political and curricular considerations about educational change	1
2	Situational factors to be considered for curricular processes of school improvement	29
3	Deliberative partnership as a new way for reform	55
4	Prospects for an innovative curriculum process	67
5	A framework for partnership-based curricular innovation	79
6	Models for innovative planning based on partnership	89
7	Putting into action deliberative partnership-based curricular innovation	115
8	Prospects for higher-order curriculum innovation and deliberative partnership	132
	References	143
	Index	158

Illustrations

Figures

1.1 Two interacting activity systems as units of the analysis	20
3.1 Paths of reform processes guided by curriculum innovation and teacher professional development	56
5.1 Activity on different system levels based on a partnership between school and university	86
6.1 Sketch of a work plan for the development of a competency matrix of given standards (translated).	95
6.2 Competence grid for the completion of topics (translated).	96
6.3 Elements of a Curriculum Workshop	100
6.4 Argumentation scheme of Toulmin (1958, p. 97)	102
7.1 The GIMMS collaborative framework (Mooney Simmie & Lang, 2012, p. 17)	118

Tables

4.1 Central aspects of teacher collaboration in schools after Huber, Ahlgrimm and Hader-Popp (2012, p. 354–355; translated by the authors)	70
6.1 Comparison of components in activity theory (Engeström, 2001) and the Curriculum Workshop	107
7.1 Main emphasis of the work in national case studies of the GIMSS project	123

Preface

Nowadays, the view of the educated person as an individual rational economic actor is widely reflected in international comparative surveys, such as OECD PISA and TALIS and in quality assurance systems of public accountability. It is dominating externally planned reform policy processes in teacher learning and schooling (Cochran-Smith et al., 2017; Hardy, 2018; Muller, 2018). In the face of globalized rhetoric and neoliberal reification underpinned by narrow instrumental principles of Human Capital Theory (Tan, 2014), questions arise about teachers' professional development and education's social responsibility for public interest values and a vibrant democracy (Lynch, 2014; Mooney Simmie & Edling, 2016, 2018). This is overshadowed by a global populism where the better argument securing reason and wisdom is under attack from a constant stream of fake news, the tyranny of metrics fixation and new soft modes of public accountability where democracy is being slowly suffocated (Browning, 2018; Muller, 2018). Specifically, in terms of schooling and teacher education, this is concerned with teachers' productive engagement in discursive meaning-making of content, sociocultural contexts and moral principles, leading to school-based curricular questions by means of deliberative partnership discourses for the enactment of new learner-centered active pedagogies, critical teacher education and other contemporary policy reforms (Ball et al., 2012; Gore et al., 2017; Gunter, 2001; Kincheloe, 2004).

Curricular questions about local considerations of educational needs and the discursive justification of these contexts, cultures and particularities are hardly ever considered (Connelly, 2013). Within a new business-like model of teacher professional learning, former understandings of good teaching as complex interplays between theory, practice, experience and research and teachers' competence in multiple knowledge forms (Mooney Simmie, Moles, & O'Grady, 2019) have been debunked in favor of the straightforward application and knowledge transfer. Teachers' subjectivities are thereby repositioned as a permanent search for a new professional identity, a new ideal teacher as a competitive entrepreneur planning risk-managed activities and predefined outcomes (Ball, 2003; Nussbaum, 2010; Skerritt, 2018).

viii Preface

This reframes critical thinking as the ability to think scientifically in a disciplinary context rather than the capability to critically reflect on the world at large linked to the view that education has an emancipatory societal function (Erikson & Erikson, 2018). A statement of learning outcomes puts a "ceiling at which students safely stop, knowing that any further achievement will not be rewarded. The more weight the learning outcome model is given, the more central this ceiling can become" (p. 5), as it embeds a "naïve conception of intellectual development implicit in a list of fixed outcomes to strive for" (p. 8).

In this way the balance point – the "open enough" discursive gaps between official (political) discourses and pedagogical discourses (Gore et al., 2017) – is distorted by the persistent epistemic dominance of performance comparisons and a national reform drive to evaluate standards and competency scales for the expedient assessment of predefined and measurable results and learning outcomes (Lingard, Sellar & Savage, 2014; Sellar & Lingard, 2013; Youdell & Mc Gimpsey, 2015). While politicians appear concerned about achievement test results and data for political and economic competitive value, they call for reform enforcement within a market-led discourse of metrics. However, policy leaders will not achieve much if they continue to adopt this dysfunctional linear rational understanding of policy as a techné of implementation (Ball et al., 2011). We will argue that what is needed is a radically different notion of teachers' practices and a radically different picture of the teacher as a professional agent and activist for a socially just and decent democratic society (Gore, 2012; Gore et al., 2017; Nussbaum, 2010).

In this book, we define the term *school-based deliberative partnership* for its practical use in understanding curriculum innovation and teacher learning. Our thinking is based on assumptions that teachers as professionals need to claim a more substantial voice as curriculum designers and policy actors in public spaces. This definition implies the following seven key principles:

- It is our understanding that good teaching and teacher professional learning are complex endeavors taking place in particular sociocultural and political contexts and settings. We understand complex as holistic teacher learning and acting that requires reflexive, collaborative and democratic procedures for a sophisticated praxis inclusive of all policy actors and stakeholders (Cochran-Smith & Lytle, 1999; Pillow, 2003; Bourdieu, 1991; Habermas, 1990).
- This situated complexity requires an advanced professional practice that includes multiple forms of knowledge and different ways of knowing (Bourdieu, 1991) that recognizes both the usefulness and limitations of large-scale empirical research findings (Opfer & Pedder, 2011) and open enough spaces for philosophical co-inquiry and questioning authority (Feldges, 2019).
- We assert that new pedagogies and reforms are never implemented in straightforward linear ways but instead involve complex, critical and creative processes of policy enactment that require teachers to do the hard work of

recontextualization, reconceptualization, interpretation and translation taking into account a rich diversity of learners, contexts, particularities and peculiarities (Ball et al., 2012).

- Schools and teachers are, therefore, positioned at the center of deliberation in public space with partners from multiple communities, a view that goes beyond the hegemonic closure inherent in singular communities of practice and/or prescriptive governance views of standards and competences. In this way, deliberation is an intense attempt of higher-order discourse with agreed rules of deliberation for justification of outcomes for deliberative democracy (Ewert, 1991). It is very different from the more usual type of argumentation practiced in university and higher education settings. It is not confined to counter-intuitive knowledge forms and involves a far more messy narrative of interaction (Nixon, 2004).

- In this regard, partners meet in school-based settings with the implication of equal treatment of all partners and an understanding that each partner has an important contribution to make to this complex epistemic puzzle. The purpose of these meetings in public space is for deliberation as shared meaning-making and justification of curriculum innovation. This requires a high level of reflexivity from all actors – not just the teachers – what Pillow (2003) calls the uncomfortable hard work of reflexivity. Bleakley (1999) argues that critical reflexivity is needed for a holistic education that is socially just and emancipatory.

- Partnership in deliberation implies a trusting sustained relationship with an equal exchange, reciprocity and mutuality. It is a prerequisite of communicative action and co-inquiry for shared meaning-making. Such a process needs to acknowledge unequal power relations and actively seek to redress imbalances. We assume as a condition of possibility communicative competence for all actors in a partnership. However, Zipin and Brennan (2003) highlight the ethical suppression of teachers' voices in contemporary times of data analytics and metrics fixation. Santoro (2017) considers the moral madness experienced by many teachers who dare to transgress and to question authority. She argues that teachers working in a feminized profession are readily dismissed by expert voices as out-of-date, lazy or burnt out and lacking resilience. Instead, she argues that many experienced teachers have become demoralized with reforms that regard teaching and teacher learning as little more than quantifiable commodities for a market-led discourse of learning.

- Deliberation for this complexity view of good teacher professional learning and innovation, involving extended social partnerships, assumes intelligent accountability for an advanced professional practice rather than the narrow technocratic modes of self-evaluation currently in vogue for public accountability in schooling (Brady, 2016, 2019a, 2019b; O'Neill, 2013; Muller, 2018).

In this way, teacher professional learning and meaning-making understood as deliberative processes, can be variously framed by complexity science (Davis & Sumara, 2007; Opfer & Pedder, 2011), by messy narratives of change in critical theory (Kincheloe, 2004; Mooney Simmie, Moles & O'Grady, 2019), by philosophy of education (Biesta, 2013; Noddings, 2007; Steel, 2018; Schwab, 1983) or as boundary crossing in system theory (Engeström, 1999). The latter approach as presented in this book involves a school-based deliberative partnership that necessitates a multiplicity of actors and institutions for a new approach to curriculum innovation and change that goes beyond teachers acting as singular communities of practice and calls on discursive rules of deliberative engagement. Deliberation between partners is described as a boundary-crossing discourse about controversial issues underpinned by the theoretical background of Engeström's (2001) *Cultural-Historical Activity Theory* (CHAT).

In view of global market rhetoric and neoliberal reification, questions arise as to the new role of the teaching profession and how this aligns with the moral and political foundations of school practices (Youdell, 2011). Teaching is viewed as a moral and political enterprise, defined not only by skills, competences and craftsmanship but also by the educationally sound value of learning opportunities and capability to interrupt the dominant hegemony of a "circle of privilege" (Angus, 2012; Ball, 2017). When we talk about a good teacher, we not only mean a competent teacher but a person who is able to make wise decisions in dynamic practices, looking toward the moral good of teaching and public interest values and demonstrating capability to pursue this democratically (Clarke & Phelan, 2017; Mooney Simmie, Moles & O'Grady, 2019).

Honesty, fairness, respect and courage are virtues that make it possible to learn from a confluence of knowledge, values and experiences. These professional virtues of teachers are part of curricular questions that are not sufficiently taken into account in the case of externally determined evidence-based reforms that lack the epistemic nuance of teaching as a complex and messy endeavor where mediation with self and practice is not sufficient and where mediation with the world is the *sine qua non* of an educator (Mooney Simmie, Moles & O'Grady, 2019). Gunter (2001) identifies the missing critical dimension of this epistemic puzzle as a combination of critical, scientific, humanistic and/or instrumental.

Deliberative curricular innovation and teacher professionalization through social partnerships in school-based activities is a relatively new and less explored area of research and is recently starting to be explored in the existing literature on teacher learning and professional development (Darling-Hammond, 2017; Livingston, 2018). It requires cross-institutional infrastructures and ontological and epistemic resources to link experiences and scientific findings from different communities (Engeström, 2001; Wenger, 1998). Multiple communities with evolved capability for authentic deliberation have the potentiality and possibility to provide "open enough" spaces for mutual understanding, intellectual quality, critical reflexivity and opening teacher learning and meaning-making outward toward the uncertain, the complex and the contested (Gore et al., 2017; Pillow, 2003; Opfer & Pedder, 2011).

This differs from an externally determined and scientifically legitimated reform concept of standards and technical certainty and convergence (Darling-Hammond, 2017). As Wenger (1998, p. 264) notes, "education concerns the opening of identities – exploring new ways of being that lie beyond our current state, whereas training aims to create an inbound trajectory targeted at competence in a specific practice." From this open stance, lessons learned from complex teaching interactions can be depicted as rather messy narratives of change within a policy ensemble of ideas and networks (Mooney Simmie, Moles & O'Grady, 2019), implying tacit knowledge (Polanyi, 1958) or hidden curricula (Jackson, 1968) that seek to reveal the "hidden hand of the powerful" (Bourdieu, 1991) and to contribute to existential freedom and autonomy rather than a performative view of freedom (Brady, 2019b).

Therefore, many routines of experienced teachers, as well as values and virtues, are not always understood as a rational matter of empirical grounding. Here we argue that cooperation and democratic deliberation of experienced teachers with other teachers, teacher educators, researchers and other non-school partners is necessary, in which experiences, disciplinary and theoretical knowledge bases and values are taken up in practice and linked in reflexive collaboration and partnership (Pillow, 2003) through *expansive learning*.

This expansive pedagogical, philosophical, professional and political pathway of teacher learning is difficult to navigate and requires not only structural and epistemic resources but the willingness of policy actors to overcome narrow roles in institutional hierarchies through new strategies of deliberative partnership (Gore, 2012; Gore et al., 2017; Lillejord & Borte, 2016; Bloomfield & Nguyen, 2015).

The comprehensive curricular approach, presented in this book, takes the side of the teacher in school practice, focusing on processes of meaning-making and *expansive learning* in teacher development understood as boundary-crossing activities between partners from diverse communities, such as teachers, teacher educators, researchers and other actors in education with their own rules, roles and responsibilities. In this way, our *expansive learning* framework positions teacher learning as a complex, relational, epistemic and political puzzle that goes well beyond a straightforward need for collaboration and instead requires discursive rules of ethical engagement and critical literacy for a socially just democratic society.

Within the increasing political clamor for expedient and measurable results and learning outcomes, teachers' voices are more often than not ethically suppressed (Zipin & Brennan, 2003; Santoro, 2017). For example, an Australian case study of an externally determined reform was presented more as a disciplinary regulation of teachers rather than a transformative concept of professionalism (Bourke, Lidstone & Ryan, 2015).

In this regard, the curricular views of Joseph Schwab (2013, reprint) are important, in particular, his argument that the flight of the curriculum field into scientific studies is often pursued as an escape from the experiential field of practice, where particularity, context and culture matters. Reform policies do not always appreciate the significant role teachers' play in their contexts and the difficulties faced in the lived reality of their practice settings (Olson, James & Lang, 1999; Fullan & Hargreaves, 1992). Programs externally imposed using a linear rational implementation, with no attention to the complex epistemology of context, culture and differential social and power relations, run the risk that teachers and administrators will be set up as key players and will be wrongly blamed when many reforms go wrong. They may also be perceived as actors who do not accept reforms, thwart, resist and/or misunderstand them (Santoro, 2017).

The curricular concept of partnership-based activities does not ignore the importance of counter-intuitive knowledge in the epistemic puzzle that is good teaching and teacher learning but rather uses it instead in an eclectic way and at the same time restricts it to an important dimension of the lived reality in a comprehensive framework of practices. It refers to processes of meaning-making and mutuality in boundary crossing between partners from multiple communities such as teachers, researchers and teacher educators (for example, schools and universities; see Young, O'Neill & Mooney Simmie, 2015).

The starting point of boundary crossing is a problem in practice with different objectives (boundary objects) or contradictions. Such a problem is developed out of practice and its genesis from a school tradition leading to a mutually agreed solution through deliberation. It is not an externally imposed problem for a reform, such as the reduction of competence deficits according to international comparative data. The dynamics for the development of innovative practice through recognition of contradictions are emphasized here as a key principle. A problem or discursive contradiction is a reason for action and not to risk further complications. In this way, it is the contradictions and discursive struggles that become policy drivers for curriculum innovation and change.

School-based deliberative partnership activities have been analyzed in different ways in a number of European teacher education and training projects and are reported in Chapter 6 and Chapter 7: for example, *Crossing Boundaries in Science Teacher Education* (CROSSNET; Hansen, Gräber & Lang, 2012) and *Gender Innovation and Mentoring in Mathematics and Science* (GIMMS; Mooney Simmie & Lang, 2012, 2017).

Critical insights from these European Comenius teacher education and training projects show the usefulness of partnership-based action and justify its selection within Engeström's (2001) *Cultural-Historical Activity Theory* for boundary-crossing as shared meaning-making in multiple communities. In this regard, the extended Curriculum Workshop became a setting for justification as one useful way of understanding the complexities involved in curriculum innovation and teacher professional learning. Taking teachers' voices into account and working within the messy complex critical narratives of a reflexive, intellectually demanding educative discourse provides an alternative model for school-based reform proposals.

Insights from these European projects open outward for a deeper understanding of the complexity of teachers' practices that seek to include the contextual, epistemic and diversity conditions and contradictions for teacher development. They raise crucial, creative and critical questions about the future and do not provide expedient solutions and predefined answers to the complex, philosophically challenging and political problems of reform policy enactment and evaluation for intelligent accountability (Cochran-Smith et al., 2017). The studies examined offer a European view on the key principles of boundary crossing partnerships for expansive teacher learning and meaning-making. This offers a novel pathway for answering Cochran-Smith et al.'s (2017) call for reclaiming teaching as an occupation and as an advanced professional practice. In the book, we consider the potentiality and possibility of this alternative framework for teacher learning and the social responsibility of education for public-interest values.

The research and development studies reported here, while conducted in several European countries, have wider implications that go beyond one continent and can assist others grappling with similar dilemmas and real-world living contradictions across the continuum of teacher education, curriculum innovation, teacher learning and professional development.

Acknowledgments

This book is based on findings and insights from a number of European teacher education and training (Comenius) projects: EUDIST (Lang et al., 2007) and CROSSNET (Hansen, Gräber & Lang, 2012), coordinated and supported by the IPN (Leibniz Institute for Science and Mathematics Education) at the University of Kiel in Germany, and the GIMMS project (Mooney Simmie & Lang, 2012, 2017), coordinated at the School of Education, Faculty of Education and Health Sciences, University of Limerick, Republic of Ireland. The main task of the IPN is to develop and support the education of the sciences and mathematics and to publish its results regularly. The School of Education at the University of Limerick is the largest higher education provider of teacher education in the post-primary sector in Ireland, supporting teaching and disseminating research at undergraduate and doctoral postgraduate level in diverse areas, such as mentoring, leadership, STEM education and critical studies.

The study refers to discussions and publications from these projects, with contributions from the case study schools and teachers across the continuum of the profession (mostly experienced teachers and some preservice teachers) and from a large number of colleagues and faculty from the IPN, the University of Limerick and other European universities and higher education institutions. These adaptations, use of project reports and feedback make the work a joint work of different individuals. However, this publication emerged from the collaboration of the authors, insofar as they are not marked as quotations.

This publication, thus, reflects only the views of the authors. In this regard, neither the IPN nor the University of Limerick nor the European Commission for Comenius projects can be held responsible for use of the information.

Chapter 1

Political and curricular considerations about educational change

The optimistic breakthrough in the western world of the 1960s and 1970s towards social modernization in the field of education can be seen as an example of an innovative new beginning. Hargreaves et al. (2010) define this turning point as "a period of cultural and spiritual awakening" after a first turning following the Second World War. With an extraordinary dynamic and intention, educational reforms, research, curriculum development and school-based explorations were planned and conducted. Many proposals for structural reforms and extensive liberalization came into being for broader access to educational institutions for the public, for greater equality of opportunities and higher responsibility of schools. In addition, topics such as in-service teacher education, the introduction of new subjects, open access of schools or experimental trials within the concept of comprehensive schools were discussed (Deutscher Bildungsrat, 1970; O'Buachalla, 1988; Clarke, 2010; Ball, 2008). In schools, traditional teaching contents were restructured, new forms of teaching such as project-based teaching were developed in cooperation with research projects and curriculum materials were developed e.g. for integrated science education. Special social groups with their own pedagogical requirements founded alternative schools in state-based or private sponsorship such as the Bielefelder Laborschule, the Glockseeschule Hannover, the Hiberniaschule in Herne, the Tvind schools in Denmark or Summerhill in England.

With these visions of new horizons, many collaborative groups arrived at their own social concerns, democratic understandings and common interests and goals for the accomplishment of self-determined results. In schools, teachers came together in groups to develop new educational materials or school-based curricular structures. They initiated collaborative structures with universities such as the PING project in Germany (Lang, 1997) or conducted projects with integrated approaches in other countries (Black & Atkin, 1996). Teachers became involved in collaborative school-university structures such as the Bielefelder Laborschule and Oberstufenkolleg as part of the newly established university (Hentig, 1971; Fuss et al., 1979) or extended the work of the school as a system of change in community education (Zimmer & Niggemeyer, 1992).

While we are not arguing for a glorious past in the field of liberal progressive education, we can state that many of the ideals of these earlier initiatives

2 Political and curricular considerations

certainly have a lot in common with the concept of deliberative partnership-based schooling for change in the education system, which is offered in this book. In both cases, the issue is social cohesion, local context, grassroots democracy and ownership, wider social, moral and political interests for public-interest values and not just market interests and discursive legitimacy of narrow claims.

By contrast, today's policy reform *intention* for innovation and change in the education sector is very different. Nowadays, the educational reform policy ensemble involving assemblages, networks and flows is primarily driven by the threat of globalized competition and human capital management without regard for cultural contexts and particularities within a much diminished view of the state in relation to public education and teacher development (Ball, 2017; Youdell & McGimpsey, 2015). Ball (2003) argues that the contemporary policy cycle, underpinned by neoliberal and neoconservative governing forms is (re)framing the policy landscape for a new regulatory discourse leading to individual and competitive entrepreneurship within small national budgets. It has moved away from education as a social responsibility for public-interest values and views the "educated" person from the narrow reductionist stance of a rational independent economic actor and the pursuit of individual and national wealth (Cochran-Smith et al., 2017; Hardy, 2018). Tan (2014) argues that while this human capital theory view of education with all aspects of public life is a deeply flawed model, it continues to gain the respect of politicians, policy-makers and researchers alike as it is a good enough model to explain a considerable number of interactions. For example, Rönnberg (2017) traces the direction of reforms in Sweden toward an edu-business by politicians and policymakers who later become independently wealthy from the systemic changes they had earlier introduced. White, Blomfield and Le Cornu (2010) confirm that within the neo-liberal macro-political framework priorities in the Australian education system have shifted from collectivism and local articulations to new forms of individualism and economic regulation and accountability:

> A rhetoric of deregulation is expressed in terms of increased market choice linked to public accountabilities and assurances. In extending its socio-economic reach into the public sphere, neo-liberalism continues to be a force that is redefining responsibilities in education, with an increasing emphasis toward the economic utility of education.
>
> (p. 181)

Harvey (2007) argues that contemporary reforms are presented as local, flexible and choice-based work in tandem with global policies (G-local) as a proxy to restore class power for a "circle of privilege". At the same time they diminish the role of the nation-state as a provider of public education and thus for education's social responsibility for public-interest values and societal benefi-cence (Lynch, 2014). Hardy (2018) gives a glimpse into the neoliberal policy of educational change as it plays out in Australia and the conception of

Political and curricular considerations 3

standardization in teacher education and learning. The loss of a culture of productive partnership as a local characteristic is a problem of individual isolation, discussed by Mawhiney (2004) under the title "The Decline of the Local". It refers to Foster's (2002, p. 11) concerned question:

> There has occurred in our society a decline of the local: A movement away from community input into the conduct of our lives and to the regulation of the state – through standards, high stake testing, funding, and so on. How should we respond if this is an important issue?

Therefore, there is a pressing need to search for new ways of educational change and teachers' practices with advanced democratic and humanitarian values. For this Hargreaves et al. (2010) propose to take positive aspects of reforms from the past into consideration, such as the changes he defined as turning to the "period of cultural and spiritual awakening":

> It is time, now more than ever, for a New Way of educational change that is suited to the dramatically new problems and challenges we are encountering. This New Way should build on the best of what we have learned from the Old Ways of the past, including those of the past decade, without retreating to or reinventing the worst of them. It should look abroad for intelligent alternatives and be especially alert to those educational and economic successes that also express and advance democratic and humanitarian values. It should attend to the advancement of the economy and the restoration of prosperity but not at the price of other educational elements that contribute to the development of personal integrity, social democracy, and human decency. It has to be concerned with the furtherance of economic profit yet also with the advancement of the human spirit.
>
> (Introduction, p. XI)

Their vision of a New Way with attention to democratic and humanitarian values requires a critical view of the current global reform policy ensemble with its erroneous trends to use *bigger, tighter* and *harder* mechanisms in the conduct of reform processes.

We will now consider each of these *bigger, tighter* and *harder* mechanisms more critically.

Bigger mechanisms in present trends of reform

According to Hargreaves et al. (2010) choice for the *bigger* in reforms is realized in recent numerous large-scale research studies with standardized tests and their impact on globalized market competition and league tables of performance:

4 Political and curricular considerations

The mechanisms of change to bring about this ideological shift were the introduction of market competition and league tables of performance between schools, a return to traditional models of curriculum and teaching through closely prescribed curriculum contents and standards sometimes accompanied by scripted and paced models of literacy and mathematics instruction, pervasive systems of educational testing that were tied to the curriculum basics and to the criteria for market competition, and intrusive systems of surveillance by external inspection. All these were linked with high-stakes consequences of public exposure, administrative intervention, and even enforced closure for schools that performed badly.

(p. VII)

In recent years, the political reform agenda in many school systems have been dominated by these bigger mechanisms, discussing international comparisons from TIMSS (Martin et al., 2012) and PISA (OECD, 2010), with more than 70 countries of the world involved and based on new narrow control systems of accountability (Tatto, 2007). The outcome from these comparative studies has resulted in the intersection of global, national and local reform policies and while they can be modified or delayed by the respective tradition of a particular country, increasing convergence is found in all cases in the direction of policy change.

Such a delayed convergence of reform policies was assumed but not confirmed by Blömeke (2007) for the Federal Republic of Germany, which had a relatively stable structure through the tradition of the German education system, developed over a long period of time and anchored in the national mentality:

Against the historical, political and socio-economic background the present change is almost surprising given the former stability of teacher education.

(p. 58)

The results and conclusions from international comparative studies were perceived as natural events, to which countries responded politically with the development of standards and competence grids. The race for measurable increases in the national ranking of performances and the soft sculpting of peer-pressure in systems of teacher appraisal (Lingard, Sellar & Savage, 2014) have left crucial questions unanswered about individual and cultural contexts and the political legitimation of learning outcomes or values. The question about "what" and "how" of learning as a quantifiable output, neglect the "why" question and the respective cultural, political and individual context. Measurable results according to formal criteria such as "enhancement of quality" and "optimization of school work" with assumptions of causal relations gained from a narrow reading of the scientific method and empirical results are more often used as starting points of educational policy decisions within a tangible fixation on metrics (Muller, 2018).

The humanistic and the critical move rapidly into the policy background due to the policy imperative for numerical criteria and the change in teaching efforts leading to a mandate for immediate and visible output of data from prescribed lesson contents. Connelly (2013) speaks of the disappearance of curricular questions in today's educational reforms in favor of a language of public accountability and predictability. In particular, quantitative criteria for the optimization of school performances play a role. Professional teaching activity is increasingly oriented towards performance measurement as a significant component of state reform processes. Teacher learning is increasingly viewed through the current mainstream lens of standardization and risk-management within an absence of the philosophy of education, the politics of teacher education and the important critical literacy role played by the arts and humanities in education viewed as a multidisciplinary field (Darling-Hammond, 2017; Feldges, 2019; Nussbaum, 2010).

According to Bos et al. (2012) empirical knowledge about the school system is today the basis for all school improvement and teacher effectiveness:

> For a lasting safeguarding and increase of the quality of lessons and school it requires reliable empirical knowledge which offers central information and starting-points for a competent support and optimization of the work at school.
>
> (S 11)

As long as there is only a quantitative increase in school performance and optimization, this statement is correct. However, it is no longer appropriate for pedagogic value decisions and in a complex teaching practice with unpredictable procedures (good teaching as a messy narrative of change; see Mooney Simmie, Moles & O'Grady, 2019), which predominates in the real-life settings in schools. In this case, situation-specific interactions and temporal sequences are decisive. They are supported by experiences, value decisions and spontaneous reactions to constantly changing situations, which cannot be fully grasped empirically or exploited in their density.

This shift towards quantitative justifications marks a shift towards a medicalized model of teacher professional learning brought about by a recent scientific revolution in data analytics, the reduction of learning content to measurable output from reliable tests and global reliance on Human Capital Theory (Tan, 2014). It is not without its critics in the academy of teacher education. According to Deng (2013) academic standards, tests and performance comparisons are developed by specialists, theorists and technologists neglecting central tasks and practices in schools. At the same time, political goals are shifting from policies for the benefit of citizens in democratic societies toward policies with a tight focus on people as human capital for national competitive interests in a system of business-like teacher identity (Biesta, 2013; Skerritt, 2018). Reith (2017) states that there have been frequent disputes between the OECD PISA coordinator, researchers and ministers of education in the past 15 years complaining about

6 Political and curricular considerations

"PISA-Testeritis", in the face of a flood of ever-new investigations test fatigue is spreading. This may be due to the increasing distance between scientific issues and the living contradictions found in practice settings, but also to an ethical turn to more normative questions about school-based practices (Amadio, Opertti & Tedesco, 2015). This is illustrated by a recent large-scale study in Norway on school-based teacher education (Postholm, 2016) and on teacher education in partnership (Lillejord & Borte, 2016), which calls for far closer cooperation with teachers and schools.

In arguing for complexity science in their (re)conceptualizing of teacher professional learning, Opfer & Pedder (2011) suggest that educational researchers have "committed an epistemological fallacy" (p. 377) by taking empirical relations between activities, tasks, structures, etc. to be "teacher learning". They go on to argue that this results from a global policy imperative that is "mechanistic and linear in response to calls for causal studies, effects and growth of linear statistical modelling" (p. 380). Instead, they view education as recursive interactions between nested sub-systems that coalesce in ways that are unpredictable yet highly patterned. In this view, the educator needs not only to consider general principles but also to pay attention to specific contexts. In this way, researchers need to consider not only findings from large-scale studies as offering partial and valuable findings (in preference to definitive solutions) but also new knowledge-of-practice generated by practitioners (teacher-researchers) in situated settings (Cochran-Smith & Lytle, 1999).

Tighter mechanisms in present trends of reform

Hargreaves et al. (2010) argue that mechanisms of *tighter* top-down control are a consequence of the *bigger* reforms:

> In any walk of life, the more that control and intervention are orchestrated from the top, the tighter the focus must become in terms of what has to be controlled. The wider the scope of action, the more that trust, decision-making, and responsibility must be devolved downwards – what is known as the principle of subsidiarity. There are simply never enough resources to permit close control of everything from above. The answer to this conundrum among large-scale reformers has been to establish a tight focus for control and intervention. Hence, the growing consensus has been to concentrate policy efforts, curriculum development, instructional training, intervention strategies, and improvement plans on raising test scores and narrowing achievement gaps in the tested basics of literacy and numeracy (mathematics) along with secondary school examination results.
>
> (p. XIV)

This tighter policy control through standardized testing and accountability in reform processes is assisted by experts and scientists relying on rigorous theories from different disciplines and data analytics. Scientific explanations from specialized sciences such as psychology, sociology, medicine, statistics, curriculum theory or economics are used in education policy to plan reforms or are expected from teachers conducting a research-based evaluation of themselves and their practices. These theories are based on generally accepted axioms or generalizations that are often fixated on behavioral sciences such as psychology and are not necessarily valid in educational practice as a multi-disciplinary field of study that needs to take wider cultural contexts and the arts and humanities (e.g. history of education and philosophy of education) into account (Nussbaum, 2010). In a similar vein, Schwab (1983) criticizes the inadequacy of theories relying on positivism in education and educational planning. It is true, that these sciences offer the possibility of a comprehensive analysis of teaching and learning processes and social deficits. They also offer support for more reflective teachers and schools drawing from counter-intuitive knowledge in their practice setting. Nevertheless, they do not adequately satisfy teaching *practice* which should address specific situations and cultural characteristics of teachers and learners at a particular time through deliberation in the sense elaborated by Schwab (1970). Besides, while positivists present as neutral objective researchers their claim of coming from nowhere is becoming harder, if not impossible, to defend (Bleakley, 1999). Explanations with generalizing research principles are external perspectives, which cannot adequately reflect the lived reality of real-world practice.

In this regard, instrumental and scientific discourses (Gunter, 2001), if taken alone, without access to humanistic discourses and critical literacy, simply fail to take into account the ways teachers not only reflect on self and practices but the multiple ways they need to mediate these insights with the world. Biesta (2013) argues that education always involves a risk, that is an encounter between humans rather than robots and, therefore, if the risk is removed there is a real danger that education itself is removed.

Attempts to overcome these tight instrumental theory-practice contradictions by reflection during and through teaching activities in the sense of Schön (1983) are attempts of professional deliberation, which are expected to solve problems rationally in a concrete situation and to a limited extent. In teaching practice, reflection as thoughtful action is dependent on past experiences, pedagogical knowledge, judgment or hidden action routines in "tacit knowledge" (Polanyi, 1958). Pillow (2003) argues in favor of a deeper reflexive view which she calls the constructive and honest feedback required of an *Uncomfortable Reflexivity*. While reflecting, questions arise for what purpose, relevance, value or democratic conviction exactly the practitioner should be reflecting (Gillies, 2017). This requires to put one's reflexive positioning in critical relation to those of others and to engage in an ethical discourse for the development of professional responsibility. Zeichner (1994) therefore draws attention to the fact that reflective practice of an individual teacher, while necessary, is not sufficient and only makes sense in the context of collaboration. In a similar vein, Gillies

8 Political and curricular considerations

(2017) proposes to make reflection more precise by inter-subjective considerations of relevant perspectives, visions or of what others would think in a given situation. He proposes to engage with peers, partners, pupils or professionals for reflective judgments.

This would come close to Engeström's (2001) idea about shared meaning-making of subjects from different communities. But the innovative professional practice is not just a matter about a reflection of undirected experiences. It entails above all questions about human values, higher-order discourse, democratic beliefs and moral considerations. As Olson (2002) argues, teachers, teacher educators and researchers need to bring such issues to the policy table in the context of systemic reform not so much to join in the "roll out" of tighter control and accountability and to offer feedback on an innovative curricular process approach.

Science is assumed to be a tool to prevent naive knowledge transfer from existing traditions based on some type of folk psychology in the lived reality of schools. Scientists are assumed to have an idea from their research evidence and results, how professional behavior in teacher education can succeed by scientific support in a lesson. Renowned educationalists in a German-Swiss project (Oser, Achtenhagen & Renold, 2006) argue:

> Since several decades teacher training programs build basically on knowledge transfer or/and transfer of traditional how-to-do-concepts about what works in the classroom. . . . It is decisive that researchers have an idea about how we can conceptualize and build a competence based teacher-training in which its actions are not only based on traditions and the always postulated field relatedness, but also on psychological and behavioral fundamental research which elucidates situations and their necessities with regard to their specific transformation through professional teaching acts. *Research must give us information about how effective such enterprises are, how much situational effects go into such actions and which action and measurement standards lead to better pathways in teacher training* (Italics from the authors).
>
> (p. 1)

However, evidence-based clinical practice positions teachers as unreflective knowledge mediators or first-order practitioners (Murray & Male, 2005). It assigns innovative planning of teaching to researchers without first-hand knowledge of schools. It does not go the way suggested by Murray and Male to develop a professional concept for the support of second-order teaching practice accompanied by reflexive collaborative work and research sharing of different communities. Through mere research-based criteria, educational objectives are reduced to quantifiable criteria with instrumental rationality and teachers are forced to follow codified education contents from outside.

There is the argument, that education with scientifically controlled teacher education and certification is better than education without scientific grounding.

However, this argument neglects the cultural-historical finding that a considerable number of reform efforts have often failed to deliver improvements (Noddings, 2007). Randi and Corno (1997) notice in a review article in the *International Handbook of Teachers and Teaching* that well-intentioned scientific innovations frequently became too restricted in duration and time and teachers frequently "domesticated" innovations into their everyday routines or worked subversively in their application. The scientific criteria of objectivity and generalizability do not meet the requirements for the deep change needed in the cultural dynamic of school life:

> Teachers recognize that schools, classrooms, and students are constantly changing. Their goals are responsive to the drivers and dynamic contexts in which they teach. They view the needs of students, classrooms, and schools as demanding immediate attention, and waiting for research and policy to invent solutions is both inefficient and foolish. . . . The complex, dynamic, and unpredictable nature of schools and classrooms requires practitioners to be innovators.
>
> (p. 1205)

Research-based concepts of innovation are used to legitimize policy representations or to delegate tasks to specialists, curriculum developers or research institutes, who transport certain convictions through scientific or technical legitimation and prepare implementations politically. Policy reform transfer from the state to schools is understood in one of at least two very different ways. First, it can be understood as a linear rational process of policy implementation, with evaluation using modes of public accountability, whereby teachers are mandated as functionaries to react to a technology of teaching using diagnosis and reporting of predetermined outcomes. Second, it can be understood as a complex policy enactment where teachers behave as policy actors and curriculum designers and makers and partake in creative and critical processes of translation, interpretation and (re)contextualization, with evaluation based on intelligent accountability (Ball et al., 2011; Brady, 2016; O'Neill, 2013).

The ambivalence of science in the service of state reform policy is highly controversial since, according to Knab (1983), it neglects the contextual reference of theories and unjustly transfers it to the field of action of the school:

> Scientifically directed curriculum research is also a preferred venue for the controversy about the role of the researcher in reform processes and the consequences of the unreflected overtaking of the practice repertoire of neighboring sciences, often dissolved from the theoretical background.
>
> (p. 699)

For those involved in a curriculum process, this scientific theorizing in school practice means that empirically-based decisions are made in advance for schools

10 Political and curricular considerations

and teachers, as for example new academic-based teaching content, psychologically-based teaching and learning methods or standards according to performance assessments, such as by OECD PISA and TALIS studies. However, justifications for these decisions have often been achieved without the proactive involvement of schools and within simplistic linear rational framing of teacher professional learning (Opfer & Pedder, 2011) neglecting "open enough" discursive spaces for deliberative and "intellectual quality" (Gore et al., 2017).

This type of external control of schools and teachers is based on cooperation between political and external research institutions. Schools are only marginally involved with feasibility studies and directed towards scientifically based constructions. Local school-based developments in communities are subordinated to a well-defined mandated and external political purpose. As a result, these narrow types of partnerships lose their local reference point and thus their social justification in communities. Through a predominantly external cooperation, formal supplier functions without discursive involvement gain importance.

Harder mechanisms in present trends of reform

Besides the *bigger* and *tighter* mechanisms in recent reform processes Hargreaves et al. (2010) add the mechanism of *harder* reliability through hard data and hard sciences instead of practical experiences:

> Data-driven improvement has become an integral part of the movement to develop schools into being professional learning communities (PLCs), where teachers use data and other evidence to inquire into their practice and its effects on students and make needed improvements together to address the shortcomings that they find. In the best or most advanced PLCs, a wide range of quantitative and qualitative data are used as a regular and effortless part of collective practice to inquire continuously into practice in the classroom, department, or entire school so as to keep improving in order to raise standards of achievement.
>
> (XVI)

While these developments have undoubtedly concentrated teachers' energy and efforts in identifying and responding to struggling students who need the most help, Hargreaves et al. (2010) point to the risk of enthusiastic adoption of data-driven instruction and school improvement. Because of the use of hard data and rigorous behavior theories, as well as accountability measures and external constructs, school reform gets into tighter mechanisms as described in the former section. Teachers' collaborative practices are re-directed toward public accounting for improved outcomes and this time is spent interrogating student test scores because of imposed high-stakes assessment and devising expedient problem-based solutions to bring about the rapid improvements that will keep the forces of external accountability at bay. Within the realist ontology of this

Process-Product paradigm, complexity is pushed aside in favor of data analytics, learning outcomes and policy compliance and there is little or no opportunity for "intelligent accountability" for a complex human endeavor (Erikson & Erikson, 2018; O'Neill, 2013; Tan, 2014).

In addition, the development of schools into what are nowadays called professional learning communities runs the risk of defining this communal unit for social co-inquiry too narrowly, and only for the school environment, neglecting the confluence of multiple knowledge forms needed for an advanced professional practice (e.g. theoretical and disciplinary and professional knowledge bases), values and experience needed to invoke an *Uncomfortable Reflexivity* in teachers' practices (Pillow, 2003) and interrogation of the differential power and social relations in a political climate expecting accountability and conformity within professional standards frameworks.

The policy imperative for expediency in this regard can be seen in the way the European Commission re-frames education as a nested system of "learning systems" with teacher professional development discursively positioned as a "learning system" nested within broader learning systems (European Commission, 2018). The philosopher Gert Biesta (2012) argues against what he calls this "empty discourse of learning" (p. 36). He goes on to argue that this construct fails to consider what content is learned, why this content is learned and who is teaching this content? Similarly, the philosopher Martha Nussbaum (2010) argues that nation-states in their thirst for profit are no longer asking the important questions in relation to curricular content, a "what works" movement appears to have overtaken arguments of "why".

The problem with the concept of a learning community reduces the view of social co-participation to a limited context of "legitimate peripheral participation" of different learners. This participation of learners in a learning community is defined as legitimate when it allows all participants access to various discursive positions and experiences, multiple learning trajectories, productive, concurrent and reciprocal learning and acknowledging differential power relations. However, what is missing is a systemic view taking place in a broader political context exerting power from outside. The symbolic danger of hegemonic closure inside a narrow view of a learning community as a convergent system looking inward was highlighted by Engeström (1999) and gave rise to a complex divergent system better understood within activity theory:

> What seems to be missing [with respect to the concept of learning community] is movement outward and in unexpected directions: questioning of authority, criticism, innovation, initiation of change. Instability and inner contradictions of practice are all but missing.
>
> (p. 12)

This latter agonistic view of democracy moves the argument forward again from former classical-humanist notions of democracy and more recent liberal progressive notions of democracy founded on compliance with the social order. Instead, activity theory has the capability to move professional practices in the direction of deep engagement with the living contradictions of practice and the wider social world order. If used in this way it can take into account the uncertainties implied in going beyond a narrow search for good teaching and teacher learning as highly predictable risk-managed activities (Hammersley-Fletcher, Clarke & McManus, 2018). This framing of the discursive boundaries in deliberative partnership is open to further development as it seeks to advance earlier work of Schwab and Habermas and the more recent critique by Chantal Mouffe (Ruitenberg, 2009).

As a general consequence, the three aspects of *bigger, tighter* and *harder* in today's policy reforms are deeply restrictive, neglecting local cultural needs and specific conditions of schools, controlling effects on the sole basis of rigorous data and unspecific scientific theories and rejecting a more open systemic view in a broader political context. Schools are limited to join in the "roll out" of top-down tighter control and accountability of predefined contents. The creative potential of schools for the development of a more open, human and vibrant democratic society remains unused. The call for better use of this potential in education requires changes in reform strategies, as suggested by Hargreaves et al. (2010) in his notion of a New Way or a deliberative partnership approach, developed here.

Considering the mechanisms of bigger, *tighter and harder*, we must be aware, that Hargreaves et al. (2010) propose their New Way of reform with a different background of *static* democratic and humanitarian values than that, followed in our book with the emphasis on *deliberative* democracy as a school-based process approach for justified curriculum innovation, grounded in discursive ethics, and professional development.

Hargreaves et al. (2010) outline with their static value assumptions a post-materialist world of a knowledge society and knowledge economy that implies mainly three aspects:

> First, the collapse of the global economy will grab people's attention into adopting educationally driven strategies like those of Finland in turning around to become successful and competitive knowledge economies.
>
> Second, at the end of the age of materialism and of "selfish" forms of capitalism . . . we will give way to goals that embrace the forms of innovation and creativity, and the identification of effective practices that are essential for advanced knowledge economies, and the virtues of empathy and community service that are integral to more "selfiess" forms of capitalism.
>
> Third, we will or should witness the decline of the district and of district driven reform. This will be replaced by districts fostering the creation and spread of promising practices. Teachers can only really learn once they get outside their own classrooms and connect with other teachers. This is one of the essential principles behind PLCs. Likewise, schools can only really

learn when they connect with other schools – including ones outside their own immediate district.

(p. XVIII)

Such a post-materialist world as a competitive knowledge economy, fostering promising practices and promoting a selfless form of eco-capitalism is a vision, which tries to overcome the assumed mechanisms of *bigger, tighter* and *harder*. But it does not tell us, how to get there or how a competitive knowledge society leads to justice independent of economic purposes, but only appears to proclaim democratic and humanitarian values as assumed and taken-for-granted. In this liberal viewpoint, democracy is not dynamic and deliberatively created by people in educational practices, but is an externally imposed construction.

In this way, the eternal question of the purpose of schooling gets opened once again when one considers schooling for social and economic purposes. Some educational theorists believe that it is not a question of shifting social and economic functions against each other, but of balancing the pendulum, which, in the present situation, strongly moves in the direction of economic dominance (Furlong, 2013). Other critical thinkers, such as McLaren (2016) and Fielding (2007), argue that schooling for a performative discourse of education as a private good for the competitive individual is irreconcilable with an organic holistic and dialectical model of relational change and communal-orientation. In the last decade, education is increasingly functionalized through competition for economic purposes and changed from education as a public good to an economic and private good (Zeichner, 2010).

In contrast to the proclamation of a post-materialist world, the deliberative approach advanced in this book gets people involved in a process of boundary crossing for shared meaning-making and ethical justification, as described in the following section. For this, the assumed mechanisms of *bigger, tighter* and *harder* can be of some use in a discourse about changes in education. They might be understood as tools in activity systems for the development of boundary objects in Engeström's (2001) *Cultural-Historical Activity Theory* (CHAT).

According to Engeström (1994), the introduction of concepts like partner-ship or collaboration in curriculum theory implies a paradigmatic change in thinking. In his contribution about teachers as collaborators he points out:

> The individualist and Cartesian bias [in reviews and overviews on teacher thinking] is manifested in our common tendency to view thinking above all as a private internal process. In psychology, it was Vygotsky who initi-ated a still ongoing revolution in this regard, maintaining, that internal, private thought is derivative of external practical and inter-individual action (Vygotsky, 1978). On this view thinking is no more seen as an autonomous process. Attention is called to the socially organized, histori-cally evolving activities in which thinking is embedded.
>
> (p. 44)

14 Political and curricular considerations

In traditional educational theorizing, this individualistic thinking manifests in the idea of teaching as the transmission of subject matter in the classroom with the role of the teacher as an autonomous practitioner working in isolation (Lortie, 1975) and learners acting as individual processors of information. Opposed to this are collaborative activities in a partnership approach for expansive learning and shared meaning-making in multiple activity systems.

But what can be meant by a partnership in a curricular process of innovation in response to the present centralized specification and accountability regime?

In some countries, competence-based curricula and standards have been developed with the primary objective of measuring performance and context-independent norms (Biesta, 2012). Responsibility in teacher education has changed from discursive accountability of equal partners to one of a market-led discourse (Cochran-Smith et al., 2017). In this respect, market-based accountability, in the interests of standardization, restricts teachers' educational efforts to technology for gaining competences and a predefined moral conservatism (Bates, 2012).

As a consequence, a partnership approach for collaborative professional development and curriculum innovation must follow a pathway different from big scientific planning far from the site of school practice, detailed empirical control through the management and narrow science systems for prediction and control and a flight from the field of practice using hard data and scientific rationalism. Innovation and creativity in school systems need more flexible conditions of teaching, learning and planning in partnership than those that have prevailed in the contemporary managerial era of test-driven and data-obsessed educational reform.

The notion of partnership is commonly understood as a sustained relationship with an equal exchange, reciprocity and mutuality achieved through a deliberative process of negotiation. Lave and Wenger's (1991) concept of professional learning communities and the assumption of social co-participation in communities is similar and holds true for a collaborative partnership. Bloomfield (2009) argues:

> Symmetry with respect to relationships requires attention to issues of mutual respect, mutual benefit and mutually agreed forms and levels of participation. Significantly, the rhetoric of 'learning communities' can convey stronger senses of such mutual endeavor, connection and shared reward.
>
> (p. 36)

But as we have learned from the previous discussion about learning communities, the symmetry of relationships is not sufficient, because it neglects mediation of practice with the world and the exerted power and social relations from outside the school system and what Bourdieu (1991) calls the "invisible hand of the powerful".

Therefore, partnership cannot be assumed as an uncontested good and this construct can be perverted and distorted in a competitive system as a governance tool and political instrument to produce ethical suppression and "silence" and compliance of practitioners in a communal subsystem (Galvin & Mooney Simmie, 2017; Santoro, 2017; Watson, 2014). This problem is discussed by Bloomfield and Nguyen (2015) for the Australian educational system, where standards of school-university partnerships are accredited as a key element to improve the quality of teacher education graduates. As a consequence, the formation and practices of partnership with the idea of social and community participation become increasingly aligned with agendas of public accountability and accreditation, and there is the risk that partnership work of this type will merely serve business-like performative and instrumental purposes. She cites Cardini (2006) with the critical comment:

> Although theoretical definitions present partnerships as a cluster of symmetrical and complementary sector partners, in practice partnerships tend to show asymmetrical and unbalanced relationships between different members; . . . in practice partnerships seem to be the instrument to implement top down central policies.
>
> (p. 398)

As a consequence of this critique of a neoliberal notion of partnership in educational planning Bloomfield and Nguyen (2015) recommend that we instead consider a wider context of community and partnership using Engeström's (1999) *Cultural-Historical Activity Theory* (CHAT). In Engestöm's activity system a community is also of central importance but this relates to a context of shared meaning-making through boundary crossing between different activity systems and of system components such as objects, mediating artifacts, rules and division of labor, for a divergent system of education that looks outward.

Specifically, the component "division of labor" is composed of a horizontal division of specialized tasks and a vertical division of hierarchies and hierarchically exerted power is made explicit and problematized. The component of "rules" considers asymmetric relations and ethical discourses between partners reflecting differential exertion of power. It is this systemic context that allows reflecting not only about school-specific partnerships that can be of positive value but also about external constraints in political power relations, that can prove detrimental to the partnership work in schools. In addition to these reflections, the collaborative systems approach in CHAT allows school-based settings for curricular planning with democratic and humanitarian values. These considerations guide our analysis and use of settings in the European projects reported here for curriculum innovation.

But we also have to consider difficulties and contestations in relation to the realization of authentic settings for curricular planning with multiple communities. One such difficulty is boundary crossing of multiple communities for

16 Political and curricular considerations

shared meaning-making with different cultural and educational backgrounds, such as teachers in schools in deliberative dialogue with teacher educators from higher education and university settings (Young, O'Neill & Mooney Simmie, 2015). In this school-university partnership situation the critical question is whose knowledge is valued, who is staging the partnership and who has the authoritative voice in relation to this and how is this mediated? While teacher educators and researchers in higher education value the specialist (decontextualized) knowledge of the academy (theoretical, professional and disciplinary knowledge base of knowledge-for-practice) they have historically placed far less value on situated professional judgments, knowledge-in-practice and possibly knowledge-of-practice (Cochran-Smith & Lytle, 1999; Santoro, 2017). Therefore, within such a partnership there are tensions and an immediate "clash" of knowledge systems. This contradiction can either become a source of curriculum innovation for a new messy narrative of change and critical reflexivity for all and/or it can become a potential site for symbolic violence (Bleakley, 1999). The key principle in CHAT suggests that deliberation for "intellectual quality" involves processes of mutual respect implying sophisticated knowledge brokerage for the achievement of agreement and ethical discourse.

Schools themselves are often not ready for higher-order co-inquiry, cooperation or deliberative communication with formal rules. According to Sawyer and Rimms-Kaufman (2007), Terhart and Klieme (2006), Steinert et al. (2006) and the OECD (2009), teachers cooperate mainly informally or through lower-order exchange of textbooks or teaching materials, less by clarifying complex pedagogical questions. In a limited sense, "partnerships" between higher education institutions and schools are often asymmetric, based on traditional, hierarchical relationships between partners, vertical lines of collaboration and stable ideas of knowledge transfer (Furlong et al., 2000). As a consequence, teaching is often carried out as a transmission in the schools according to given content, rules, roles and responsibilities and fails to become transformative and inclusive of co-inquiry with diverse others.

According to Murray and Male (2005, p. 126), this corresponds to a first-order instruction process: "First order teachers teach subjects to their pupils and students, while second-order teachers induce their students into the practices and discourses of the school". Higher-order innovation with settings for the cooperation of partners with equal rights, based on well-founded discursive rules of agreement, is a complex undertaking involving teachers and others from different communities working together in more symmetric partnership. This form of an innovation process, however, ensures that curriculum innovation through school participation allows a legitimate claim and realization.

For this purpose, an appropriate curricular model of innovation through partnership needs to be developed for complex interacting systems with higher-order innovation and mutual respect in a school system, as proposed by Bloomfield and Nguyen (2015). They emphasize the collaboration of different professional stakeholders with high quality of interactions and communication and facilitating conditions in interacting activity systems on the basis of Engeström's (2001) *Cultural-Historical Activity Theory* (CHAT) as third space:

> The partnership is arguably stronger if it is based within and around the professional experience and the professional learning of all parties. Understanding professional experience through the perspective of activity theory can enable all stakeholders to identify the core issues of contradictions from the professional experience. This then can be seen as the foundation to initiate the partnership between school and university. The primary focus of a partnership, in our view, is on developing a third space where such different elements of the two systems come into view and can be renegotiated.
>
> (p. 34)

This sophisticated brokerage approach not only promises to meet policy demands for specific outcomes but involves participants in a democratic and deliberative discourse without pressure from *bigger, higher* and *tighter* mechanisms, acknowledging problems, a diversity of views and a multiplicity of experiences and knowledge forms. The arguments for this endeavor will be further elaborated in the chapters that follow.

A deliberative turn for teacher education as boundary crossing

With the phenomena of boundaries in a system of education, many constructs can be examined beyond well-known forms of differentiation according to subjects, age and achievement groups: boundaries between school and nonschool education, between teachers and learners, institutional boundaries between school, teacher education and educational administration, boundaries through disability or social developments and much more. Boundaries are necessary, they regulate institutional and interpersonal exchange, give shelter and protected spaces in which the self can unfold and give feelings of security and belonging. Boundaries of disciplinary knowledge are required in order to deepen insights with a specific methodology or a specific knowledge potential and to acquire reliable expertise.

But – and this is the other side of the coin – boundaries can also restrict, obscure, limit, discriminate and hinder. They exclude the strange and foreign, they discriminate against people who are in any way different, and thus can hinder development. To overcome these limitations, one needs boundary crossing, the contact and exchange with other cultures, other standpoints, the external view and different perspectives. Only with a change of perspective and the view of other perspectives is there the real possibility of an insight into innovation.

18 Political and curricular considerations

Boundaries in system theory define the difference between the environment and a system (Krohn and Küppers, 1990). Self-organized social systems with open boundaries regulate the relation between system and environment. If there are several systems each system is separated from the environment of the other systems by a boundary. A boundary is significant for the maintenance of a system. In a social system, the intra-system relations of a group of persons are defined in a community, separated from other communities by boundaries. Intersystem relations between communities subsume boundary-crossing activities.

To exemplify this, the science community is taken as a self-organized social system of scientists in a community producing knowledge about a limited domain in an environment. This system defines an operationally closed system with constructed boundaries of science communities defining an environment. The outer rim of a system at the boundaries is an open social space that influences the dynamics of a system by feedback mechanisms or disturbances. At the outer rim of the system "hybrid-communities" from different domains such as other sciences, politics and economy come together with the potential for innovation and change.

Boundary crossing for curricular innovation is a concept aimed at overcoming "problems" in a system, problematizing a contradiction in professional practice (Postholm, 2015), by seeking a common understanding to be generated in a third space identified at the interstices between multiple communities (Engeström, 2001; Akkerman & Bakker, 2011). The "problems" in the discussion as negotiated between the various actors are characterized as boundary objects in *Cultural-Historical Activity Theory* (CHAT; Engeström, 2001).

According to Star and Griesemer (1989), a boundary object is useful for the analysis of objects of overlapping social systems. According to Star (1989, p. 46), they are plastic concepts with a common identity at different standpoints:

> Boundary objects are both plastic enough to adapt to local needs and constraints of the several parties employing them, yet robust enough to maintain a common identity across sites.

The concept was originally developed for scientific classifications of vertebrates as objects of collaboration between different types of persons. The concept of a boundary object is a tool for identifying common activities. Tensions in relation to the importance of the boundary object are part of what is created in the coordination of different interests.

A theoretical framework of CHAT with contradictory actions for an educational innovation builds upon sociocultural discontinuities such as gender or minority problems or contradictions in or between communities of teachers, teacher educators and other policy actors (Akkerman & Bakker, 2011). Within this framework, a deliberative decision is prepared by deliberating across boundaries within or between different activity systems – a controversy or a practical problem.

CHAT is a sophisticated but less known approach in education research. Therefore, we offer a gradual elaboration of this construct in different sections of the book. In a first step, the basic structure and concepts of activity theory will be introduced here for the elaboration of a framework for school-based deliberative partnership. This helps to understand the theoretical language for the specification of the framework and its implications for curriculum innovation. In a second step, further differentiation of activity theory will be given in Chapter 5 with different levels of contradictions and multiple communities for the analysis of outcomes in different projects.

Activity theory was first formulated by the Russian psychologist Vygotsky and later substantially developed to a higher degree as a more extensive form, a second and third generation approach. In the original theory, Vygotsky described actions of the individual as mediated where learning takes place – in the outer rim where our thinking is stretched and where we are emotionally held in an uncomfortable space by our teacher in what he called the zone of proximal development. The theory suggests that the role of the teacher as an educator is to move students into this outer zone of proximal development and hold them there long enough for something new to be learned.

In the second generation, Leont'ev extended the first individual perspective to the collective.

Finally, in the 1990s, the third generation of related concepts as *Cultural-Historical Activity Theory* (CHAT) was developed with the idea of multiple interactive systems and the concept of boundary crossing. This latter form of activity theory represented a connection of the systems as a network reflecting postmodern society. As far as individuals are represented in single parts of the system, they are not limited to their output or reproduction but contribute to society through different exchange functions between the different systems that constitute a society. It contains contradictions that lead to dialogue and power questions beyond the individual and his relationship with the other elements of CHAT.

Roth and Lee (2007) perceive the potential of CHAT, opening up new avenues for educational research and practical questions of educational psychology. CHAT attempts to analyze and shape complex relationships, habits, beliefs, practices, norms and values of different communities by means of components. This is the case in teacher education when teachers, teacher educators, researchers and other participants realize school-related changes through deliberation in a trusting climate. Participants from different *communities* as *subjects* of the system agree on an *object* of change, a curricular innovation with *mediating tools* and *artifacts* taking into account *accepted rules* and a *division of labor* (Engeström & Sannino, 2010). CHAT works with contradictions and the need to seek agreement for a better solution.

The components and their relationships within a system are represented by triangles with a subject-object relationship in the center. A complete system consists of all possible relationships between a subject, its membership in a community, an object of the conflict, tools for this activity, recognition of regulatory or ethical rules of engagement and division of labor. A network of different systems consists of two or more such triangles (Figure 1.1):

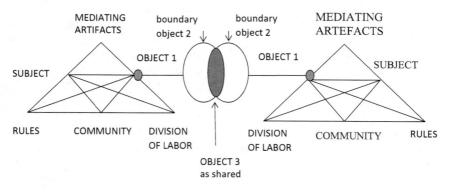

Figure 1.1 Two interacting activity systems as units of the analysis (Engeström, 2001, p. 131)

The connecting element of such a network is the agreement (shared boundary object 3) for the communication about the objects to be treated of each system (boundary objects 2).

For the purpose of illustrating the components, the following explanations are made:

The *subject* as a component is defined by a person or persons involved in the central activity (Engeström, 2001). It is possible to use this component as an analytical anchor to design the entire activity of the system. In education, this component refers to a student or group of students from any level. Teachers and teacher educators can also be identified as subjects.

An *object* refers to the problem space in which the activity is directed and transformed by means of physical and symbolic tools. The object leads to making certain meanings in the behavior of the subject. If, for example, the subject of the activity is a teacher or other person in the field of education, then the object of the activity can be described as a goal of improving teaching, practical learning or developing the technical skills of students. If the subject of the activity is a student, then the object can be described as a short-term goal for understanding algorithms or as a formative assessment to solve problems.

The *instruments*, mediating artifacts or tools are material things and mental constructions for the use of a transformation process. There are two types of instruments: psychological tools for transforming behavior and material tools to transform the environment. It can be used individually as a language, gestures, group work, concept, strategy or computer technology, software, interactive whiteboards, dictionary or combined.

The *community* consists of subjects involved in a pedagogical activity in an institution or group or additional persons associated with a common object. The members of the community usually meet in one place at the same time. In a classroom, the community is represented by a teacher and students. In a larger macro context, members of the family, friends, other educational administration representatives and political decision-makers can be involved. The community ties individuals together through social *rules* and *division of labor*.

The *rules* consist of norms, conventions or social traditions defined by the community and regulations for exchange. There are implicit and explicit rules. Implicit rules refer to permissible or inadmissible behavior to regulate arguments and opportunities to discuss in the community. Examples of implicit rules are: to raise a hand when a teacher asks a question or to speak in German, where this is the official teaching language. Explicit rules can be explicitly defined by teachers or school authorities. Examples of this are tests and curricula.

The component of the *division of labor* distinguishes work among members of a community according to a vertical or horizontal dimension. The horizontal dimension refers to the negotiation of basic tasks and responsibilities between community members. Power relationships and authority define the vertical dimension. Examples of a division of labor in the school are assignments of tasks or cooperation agreements among members of a community, based on hierarchies in authority: students, teachers, coordinators, administrators.

Boundary crossing in activity theory differs from a consensus process in that it searches for agreement for a boundary object by a discursive deliberation of equal partners in public space. This discursive commitment makes it possible for actors involved to find common ground in a dissent, despite alternative positions and outside of institutionalized procedures.

Engeström's CHAT model of multiple activity systems, elaborated in more detail for different levels of contradiction in Chapter 5, provides a way to present and analyze complex forms of deliberation and learning in different sociocultural contexts of professional experience as contestation and tension across distinct fields and practices. This complexity can be represented through multiple participants within and across communities and the diversity of discursive fields and practices linked to rules, roles and divisions of labor. This model offers a way of looking at different actions within a complex system such as processes of change in professional development and curriculum innovation.

Curricular presuppositions and concepts for collaboration in partnership

Curricular considerations are according to Amadio et al. (2015) necessary for the planning of innovation or reform. In other words, the planning of innovation in a curriculum is a blueprint for the realization of a reform: "More attention to the role of the curriculum seems necessary not only since successful educational reforms depend on sound curricular proposals" (p. 8).

22 Political and curricular considerations

In order to judge the suitability of a model of curricular innovation, a systematic overview of curricular theories can be helpful. For this we will not refer to the widely used but restricted notion of curriculum as a defined sequence of learning (study program), but to a more extended construct of the curriculum with social, cultural, personal or every-day-life relations, as described by Amadio et al. (2015):

> While the disciplinary approach is still predominant, it is observable that the curriculum has begun to occupy a major place in the discussions, agreements and dissensions around what society it is sought to construct and achieve for the future generations. . . . The spaces of curriculum legitimation increasingly involve the political, social and economic stakeholders, the media and the social networks through, for example, public consultations, parliamentary debates and commissions or boards made up of trade-union representatives, employers' organizations, professional associations and sectors of civil society. Dialogue on change and curriculum content has expanded and it no longer seems possible to maintain that they are themes exclusively incumbent on the educational authorities, the disciplinary specialists and teachers' unions, with the marginal participation of learners, citizens and society as a whole.
>
> (p. 4)

Hameyer (1983a) and, more recently, Smith (2000) have made proposals for this extended notion of the curriculum. Hameyer (1983b) assumes that general curriculum theories deal with key questions and basic categories of education. However, these theories cannot be used in the traditional sense by fixed premises and derivations for practice, but are insufficient in the sense of Schwab (2013, reprint), since reality can only be viewed as a theory object from a selected perspective. This means that curriculum theories are limited to the social genesis of education, with statements about the curriculum *process*, without predefining ideals about the educational objectives to be achieved. According to Hameyer (1983b), in curriculum theory, an object of education is extended to those aspects of the curriculum, which focus on the processes of production and realization of curricular innovations. According to Frey (1983), these educational objectives are consolidated as laws, syllabi, examinations or textbooks and are to be handled through an innovative curriculum process. Factors of this procedural curriculum understanding are the selection of persons, use of information resources, working conditions, forms of interaction, ways of qualifying the lesson plans, evaluation, the relationship between law and action and the importance of research and innovation practice.

In this process, according to Knab (1969), teachers need to be included in curriculum development in the sense of democratization and participation. The process of finding practical solutions in the field of education needs to consider alternative possibilities for action and the associated consequences, costs and feasibility.

For this, the method of practical deliberation is proposed by Schwab (2013, reprint). It is fundamental to the subject of curriculum innovation and will be resumed at a later stage. It also plays a role in the classification of curriculum theories as syllabus, product, process and practice of Smith (2000) emphasizing the structural context or milieu.

While curriculum approaches as a syllabus, course of study or product are based on traditional notions of a theory as a closed system of knowledge transmission or technology for the achievement of given goals, the context-dependent curricular approach (Cornbleth, 1990), which takes into account local characteristics of schools according to Mawhinney (2004), is open to social relationships such as teacher-student interactions, collaborative teacher education and class organization and takes into account hidden regulatory influences found in differential power relations ("hidden curriculum", Jackson, 1968).

The contextual reference can be interpreted as an effect in a complex structural and sociocultural system with subsystems. *Structural* components are, in particular, control mechanisms of a market and bureaucracy in delimited areas and cultural traditions of opinions, values and priorities. They are stable systems with closed system boundaries and resistances for change. *Sociocultural* components, on the other hand, are subject to constant change through social, political or economic conditions. They are conceived as a fundamental potential for curricular change (Cornbleth, 1990):

> Curriculum construction is an ongoing social activity shaped by various contextual influences within and beyond the classroom and accomplished interactively, primarily by teachers and students. Curriculum is not a tangible product but the actual, day-to-day interactions of students, teacher, knowledge and milieu.
>
> (p. 89)

This meaning of sociocultural context in educational practice is emphasized by Connell (2016) for the professional behavior of good teachers. It is not the neoliberal atmosphere of competition and standardized performance comparison between individuals, which is responsible for the dynamic development of good lessons but the collective work and professional culture at schools. The work of a single teacher depends to a high degree on what colleagues, other partners and students do or plan together.

This change of curricular practice in a sociocultural context is a complex process, which is related to partially divergent communication of partners involved, which cannot be controlled by bureaucratic controls or quantitative measurement of competencies and takes into account unpredictable informal or collateral learning resulting from a "hidden curriculum" (Jackson, 1968) and the need to "reveal the hand of the powerful" (Bourdieu, 1991). Mooney Simmie et al. (2019) question the closing of discursive gaps through narrow modes of accountability:

24 Political and curricular considerations

Conclusions position 'good teaching' within the super-complexity of a messy narrative of change and flows enacted with a diversity of inquirers and institutions. The study questions the role of state inspectors as arbiters of 'good teaching' and challenges the academy of teacher education in assuring productive discursive gaps for education as a social responsibility for public-interest values.

(p. 1)

For an innovative partnership approach the context, however, cannot be related arbitrarily to wide ranges in educational systems, but only makes sense for local school interactions with personal relations in communities. This idea about a curriculum-in-context is emphasized by Cornbleth (1990) and is related to a local practice mentioned by Mawhinney (2004). However, within a sociological perspective, it is understood that schools and partnership institutions are not coming together by chance and instead define themselves within broader ideological and societal governing forms (Youdell & McGimpsey, 2015).

The preferred concept of curricular innovation in this book emphasizes school-based activity in partnership in context-dependent processes. In these processes teachers as curriculum designers and planners (Clandinin & Connelly, 1987) play a specific role as partners of colleagues, students and other educational stakeholders from multiple communities, particularly teacher educators, educational researchers or politicians. Respectively Olson (2002) states that teachers must become proactively involved as moral agents especially with questions about values, morals and tradition in deliberative or reflective practice and collaborative partnership in school practice and policy:

These professional practices entail questions about human values, beliefs and moral considerations. Teachers need to be able to bring such issues to the policy table in the context of systemic reform not so much to join in the 'roll out' as to offer feedback on the purposes and methods themselves.

(p. 133)

In this regard, Brady (2016, 2019a, 2019b), Bloomfield and Nguyen (2015) and Hargreaves (2000) point at a critical aspect of school-based activities, such as self-assessment or partnership, that have the potential to be worthwhile endeavors but can be misleading, if criteria are not internally generated but externally imposed leading to debasement of the ideal of existential freedom and autonomy. For the purpose of worthwhile activities, the possibilities of collaboration and partnership must be discussed. In higher education institutes the accepted language of argumentation is challenged in a school-university partnership using CHAT and instead, the "change" required needs to be (re)framed, with respect of multiple ways of knowing and for epistemic justice, in terms of reflexive change on all sides. In schools, often limited by weak collaborative capabilities of the teachers in terms of higher-order collaboration barriers in the physical structure or culture (e.g. a culture of imitation and compliance) need to be challenged and addressed (Sawyer et al., 2007; Terhart & Klieme, 2006; Steinert et al., 2006; OECD, 2008). Moreover, it needs to be agreed, that the partnership activity as an educative space is not for the purpose of disciplinary regulation of teachers for the realization of predefined outcomes and governance (Watson, 2014) but for authentic partnership-based collaboration for school-based innovation. Here the concept of *Productive Mentoring* (Mooney Simmie & Moles, 2011) provides a special meaning as co-inquiry, critical thinking and care for authentic and vibrant democratization.

Considering partnership-based collaboration for justified curriculum innovation, one has to care about the selection of participants from different communities. Objective criteria for a choice are hard to find. In the Curriculum Workshop, presented in Chapter 6, pragmatic rules played a role, such as the appropriate number of participants, availability, spread of different communities and competences, suitability for the educational area of the innovation, personal relations, personal integrity and sound judgment of "good companions" (Arendt, 2013).

According to Murray (2014), teachers engaged in teacher education as second-order practitioners are of special importance for policy impulses for curricular innovation. These teacher educators have both, professional content knowledge for teaching and professional knowledge and skills in pedagogical interactions with adults and researchers.

> Such efforts may well help teacher educators to gain louder and more powerful voices in policy debates about teacher education. That in turn might assist policy makers in recognizing the strong and irreplaceable contributions we make to high quality teacher education and schooling.
>
> (p. 7)

Preparatory annotations about the structure of the book

In this chapter, we first discussed the current policy imperative of educational change and the living contradictions found when we think about teacher professional learning and the various understandings between education and democracy. Second, we highlighted the special value of a democratic deliberative turn as a process of curriculum innovation through boundary crossing partnership. We then specified the kind of deliberative turn in terms of Engeström's activity theory and we will discuss this in greater detail in Chapters 3 and 4.

In the next chapter, we begin with reflections about the present state of subject-related and structural questions that are of particular importance for educational practice and teacher education. These questions are shaped in today's times, especially by public accountability of school performance in international comparative studies inside a neoliberal atmosphere of decision making and need for teacher professionalization and curriculum innovation.

26 Political and curricular considerations

This means that policy issues must be taken into account under socio-economic perspectives of neoliberalism and neo-conservatism, as well as sociocultural issues and a school structure with well-defined boundaries. These questions will be discussed in the context of boundary crossing in education policy, teacher professionalization, teaching content and institutional interaction. In this way, the curricular process of innovation through the actions of different boundary-crossing communities is preferred in contrast to the design of a curricular product.

Considering divergent policy issues, different pathways of curriculum innovation are outlined as externally-controlled processes or school-based reform processes in Chapter 3. The school-based process, involving partnership, requires higher-order collaboration and deliberation in school practice and needs to be discussed with the perspective of justification of a curriculum innovation. This discussion leads to the construct of boundary crossing in an extended Curriculum Workshop for justification in Chapter 6.

For the understanding of curriculum innovation as a process of boundary crossing, critical considerations and frameworks for curriculum theory are presented with applications and analyses from case studies of two European Comenius teacher education and training projects CROSSNET (*Crossing Boundaries in Science Teacher Education*, Hansen, Gräber & Lang, 2012) and GIMMS (*Gender Innovation and Mentoring in Mathematics and Science*, Mooney Simmie & Lang, 2012, 2017) from 2006 to 2009 and related findings from an Irish teacher education research and development project PLUS (*Partnership in Learning between University and School*) (Costello, 2017; Young, O'Neill & Mooney Simmie, 2015).

Deliberative partnership is discussed in Chapter 5 as boundary-crossing collaboration, taking into account components of *Cultural-Historical Activity Theory* (CHAT; Engeström, 2001; Edwards, 2010). CHAT is an extension of the original learning theory of Vygotsky to a collaborative approach with structural determinants useful for pertinent curricular questions.

An appropriate boundary-crossing collaboration of multiple communities within the CHAT framework allows affordances for processes of educational change. This framework is basic for change but needs for our purposes of curricular justification some specification through discursive rules for deliberation as elaborated in the Curriculum Workshop (Chapter 6). It is an experimental release of practical action in the school (Schwab, 2013, reprint). A complex framework from CHAT, adapted forms of boundary crossing and procedural questions of deliberation, are correspondingly offered for the proposed topic of curricular innovation and teacher professional development through partnership-based school activities.

Successful use of CHAT in school-based teacher education was realized in a study of Postholm (2016) undertaken by the Norwegian government. An assumption is that school-based development is due to a collective practice. In this CHAT activity systems with different components are interacting. For the study of curricular innovation, it is important that problems or living contradictions in the activity systems are the basis for change.

In the Postholm (2016) study, contradictions were developed through a collaboration of teacher educators from universities, teacher-leaders and other teachers working for shared meaning-making. Contradictions arose between the offerings of the teacher educators and the insights offered by the teachers. The scientific offer is an intervention of the teacher educators as researchers, which partly leads to a contradiction of teachers, since the groups have different goals. These contradictions, however, led to discourses as a form of boundary crossing to further development of a common idea from separate visions. In addition, there was an impetus for the development of teachers and teacher educators.

As a result, not only the teachers involved were able to put into practice new ideas, but teacher educators from the university became familiar with the lived reality of the school. The study found that the activities of both groups led to changes in both institutions and that research and practice could be combined for mutual benefit.

This study is of particular relevance for the analysis of partnership-based school activities in the European projects CROSSNET and GIMMS, presented later in this book in Chapter 6 and Chapter 7. It points to the importance of contradictions for deliberation of curricular innovation through boundary crossing. Many attempts to realize innovation at school are based on a different understanding of scientifically grounded policy implementation, in which research-based concepts are offered for testing in schools without the dynamics of discourse about problems or contradictions and where no mutually agreed developments from both sides are reflexively considered and taken into account.

In the case studies of the European project CROSSNET, innovation in science teaching was conducted and analyzed as boundary-crossing collaboration in multiple activity systems with a setting of an extended Curriculum Workshop for curriculum justification. This complex structure of boundary crossing was difficult to introduce in school practice.

The concept of boundary crossing was adapted with different modifications in the GIMMS case studies in Chapter 7. In this project, national coordinators and teacher educators were introduced into the concept of collaboration as boundary crossing for the planning of pedagogical innovation with an outcome of Productive Mentoring (Mooney Simmie & Moles, 2011) and Gender Awareness with practicing teachers (Mooney Simmie & Lang, 2012, 2017). This concept was later used in Ireland for teacher professional learning based on school-university partnerships where teachers engaged in dialogue and discursive ethics with teacher educators and researchers-in-residence (Costello, 2017; Young, O'Neill & Mooney Simmie, 2015).

In summary, the case studies discussed in the book show different successes, contestations and contradictions with school-based curricular innovation based on deliberative democratic partnership and open a discussion outward about limits and transformative possibilities. As a consequence, this expansive learning system with living contradictions in activity systems according to Engeström (2001) and its processes of boundary crossing, have demonstrated the capability to move beyond singular communities of practice.

Chapter 2

Situational factors to be considered for curricular processes of school improvement

The focus of this chapter is on the curricular *process* of educational renewal based on deliberative partnership in teacher education and professional development (Loughran, 2012) within the current context of global competition and its reliance on traditional disciplinary content, school structure, external control of effectiveness and neoliberal policy. This process emphasizes procedures about how and with what justification teaching content gains access in school systems or how curriculum processes guide reforms. It is closely related to Schwab's (1983) notion of a curriculum:

> Curriculum is what is successfully conveyed in differing degrees to different students, by committed teachers using appropriate materials and actions, of legitimated bodies of knowledge, skill, taste, and propensity to act and react, which are chosen for instruction after serious reflection and communal decision.
>
> (p. 240)

In this definition a basic curricular framework emerges, that is central for the educational situation and its control for development: the aspect of "legitimated bodies of knowledge, skill, taste, and propensity to act and react" refers to the use of educational content and methods – usually defined in subjects – and structure for schooling with fixed rules for learning and educational development – usually organized through grouping of students in classes, types of schools or achievements. The aspect of "serious reflection and communal decision" circumscribes the political situation of control directing the educational effects through measurements, accountability or political ideology.

These aspects of subjects, structural conditions and external constraints through public accountability and political directions defining the situation need to be considered for curricular planning of school improvement. They are points of departure for curricular processes that need to be taken into account for different perspectives of education. They will be discussed here in detail illuminating directions of policy or deliberative democracy in educational systems, serving the public good through the proximity of teachers with legitimate

30 Situational factors to be considered

persons. At the center of this discussion is the role of teachers as professionals in a deliberative discourse about change in contrast to a top-down approach (Schwab, 1983):

> Curriculum is not decided in Moscow and telegraphed to the provinces. . . . It arises at home, seeded, watered, and cultivated by some or all of the teachers who might be involved in its institution.

(p. 258)

The importance of teachers as partners is widely recognized for the policy enforcement of quality improvement as well as by self-organized partnerships for innovation of practice. In the OECD study "Teachers Matter" (OECD, 2004, p. 7), the following is stated: "Teachers are central to school improvement efforts". However, there is a growing literature that questions this positioning of school and teachers as a relentless global policy drive to reframe education as competitive individualism and to pay lip service to education as a social responsibility for authentic democratization and solidarity (Ball, 2003; Biesta, Priestley & Robinson, 2017). The arguments suggest that positioning the "teacher" as the most important quality player in the education endeavor fails to take shared responsibility for education achievement into account and places teachers in the firing line for blame when school reforms fail, a well-documented outcome in the field of education (Noddings, 2012).

The situational factors in a global context do not so much consider the local curriculum that "arises at home", as Schwab (1983) points out, but focus on the increase of external constraints controlling content and structure. There are numerous studies on the effects of teachers' subject knowledge and teaching methods for student performance. These effects are verified by indicators of teacher competences, for example from the National Research Council (Murnane & Raizen, 1988) or the Ständige Konferenz der Kultusminister (Kultusminister-Konferenz, 2005). Similar attempts are made in Germany in the national program "Qualitätsoffensive Lehrerbildung" (BMBF, 2016), a top-down national initiative on teacher quality improvement, planned to run until 2023. This program focuses on all higher education providers and focuses on improvement in teacher education. It is planned to coordinate teacher education more closely and to promote digital technologies. It is intended that competencies for future teachers will be aligned with characteristics of "best practices" of good teaching and will outline criteria of possibilities for action, individual assumptions and different cognitive, but also metacognitive and motivational features. The involvement of professional teachers as partners is not the focus of this planning, but a renewal of the teaching staff, prepared for new requirements, through what is understood as a foreseeable generational change.

The German word "Offensive" means an attack on a boundary and hence no partnership. Correspondingly, this does not involve a boundary-crossing understanding of partnership, but an exercise of power to overcome boundaries. Such a model can hardly be of beneficial value for a generation of innovation in teacher education without the involvement of teachers, as Olson, James and Lang (1999) and others repeatedly observed in various investigations.

Due to the complexity of teaching and the contentious knowledge base of what makes good teachers, these attempts to create competences and their evaluation while maybe necessary are incomplete for curricular innovation. They fail to take into account the complexity, cultural contexts, structural constraints, the necessary discursive spaces for philosophical co-inquiry and challenging authority (Feldges, 2019), the place of theory in teacher education and the differential power relations between policy actors (Timperley et al., 2007). With characteristics of good teachers and measurable criteria of competence, there might be a high probability of achieving indicators of good teaching, but not the ability of good teachers to give feedback and contribute to the development of curricular innovation using higher-order pedagogical dialogue as indicated in the OECD (2013) *Teaching and Learning International Survey* TALIS (2013). In addition, these indicators do not fully represent what people of diverse talents and temperaments do, a waste of potential as Darling-Hammond (1987, p. 45) assumes: "We do not have the luxury of squandering teaching talent by limiting its use on the basis of poor proxies for ability that can never really capture the demands of work and the potential of diverse workers".

Personal and situational factors of professional development in messy classroom narratives, political influences and leadership qualities are far harder to grasp. Moreover, it is difficult to determine teacher quality by the mere involvement of teachers in planning processes. Teachers need to be involved in planning and engage in critical, creative and challenging dialogical processes in order to effect authentic change and to justify their selections. This productive engagement of teachers, e.g. in collaborative teams according to Schwab (1983) and acting as "curriculum makers" according to Clandinin and Connelly (1992), are particularly viewed as promising and worthwhile. However, this close-to-school participation does not play a recognized role in reform policies due to current dominant hegemonic interactions between politicians and a number of career-minded researchers and academics.

Although curriculum research is being replaced by questions of OECD PISA comparability of performance and accountability, its relevance is still remarkable (Connelly, 2013) as discussed in a special edition of the *Journal of Curriculum Studies* (2013) by various contributions. In particular, these contributions point to the actual task of school for the broader welfare of people in a democratic society, with the subordination of disciplinary knowledge in school subjects and lowering of the need for theoretical knowledge amid the growing national interest to increase human capital for competitiveness.

Teacher education and teacher professional learning, which are intended to meet these demands are faced with multiple, contradictory and difficult decisions. They need to take into account a vast array of knowledge, skills, dispositions and

32 Situational factors to be considered

capabilities such as knowledge and knower dispositions for an emancipatory practice of reflexivity for human existential possibility and development, subject matter knowledge, knowledge of the foundational disciplines in the cross-disciplinary field of education, pedagogical knowledge, theoretical knowledge and research, supporting teacher education as a continuum, social needs of students, the needs of parents, the requirements of a vibrant democratic society, market requirements for suitable qualifications as well as standards and the professional knowledge base.

In order to accomplish these contradictory tasks, it is particularly important to consider teachers as policy actors in education and not as third-party technicians that deliver teaching behavior for prescribed learning achievements in predefined school environments. Teachers as actors need substantial flexibility and autonomy in order to cross boundaries of restrictive subject knowledge and prescribed school regulations. This is not easy, because teachers are primarily equipped in Initial Teacher Education with basic disciplinary subject knowledge and skills to attain predefined goals at school. They are thought to be accountable for learning outcomes within these limits and not to develop a professionality for innovative content or school structures for a justified educational context. This professionality has to be developed individually and in a collaborative discourse with additional readiness for discursive communication in multiple communities of co-inquiry. Besides, increased freedom and autonomy for teachers are nowadays subsumed within a neoliberal framing of a discourse of performativity rather than a more existential understanding of professionality (Ball, 2003; Brady, 2019b).

Doctors, lawyers or engineers are recognized as professionals, who make autonomous decisions according to their profession, scientific knowledge and techniques and make the right decisions for their clients. They are largely free from external nonprofessional controls. For example, doctors are subject to personal responsibility and the collective consciousness of the Hippocrates oath for the welfare of their patients. For teachers, this concept of professionalism must be used in an extended framework because the criterion of the correctness of decisions and actions for the well-being of the students is not as clear as for doctors who can point to real consequences in the recovery of ill patients. Identification of student needs is not clear cut as in a medical intervention nor is it the clear result of an action. For a professional teacher, there is no fixed initial state of a student as with a patient with an illness and no associated welfare as with a cure. Activities in education are diffuse and extended and do not come from the deficit position of diagnosis of an illness and instead require a far greater nuance, complexity and understanding than those of a medical practitioner. Unlike a medicalized practice, teachers are concerned with multiple contradictory tasks such as passing on culture and heritage as well as making space for imagination and human potential to be found by the student and making space for something new to burst through, what Biesta (2013) has already described as the "beautiful risk" of education. Teachers educative work practices move between the threshold of personal and public spheres, and in this way, teachers, teacher educators and educational researchers all need to go beyond a reflective practice to much deeper deliberative understandings (Bleakley, 1999; Pillow, 2003).

Nonetheless, professionalism is inherent in the field of education, since adequate personal actions, the use of scientific knowledge, interactions and reassurances have led to successes recognized in the public domain. In the case of recognizable successes of teacher professionalism, there is always personal uncertainty, since feedback is generally not confirmed externally and conformity with official criteria or cultural circumstances is not always clear. Nonetheless, professional successes of action are subject not only to subjective opinions but can be confirmed in cooperative efforts and can refer to features of autonomy inclusive of background. In spite of this rather "wobbly" starting situation, a defense of one's professionalism is important for teachers, in order to justify teachers' selections, to support the "intellectual quality" of such a complex epistemology (Gore et al., 2017) and to keep democratic control of actions in the context of the education system and thereby limit or indeed obviate the need for external regulation (Bourke, Lidstone & Ryan, 2015).

In educational systems, regulation of activities and restrictions of teacher professionalism are to be taken into account by various systems of curricular justification, which are discussed in the following paragraphs. They contain conditions for the realization of innovation through a boundary-crossing partnership between teachers and other policy actors, such as teacher educators and researchers at the university setting (Young et al., 2015).

The changing role of school subjects and educational policy

Subjects are used for the specification of lesson content, learning objectives and teacher education programs. They are structures based on science disciplines or fields of practice, to a lesser degree on controversial issues in the humanities, arranged in documents like "Lehrplan" for "Didaktik" (course of study) in the German-speaking humanistic tradition or "curricula" in the Anglo-American utilitarian context about worth of knowledge (Horlacher, 2018). These documents put a cultural emphasis on disciplinary perspectives and fields of practice in education (Hopmann & Riquarts, 1995), but are coming close to a utilitarian curricular perspective today, when they agree on present concepts of competency structures as in the Swiss "Competency oriented Lehrplan_21" (Horlacher, 2018).

The differences with respect to the role of disciplinary knowledge in schooling become less relevant, if the perspective changes from fixed documents for policy planning to a *process* approach for school improvement, as elaborated here, where a general principle unites different aspects of the use of subjects. This general principle as a process approach for curricular innovation was first claimed by Hameyer, Frey and Haft (1983, translated from German):

There are fixed components for Didaktik and curriculum research (with the meaning of curriculum as a process): selected persons, use of information resources, conditions of work, interaction of participants, the kind of qualification of educational planning, the kind of evaluation, the relation of justice and action and the status of research for innovation in practice. These factors are determinants of Bildung and should be realized as fixed components of Didaktik and curriculum research. As a consequence, Didaktik is not only a theory of lesson content or objectives for Bildung, but also a theory of processes and history. . . . In contrast to the classical theory of didactics in the 60's and before, curriculum theory then deals mainly with processes and factors for the development of Bildung. Topics like *curriculum processes, models for justification and evaluation of innovation procedures* need to be mentioned.

(p. 17)

Referring to this process-oriented concept, Hopmann and Riquarts (1995 p. 20) agree in a comparative study of Didaktik and Curriculum, "from the point of object, no purposeful line can be drawn to distinguish curriculum from didaktik".

The subjects as parts of Didaktik or curriculum are usually defined in line with a disciplinary logic or cultural assumptions and societal expectations for schooling with boundaries between different fields. Atkin and Black (2003) describe the problems of subject matter boundaries for separate courses in science teaching pointing to a lack of a comprehensive curriculum plan for application in daily life, inclusion of social issues or cross-disciplinary themes:

The common pattern at the secondary school level in the United States and the United Kingdom is to teach separate courses in biology, chemistry, physics, and earth sciences, usually with little attempt to underscore connections among these disciplines. Rarer yet are attempts to teach about links between science and other school subjects such as history, economics, or art. In the United Kingdom, the list of prescribed subjects is set out in legislation as if they were both freestanding and self-evident. . . . The formulation of national standards in the United States is also approached subject by subject, with no overall plan. Yet there are other ways. For example, the curriculum documents produced in both Norway and Finland set out a clear, inclusive educational and curriculum philosophy, so that it is possible to discern, for science as for other subjects, their specific contribution to a general conception of the purpose of schooling.

(p. 56)

However, the policy imperative for a deliberative curricular vision in school systems is not readily accepted. Instead technocratic conceptions and techniques of verifiable knowledge transfer as instruction are preferred in the mainstream literature (Biesta & Miedema, 2002). This emphasis on instruction rather than pedagogy may continue despite a new vision of a digital era, changing traditional teaching through digital classroom strategies: Cuban (2001) in his book entitled *Oversold and Underused Computers* in the Classroom – and similarly Gibson (2005) – observed that teachers typically maintained traditional models of teaching and learning rather than altering existing classroom practice through ICT equipment.

In this way, reforms simply become mechanisms for reproduction (Bourdieu & Passeron, 1977), rather than curricular designs for future developments or alternative perspectives. Sometimes they are even behind a cultural development giving rise to political demands for change or scientific statements about deficiencies.

Reforms that intend a change beyond mere reproduction of society need to overcome the static view of Lehrplan or curriculum as predefined policy documents. One alternative is the adoption of curricular *processes* for democratization as claimed by Hameyer (1983a) and specified for change in deliberative democracy, elaborated here. A curricular process allows an open dynamic for improvement crossing boundaries of traditions and political constraints.

In the past, a curricular process approach gained no substantial consideration in educational practice, because traditional subjects, standards or competencies were continuously defined, protected by authorities in governments, federations, churches, teacher or science associations. Only occasionally changes of teaching content were proclaimed, because a lack of relevance for everyday requirements, applicability or demands for future development of society in a global, digital or knowledge-driven world (Sjöberg, 2012; Solomon & Thomas, 1999; Buchberger et al., 2000; Krainer & Kühnelt, 2002; Eijkelhof & Lijnse, 1988; Olson & Lang, 2003). Terhart (2013) reminds us, to consider at least the dynamic of disciplines and their socially constructed boundaries. Hesse, Graoffsky and Hron (1995) and Zell and Malacinski (1994) point to the positive aspects of expansive learning activities beyond narrow boundaries of subjects in cooperative learning, metacognitive planning and narrow scientific views of critical thinking.

There are policy imperatives to dissolve learning in school from disciplinary knowledge frameworks and to replace it with new content or redirect it by crossing boundaries of the traditional subject matter. This is a controversial reform movement and there is concern with the loss of disciplinary and theoretical knowledge bases from the school system and their replacement with a rather "empty discourse of learning" (Biesta, 2012, p. 35), a practice turn toward skills and dispositions, knowing "what works" but without the intellectual toolkit needed to engage with the bigger landscape of "why" and "how". This, it is argued, repositions the teacher as a functionary and a problem-solver and no longer a critical thinker and problem-poser mediating self and practice with the wider world (Lim, 2014).

The separation of subjects is strongly related to a scientific system with long traditions and interests and is structurally anchored in education systems. In the

36 Situational factors to be considered

1960s, the structure of disciplines in universities and their translation into school subjects celebrated many successes in schools. Scholars and philosophers working in universities suggested valid fields of disciplinary knowledge that were translated for use as school subjects. Scientific, technical and mathematical subjects gained huge importance due to the space race for technological and political supremacy in the Cold War and were appraised in education planning. In 1970, the German Education Council (Bildungsrat) defined the topic of the subject structure in the structural plan for the education system and the comprehensive educational plan. This structure was fixed and remains valid for the present time. According to this, educational elements in teacher education should be the foundational disciplines, all based on scientific principles of research. Disciplinary knowledge needed to be complemented by didactics, theoretical knowledge in the social sciences and practical experience. These additions played a decisive role in curriculum revision. This did not only connect subject structures to scientific knowledge but also related curricular innovation to societal topics.

These traditions are reflected not only in common sense opinions about tasks of teaching in schools, but also through teacher education in universities with solid demarcation lines drawn between scientific disciplines and as a consequence between courses for teacher education, syllabi, schoolbooks and teaching materials, school equipment, qualification requirements for professions, identifications, social appreciations and many others. These disciplinary lines cannot simply be suspended with no justified rationale and education debate, since the qualifications of teachers and teacher educators in higher education institutions continue to prevail. However, from the canonical traditions of subject disciplinary knowledge, something new can emerge that leads to new content structures and new spaces for different ways of knowing to be recognized and acknowledged. This is a central component of the content-based innovation of teaching. It is not only about changes in content but also of related structures or systemic changes (Olson, 2002) as presented in the following chapter.

A substantial critical reflection on subject boundaries was initiated by the OECD study SMTE (*Innovation in Science, Mathematics and Technology Education*) with the title "Changing the Subject" (Black & Atkin, 1996; Atkin, 1998; Olson, James & Lang, 1999). In 23 projects from 13 nations, an extension of subject-related knowledge was presented, critically assessed and analyzed in a cross-case study. In the projects described, curriculum materials were developed for topics that took into account social aspects and student interests beyond the disciplinary framework. In this way, teachers were challenged to develop innovative practices beyond subject knowledge. Changes were often developed by research institutes, with teachers as participants but not equal partners. An exception was the German PING project (Lauterbach, 1992) in which a teacher-led collaboration with universities was achieved. As a result, the subject matter in these case studies was connected and helped students to understand how disciplinary knowledge relates to personal and community life and how it corresponds with what practicing scientists really do. The authors experienced this as a sharp contrast to reforms 40 years ago, emphasizing topics of advanced research from university sciences.

According to Olson, James and Lang (1999), the innovation provided an epistemic puzzle for teachers because of the uncertainty and risk of having ready answers as experts in their field, but instead opening their understanding as a tutor for their students. Teachers could no longer rely solely on expert knowledge and routines but were encouraged to discuss the value of science and technology in society and responsible action. In addition, the boundary crossing of their own disciplinary area, such as science and the nature of science required partnership with other teachers, teacher educators and researchers. This participation in a research-led community required an understanding of scientific work with appropriate feedback for the curricular innovation process. Olson, James and Lang (1999) note that, in contrast to previously prescribed innovations – such as the "teacher-proof" projects in the 1960s – this type of partnership action has brought about fundamental changes:

> Reform processes which did not enter into dialogue with teachers were the less successful in consequence. We can see in SMTE vigorous efforts to involve teachers and students in the process of change, in consequence of which the culture of the teacher and of the classroom is better understood.
>
> (p. 74)

In a similar way, different approaches about subject integration tried to overcome the narrow limits of subjects. Integrated curricula emphasize student's needs, topics about a life-world or a social context, that put different parts of subjects together. For this, teachers needed support to change their routines and teacher educators and researchers were challenged in this regard. In addition, questions about the nature and curricular structure of schools were raised.

These approaches such as General Curriculum (Jenkins, 1972), Liberal Education (Donnelly, 2002), Science Technology Society STS (Solomon & Aikenhead, 1994), Humanistic Science Curriculum (Aikenhead, 2003), Interdisciplinary Education (Drake, 1998), or Progressive Education (Terhart, 2000) can provide us with some instructive insights. Jenkins notes that in the past, these approaches were generally unable to exert a substantive lasting influence on educational reforms, and only a few survived.

Questions from real life were often excluded in schools and classrooms, because they were ambiguous, messy and not clearly structured. In the school context with recurrent interests of subjective expectations from a life world, prescribed syllabi and regulations, coverage of the teaching material, attainment of quality criteria or preferences of the teachers there is little or no room for pondering real-world questions (Knab, 1983).

38 Situational factors to be considered

These questions about "real problems" require an open discourse on the legitimacy of certain values in a deliberative system. Mawhinney (2004) assumes that deliberation as a practice could diminish externally imposed rationality and alienation. Deliberation is based on the exchange of arguments and joint meaning-making of public affairs. The concept of deliberation is adopted by Schwab (2013) as an experimental trial in school practice. For teachers, this type of deliberation involves a communicative reflection of practice in the classroom, which has the capability to question un-reflected educational policy regulations.

The current discussions on standards – reduced to core areas of language, mathematics, sciences and technology – have shifted the starting point of planning from disciplinary knowledge to intended outcomes and competences (Marcel, 2013). The material basis for attaining these competencies is, however, as usual, scientific knowledge and methods. According to Green and Luke (2006), a "psychologization of the subject content" has developed in North America through the influence of behaviorist and cognitive learning theories. Doyle and Westbury (1992, p. 137) confirm, that "none of the many forms of traditional American educational sciences have given serious attention to the school subject or teaching content as a starting point for educational considerations". The content of subjects is mainly used as a means to an end for administrative control of achievements of cognitive learning goals and less to follow didactic rules in subjects (Au, 2014).

However, a one-sided orientation to disciplines or their goal-oriented superposition of behavioral skills is questioned by a recent "practice turn" of sociocultural learning that challenges the conceptualization of subjects and behavioral learning objects (Green & Luke, 2006). A valuable basis for this practice turn is seen in the work of Lave and Wenger (1991) about the participation in learning communities and of Vygotsky (1978) about socially constructed dialogic knowledge. As a consequence of this social aspect, learners in a community are encouraged to participate in discourses about what counts as knowledge of a discipline. Scientific disciplines are defined as social endeavors in which participants collaborate and compete by debating what should be accepted as knowledge. In this regard a two-sided change of traditional disciplinary learning is required: a change from prescribed learning content to a community-based mutually agreed content and a change from hard science content to a socially constructed content in scientific communities.

This practice turn is associated with Engeström's activity theory. It emphasizes shared meaning-making as boundary crossing of physical or mental objects in communities in a sociocultural context. This implies negotiation of knowledge and thinking as artifacts and justification of knowledge claims in a deliberative discourse. It is a broad concept that can be adapted to different efforts in curricular innovation such as approaches of integrated subjects.

As Terhart (1999) notes, teachers generally teach subjects without sufficient reference to other subjects unless they are in a cooperative relationship with colleagues. A prerequisite for a critical revision of specialist knowledge is, therefore, cooperation, in which one's expertise is linked to other knowledge or more comprehensively with a curricular concept for integration.

A critical revision of disciplinary knowledge in professional teaching practice is not only dependent on the linking of expertise from different areas, but also has to consider other components of education in addition to knowledge. This includes a new representation of knowledge in suitable value and target systems of education, a practice repertoire for imparting new content and new forms of interaction with students, colleagues, parents, teacher educators or educational researchers. It also requires a place for theoretical knowledge for understanding the bigger system questions and the capability to interrupt the discourse. The task of restructuring specialized knowledge thus requires work at various points in a curricular system: boundary crossing to other subjects and an orientation towards new objects, action repertoires of teaching practice and interactions. For this, hardly any support is offered in a school system. In the academic field, knowledge for pedagogical content is offered separately as isolated knowledge. In school practice, teachers need to be able to combine these knowledge fragments or resort to the occasional elaboration of curriculum materials.

Obviously, teachers are challenged to expand the scope of teaching and to re-evaluate teaching materials. The canonical teaching materials of former times need to be subjected to critical analysis and new views from a sociocultural perspective and the purposes of materials need to be expressed. New questions about materials arise such as the social process of searching for valid knowledge in argumentation and material demonstration, of disciplinary boundaries in education or the kind of boundary crossing in a search for knowledge and dispositions that count. According to Green and Luke (2006), questions about social and material aspects are closely connected in the sciences. The material aspect of "nature's voice" is not independent of social aspects, brought to the table by scientists and their conviction about theories:

> The ways scientists frame, measure, and represent nature to support arguments are directly related to the theoretical notions they are asserting. However, this does not mean that we can make whatever we want of nature's behavior. . . . Making nature's behavior apparent for peers to support arguments about theory is the second aspect of material practice.
>
> (p. 14)

These processes take place on a local level and between different groups in public presentations and publications. They give insights about knowledge claims that are challenges for discursive learning in schools, very different from traditional learning of facts. In short, teachers are confronted with discursive challenges and must relate this to their practices. In this way, teachers become active agents in reconstructing curricula and become curriculum designers, engaging with other teachers and various policy actors in a common approach of deliberation for new strategies of expansive learning.

Change of this nature is not easy and straightforward. There are practical as well as political problems, especially about questions of normative implications concerning goals and values (Youdell, 2011). A political privilege of normative regulation does not lead to any solution if the justification of norms is only proclaimed as a natural right and not valid as an ethical discourse. A discursive justification is necessary to negotiate normative positions as consistent meanings within an appropriate framework (Oser, 1992).

In a partnership approach based on Engeström's (2001) *Cultural-Historical Activity Theory* (CHAT), the possibility exists to realize this discursive justification by mutual understanding in ethical discourse. For this purpose, the extended Curriculum Workshop is offered in Chapter 6. With this method, not only school-based changes are justified in a discourse, but teachers and participants from other communities are involved in a process of understanding in a self-determined process. As a result, all participants can identify themselves with curricular changes they have developed and can represent these changes in a sustainable manner.

Structural conditions of an educational system

Educational systems are usually structured in complex hierarchies depending on power relations, networks and administrative responsibilities. They are polycentric with numerous means of influence, where power is distributed and decisions are negotiated. An educational system cannot be governed from one point by legislation only, authorities have in former times generally regulated through indirect forms of power and high trust modes of evaluation. Nowadays, there is a growing epistemic dominance of supranational policy agencies such as research institutions or commissions from professional groups, OECD, EU or others, all soft-sculpting new approaches to teaching and teacher professional learning through peer pressure and new low trust modes of public accountability (Sellar & Lingard, 2013).

Personal, dialogic relations in a local context (Freire, 1970) with the perspective of equity and transformative or distributed leadership are the exceptions (Shields, 2016), although they promise more productive ways of improvement through collaboration across boundaries. They can consider problems of social inequality and educational disadvantage and can take a critical stance in relation to governance intending to promote transformation and change.

Within these complex structures, substructures exist with boundaries between subsystems and their environments (Krohn & Küppers, 1990). These boundaries are significant for the maintenance of a system, but as well for innovation or inconsistencies of a system and its environment.

For an educational system, this means a tendency to maintain existing structures. For example, subject disciplinary knowledge, discussed in the last section, is defended by communities of subject teachers who question the value of educating young people with skills in what is supposedly a knowledge world. Their pleas often go unheard, written off by more knowledgeable others in education as fear of change, resistance to new approaches and as laziness (Santoro, 2017). In a similar way, educational researchers who engage in communal-oriented work with teachers often cling to their scientific expertise, their power of argumentation and use of reason, facts and logic and reject engaging in the messy narrative of change required in boundary crossing work such as, the celebration and inclusion of multiple forms of knowledge for situated professional judgments (Nixon, 2004).

These constructs of systems and subsystems, separated by boundaries, are interacting in a network of knots and relations, each embedded in an environment or context with specific impacts of sociocultural, political or economic developments or governance. This means internal regulations within the boundaries of a system, such as a classroom, internal agreement, activities and interactions among participants, and in addition, dealing with external impacts from administration, parents, market requirements or other forces.

Applied to Engeström's (2001) theory of CHAT this becomes meaning-making for educational change between subjects of a community about objects in a situation defined by "artifacts", "rules" and "division of labor" in an external environment as an incentive of boundary crossing. As a consequence, "rules" can be implicit as norms, agreements, policies or conventions of a community or explicit as governmental legislation, guidelines or prescription. The same is true for "division of labor", which refers to both the horizontal division of tasks and the hierarchical status relations between actors due to an internal agreement or external impact. In other words, the situation of meaning-making about a problem in education can be more or less due to the development within a system or from outside.

This view from CHAT is more appropriate for a curricular process approach of innovation than models with static structures for restructuring or market regulation (Papagiannis, Easton & Owens, 1992). It takes into account various interacting driving forces for boundary crossing between activity systems. In our case of school-based deliberation, the focus is on schools as systems, with a special concern of teachers, in an educational environment of other systems such as teacher education, administration, research, policy and/or neoliberal market forces.

School-based deliberation is the starting point for meaning-making about curriculum innovation with an agreement about "rules" and "divisions of labor" and from the perspective of a justified curriculum discourse for reform. This starting point is viewed as a knot in a networked structure in an educational system, relating to other subsystems across boundaries such as faculties of teachers within or between schools, institutions of teacher education, educational research or administration and other educational establishments. Such a structure of subsystems and boundaries is the basis of curriculum innovation as boundary crossing in a CHAT model. It can be useful for planning of reforms on a large national scale but works equally well for local changes. As a process approach, it depends on teacher professional development of knowledge and skills but especially of higher-order deliberative partnership.

Neoliberal tendencies nowadays do not generally question structures with fixed boundaries but introduce a centralized strong leadership for output control and competition with public accountability measures for centrally imposed standards. In this regard, professional leadership within schools has come to be understood within narrow limits of predefined standards. Gunter (2001) and others (Biesta, 2013; Nussbaum, 2010) argue that this narrow "scientistic" approach eschews the "critical" and the ongoing need to think for oneself and to question systems and authority rather than merely following technocratic prescriptions, values and norms laid down by policymakers and researchers. For system change, therefore, a process approach for boundary crossing and discursive justification of changes is necessary.

Boundary crossing implies the interaction of multiple professionals with different people as subjects in activity systems, taking responsibility for the procedure of the process and outcomes. Edwards (2017) defines this as relational work in professional interaction and successful leadership. Leadership plays a special role for responding to complex problems, which is not defined by individual decisions or actions, but by interactions between subjects as leaders in different communities and other agents in specific settings for shared meaning-making on the basis of common knowledge, not violating norms of equality and independence. Thus teacher-leaders engage in relational work interpreting, translating and expanding work relationally with others on complex problems, learning how to negotiate culture and handle disequilibrium, create opportunities and support for social and professional learning and engagement in collaboration (Ball, 2003; Kincheloe, 2004).

In a similar way, Spillane (2015) uses the concept of distributed leadership in activity theory for exchange between members of communities with a shared sense of identity and common norms, routines and tools of communication. Spillane did not adopt all aspects of Engeström's CHAT model with interacting activity systems and reduced the components of tools, rules and division of labor to a general expression of a situation (Ho, Chen & Ng, 2015).

In the Curriculum Workshop, described in Chapter 6, this kind of leadership can be identified as "brokerage" in a complex situation with controversial issues and the identification of leaders in school communities as interacting activity systems.

Structural issues can change, on a large scale for society and individual life depending on political influence and pressure. To this end, one needs only to recall the warning of the philosopher and educator Picht (1964) about the danger of an upcoming catastrophe for the development of education, of Dahrendorf (1965) about the civil right for education or of PISA (OECD,

2012) on the social dependency of school performance. They all led to political decisions about the structural planning of teacher requirements, expansion and equality of opportunities. The speculations of these decisions were aimed at labor markets in terms of educational economics, regulating the supply and demand of "human capital" and avoiding social crises.

In addition to these structural changes on a large scale, there are also local changes that are intended to reorient education. These relate, for example, to school types, classes, grades, courses, religious affiliations or gender, students' educational career, interactions within and between schools and related institutions, entitlements to access, powers for decision-making and assignment of resources. All such conditions are regulated in detail and fixed in social structures by modes of governance (Youdell & McGimpsey, 2015). There are hardly free choices, only options from given alternatives.

These structural conditions of a school system consist of a network with a multitude of boundaries, which cannot be exceeded arbitrarily and require authorization or legitimation. Boundary crossing as structural innovation is a system question, which not only requires renewals at a node of an interlaced system but also puts into question the interaction of the entire network. An example of such a change of boundaries in a system is the change of boundaries between school types with the consequence of many other changes such as the sorting and stratification of students, boundaries between subjects or licensing for teaching.

Boundary crossing in conservative structures is a substantial topic for innovation in partnership. It requires an understanding of different communities involved in schooling and higher education institutes. However, this is one of the main points for reluctance to innovation through boundary crossing in the education sector. Due to the often-secured boundaries and isolations by cellular structures (Lortie, 1975) school participants are often not adequately equipped with suitable communicative competences for deliberative meaning-making across multiple communities. Participants in higher education use a form of argumentation that merely serves to preserve the interests of the academy.

In their professional activities, teachers often work on their own and only in exceptional cases are other adults or supervisors present and often only in the role as guests. Consequently, teachers often act autonomously in their teaching activities. Teaching is to a large extent a matter of privacy and takes place independently of exchange with colleagues.

Even in the case of existing motivation for cooperation, the effort for coordination and realization to overcome the cellular boundaries of classrooms is so high that it is relatively rare to achieve substantive higher-order cooperation. However, there has been less attention paid to legitimate concerns of teachers and less attention to the lowering of power relations so that spaces for authentic democratization can become realized in practice (Brady, 2016).

Under the given structural conditions, there is only the possibility of small-scale local boundary crossing in areas within the framework of given structures and networking. These accessible passages need to be found and used for elaboration. They arise repeatedly by shifting boundaries through policy decisions. As an example, the decision on the admission of comprehensive schools in Germany may be taken here. As a result, the boundaries of the tripartite school system were offset to varying degrees. In some schools, open-mindedness allowed students the flexibility to find their way through the school, without constraints or partaking in learning courses. This led to the possibility of a series of innovations to overcome the placement of students, the rigid stipulation of courses or integrated educational offers.

In addition, innovative projects can be used to enter new terrain beyond fixed boundaries of existing structures and prescriptions. Teachers and leaders will be expected to demonstrate the commitment to cooperate and engage in the expansive work involved in these discursive spaces. This can be of great significance if small-scale local partnerships acting as nodes in a network modify related structures or develop distributed intelligence. An extension of these local curricular innovations is also possible through the inclusion of communities in partnership-based processes, albeit limited and with limitations of the innovations.

Systems for control and accountability of schools

Educational content and school structures are a result of historical development in different societies, of public and private interests and investments and respective expectations for social, cultural and economic justifications. Arguments about the purposes of public schooling that speak only to emancipation, individual enlightenment or "Bildung" traditionally fail to bring public investment. There has always been a policy imperative for the kind of worker needed in the labor market and/or the type of citizen needed for a democratic society.

However, what has changed in the last decade, has been the colonization of the field of education by *Human Capital Theory* (Tan, 2014) which reduces the purposes of education to the development of competitive individualism for national economic success. Concerns for human emancipation and the necessary problem-posing necessary for a vibrant democratic society, when mentioned, are all relegated to a subordinated policy intention.

School structures are defined by political or administrative decisions and controlled by committees, legislators, supervisors or financial regulations. These controls are furthermore related to external criteria outside the school system, such as accountability for economic purposes, global competition in international league tables or benefits for private enterprises such as companies, foundations, churches or charter schools (Mooney Simmie & Edling, 2018). While accountability is needed, it has fallen inside the hegemonic closure of "public accountability" rather than "intelligent accountability" for informed judgements commensurate with a complex critical epistemology of teacher education (Gore et al., 2017; Kincheloe, 2004; O'Neill, 2013).

In a contribution about the reform of the school system, Olson (2002) notes that teachers and schools are increasingly subject to the pressure of politics to promote human capital in the face of global competition through TIMSS and PISA:

> Pressures for school reform have intensified as national and multinational test scores become part of the political debates about productivity and the globalisation of educational objectives. . . . Data are used to advance theoretical and political agendas that imply images of teacher professional practice as much they do of student achievement.
>
> (p. 132)

After the PISA country rankings in the year 2000, showing deficits in student performances in countries like Germany or the United States, programs were established to intensify performance measurement and to change subject matter content and methods. In addition, analyses for the political support of reform was offered by members of the OECD PISA working group (Harlen, 1999). An intensive reform movement was triggered to improve student learning.

The situation was different at the level of teacher education and the school. On this level, relevant for the deepest and extended changes, one was partially shocked and skeptical about announced innovations. One of these measures, introduced because of poor international results, was the introduction of standards in many countries. National educational standards define competencies that students should have at the end of a defined grade. Policymakers put more responsibility in the hands of the teaching staff in the schools. However, according to Sellar and Lingard (2013), the epistemic dominance of the OECD is enacted through a clever policy ensemble of soft sculpting and peer pressure that seeks to remake the change to standards, competences and self-evaluation acceptable for teachers (Ball, 2003; Brady, 2016).

Prior to the publication of standards, teaching has usually been oriented on subject matter content as input, related to subjects and grades, describing what is to be taught and when. These syllabi about content were designed to provide the teacher with a secure sequence for cumulative knowledge and secure handling of classroom preparation. The new competences according to the standards give, instead, the desired outcome. Since the introduction of standards, controversial ideas about the question of planning, organization, design and reflection developed. Thus, the planning and conduct of teaching-learning processes are no longer defined exclusively as an individual task of a teacher, but rather as a curricular framework based on new models of cooperation. The literature suggests these new models need to be based on deliberation rather than functionality and instrumentalism.

It is obvious that the OECD PISA project offers a comparative performance measurement of the international market economy, which does not leave the educational sphere untouched. According to the principle of New Public

46 Situational factors to be considered

Management of this market-oriented philosophy, the public sector is to be made efficient by higher quality, transparency, accountability and "value for money" as Sjöberg (2015) states:

> The term New Public Management is used to describe this market driven philosophy which is supposed to make the public sector more efficient. Terms like quality, efficiency, transparency, accountability and – value for money are among the (often positively laden) terms that are used in these policy reforms.
>
> (p. 115)

Nowadays, market thinking does not only apply to areas of commerce and the financial world but to all public services like schools and universities, health care and cultural offers, operated as edu-businesses in competition with private providers. This applies to local areas as well as to a globalized world market with large multinational enterprises and the perceived requirements of a flexible labor market. The precondition for this flexibility and interchangeability are standards with comparable test systems and calls for higher qualifications. The ideological governing forms of this system are bringing schools, teachers and students under the control of competition for individual success in a market-led discourse rather than supporting critical consciousness, solidarity and a deliberative approach of public education (Giroux, 2015).

The impact of the OECD on the development of national education systems worldwide is presented convincingly by Tröhler (2014). During the Cold War, and after the Sputnik shock in 1957, foundations were laid in the western alliance to transform education from a cultural system to a competitive system of science and technology. For the first time in the United States, standards were defined by experts for the unification and comparability of school performances in order to elevate the level of scientific and technical knowledge not only in the United States but in Western countries. Through specific rhetoric of the avoidance of political taboos such as war, iron curtain or democracy, a program of performance measurement was implemented with supposedly neutral terms of standardization and accountability (Tröhler, 2014, p. 1): "The new iron cage of accountability was based on omitting controversial topics".

Initial US testing systems (NAEP) for comparative studies were later applied in the first OECD PISA studies. According to Tröhler, the seemingly nonideological premises are the belief in experts, skepticism towards democracy, trust in numbers and a strategy of competition in the eternal East-West conflict. The implementation of the OECD results occurred on the pretext of neutrality at ministerial level with trained staff. Through this centralization, it was possible to avoid challenging local cultural contexts and to hinder them by local counter-defenses. In the background, however, was the interest of the West to upgrade education with scientific and technical knowledge for the defeat of the East.

Situational factors to be considered   47

The call for improvement of learning is not in itself bad and neither is the call to teachers to use knowledge from research in their practice. However, with the means of centralization, normative values and different ways of knowing become lost e.g. the culture of local communities with the support of educated, helpful, caring persons (Mawhinney, 2004):

> The decline of the local in the conduct of . . . schools is a decline in the promise of a truly democratic regime. . . . Standards of productivity, economics, consumerism, and technology . . . are driving out the ability of the local to develop virtuous citizens, who care about their children and the environment.
>
> (p. 194)

Due to the shift in the political focus in education, Page (2003) points out that democratic and humanization aspects are increasingly lost:

> Education is justified more and more in terms of its serving the national interests, not because it is in the interest of youth, not because intellectual inquiry is important for a democratic society, and certainly not because education is fundamental to what makes us human and is therefore its own justification.
>
> (p. 10)

Similarly, Aikenhead (2003) notes that the goals of the traditional school are narrowly oriented to defined positions and international tests underpin these positions and do not take into account socially significant results. Olson (2004) argues that it is a central task of education to promote people in their development as emancipated citizens.

In recent times, concerns have been voiced about the one-sided orientation of education to national interests within the draft of the newly proposed *Transatlantic Trade Agreement* TTIP. McLaren (2016) shows how the international race to the top views education using the exchange value of a commodity and is currently dominated by what he calls the "behemoth of giant capitalism". The president of the University of Hamburg, Lenzen (2015), pointed out that with TTIP education is finally and fully released as a commodity in a volatile market. Educational firms e.g. the big IT companies such as Microsoft or Dell will be given the right to make educational investments and to challenge government measures in international courts for any attempted profit restrictions. TTIP has been rejected to date by the Trump government on 22.1. 2017. Otherwise, there would be the danger that Europe would lead the US situation of market conquest, as Giroux (2015) describes in an example:

> Many students in Florida sign up for classes and are quite surprised when they find themselves in what are called virtual classrooms. . . . The only

48 Situational factors to be considered

value this approach to pedagogy seems to have is that it means school districts spend less on teachers and buildings. Unfortunately, this approach to teaching is less about learning than about a deep-seated disdain for teachers, students, and critical modes of education. It is also an approach to teaching supported by billionaire reformer Bill Gates, who stands to make millions in profits selling online courses to schools.

(p. 4)

This tendency in politics to promote education as a commodity and not to develop it as a cultural legacy brings market mechanisms into play which focus on performative discourses of a high-performance learning organization, with competitiveness, globalization or measurable comparison. Taylorism found in industrialization in former times reappears. Au (2014) defines this as New Taylorism in the US-American school system. The standardization for checking the products of the education system plays a special role.

In European countries, similar to the United States, efforts to introduce standardization, output-oriented education and quality controls have advanced, but the market economy of this standardization through fierce competition in the production of products and the repression of public interests has not yet reached the extent found in the United States. According to Holland-Letz (2011), educational systems are influenced by the rules of market economy and competition by hidden privatization of state areas from within. Neoliberal forces carry the dogma "private is better than state" into the education system and try to transform schools into enterprises and to control them as such (Mooney Simmie, 2012).

According to Dedering (2015), in the Federal Republic of Germany, foundations with an operational character play a particular role to promote "accountability of education" by New Public Management, making their claim in the area of education policy and teaching. Similarly, in England, privatization by foundations is strongly advanced and private schools are promoted according to the American model of charter schools (Holland-Letz, 2011). Holland-Letz (2011, p. 8) points out, foundations in the education system have extra money by means of considerable tax savings, with which "the rich as householders in their own foundations determine like absolutist princes whom they do good to and to whom they refuse it". In the same way as in the United States through Microsoft, the Bertelsmann Foundation in Germany uses the introduction of digital technology in schools, to evaluate school quality in education, selling software, devices and training. In Ireland, this neoliberal imaginary is found in the new way teacher identity is (re)constructed and how this new subjectivity foregrounds social constructivism, professionalism and knowledge application and debunks theory-practice and theoretical and disciplinary knowledge forms (Skerritt, 2018).

With the creation of a market economy by standardization, however, there is an inherent danger of the loss of humanist culture in European countries. This will be described in the next chapter under the subject of neoliberalism, using as an example the United States.

Au (2011) sees the rationale for the New Taylorism as an attempt to strengthen top-down control of schools more effectively. In order to promote students' performance, control mechanisms such as tests, school reports, rewards and sanctions must be used as instruments for effective behavior change to be applied by principals or teachers. This does not only apply to schools, but also to other organizations, in order to give leadership at the top the opportunity to bring people to the desired behavior according to their aims. The public-school system, like other organizations, can readily be organized in this respect. By means of test results, the output of teachers and students can be checked according to given standards. Standardized tests provide a form of remote control, which can guide the activities in school practice through the management and regulatory powers of the administrations.

According to Au, in today's neoliberal globalization the perspective of Taylorism has changed from earlier industrialization. In contrast to the former organization of factory production, New Taylorism is defined today by an account of the measurable results of neoconservative objectives for the privatization of schools and the use of productive knowledge. In the current context, new Taylorism is a tool of neoconservative policy of neoliberalism, which is discussed in the following paragraphs rather than part of a process of democratizing the education sector.

Neoliberalism: free market criteria for a human capital theory argument

The ideas on neoliberalism, developed by Giroux (2015, 2005) are fundamental for understanding the orientation of an education system under market-based premises and need to be presented here in greater detail in order to illustrate curricular alternatives.

In modern usage, neoliberalism is a market-fundamentalist policy concept (Schmeichel, Sharma & Pittard, 2017) that does not solve social and ecological problems but rather exacerbates them. Giroux sees it as a widespread and dangerous ideology of the twenty-first century, not only in the United States. He fears that this market-led discourse of education will subordinate democracy to the market fundamentalism of neoliberalism and determine a new type of economy and politics in many parts of the world. The principles of neoliberalism originated in the 1980s and started in Thatcher's United Kingdom and Reagan's United States (Harvey, 2007). As an ideological formulation, neoliberalism values individual competition over all modes of cooperation, private services over public services and focuses on competitive individuals as "entrepreneurs" rather than any notion of society or solidarity. It operates within a much-diminished view of the role of the state and this is especially seen in the diminution of education as a public service.

The value of a rich and vibrant democracy, public welfare or the concept of the Social Welfare State have all become subordinated to a maximization of profits or the power and the interests of giant corporations (McLaren, 2016). The new concept of a Social Investment State releases the state from care and social needs of the most vulnerable people in society and from direct moral responsibility to respond to and deal with social injustices. Instead, deregulation, profit maximization and privatization were allowed in favor of the supremacy of unfettered markets (Tan, 2014). Authentic partnership and cooperation, as opposed to functional modes of a partnership, are lost due to the competitive spirit of "Survival of the Fittest".

The policy imperative pointing toward this market fundamentalism in education systems was prepared by the work of the OECD and underpinned by European legislative structures, such as the Lisbon Treaty. In the OECD report, entitled "Teachers Matter", the effectiveness of teachers is underlined for the impact on school learning, greater than students' potential and social background, but mainly highlighted for the great potential of political influence. Formally this finding has received broad mainstream approval. For educational policy in many countries, however, this realization was not understood as a call for improvement promoted by resources and support for teacher education, but by controlling teacher quality through new top-down public modes of accountability (Bourke, Lidstone & Ryan, 2015). This included the development of standards for the competence of teachers and students and their examination by means of measurement instruments and "datafication". According to Tatto (2007), teacher education is seen as an effect, manifesting its success in student achievements:

> In many cases these reports reveal, that innovation in teacher preparation – often induced as a consequence of curriculum reform – have rarely been subjected to rigorous scrutiny in their own right, and that effects of these changes are expected to manifest in pupils' learning rather than more immediately in teachers' knowledge and practice.
>
> (p. 10)

Through such disciplinary regulations, schooling is instrumentalized within the terrors of performativity to reproduce a society proficient in technological and economic competition in the immediate (Ball, 2003; Youdell, 2011). In this way, the cross-disciplinary field of education has been redefined as "learning systems" (European Commission, 2018) and is no longer recognized as an active part of an evolving culture or potential for human emancipation and democratic forms of associated living (Browning, 2018; Nussbaum, 2010).

According to Giroux, this pedagogy of oppression is enforced by rules of neoliberalism and supported by neoconservatives and unwittingly by civil society that appears to see everything in terms of narrow modes of public accountability and a fixation on metrics. This way of schooling is killing

Situational factors to be considered 51

imagination and aesthetics and instead promotes a dull way of memorizing for an intensive labor market, which restricts development to committed action. The aim of a market-led discourse prevents the development of inner convictions and subordinates equality, justice and the search for truth in public schooling as important goals.

According to Giroux and other critical theorists in the field of education, economic policies for the benefit of bankers, corporations and the financial elite lead to massive injustices with regard to the distribution of wealth and income in society and negatively impact people's attitudes towards public schooling and the wholesome needs of young people. As the market economy is transformed by the influence of private corporations, investment in education as a public good is replaced by an overstated emphasis on education as a private good for an edu-business, an investment in economic and human capital (Rönnberg, 2017; Tan, 2014). Uncontrolled market fundamentalism destroys hopes in the social and political infrastructure of a vibrant democracy and the shaping of a new education future for the benefit of all.

The infrastructure of the education system has been strongly attacked since the 1980s especially in the United States (Giroux, 2015) and in England (Ball, 2008), with the advent of market fundamentalism and the growing neglect of the social welfare state, public good and public values (Lynch, 2014). Infrastructure is understood instead to be connected to the material and the financial. Intellectual resources, disciplinary and theoretical knowledge bases necessary for the school to function in ways to ensure teachers' autonomy and situated judgments, to allow trade unions, meaningful curricula and pedagogy to advance young people as creative, critical and committed citizens in an authentic democracy are denied.

An atmosphere of thoughtlessness, indifference and fear that thinking itself is dangerous, will produce a basis for adapting students to a totalitarian regime rather than a vibrant democracy (Arendt, 2001; 2013).

Against the antidemocratic reforms of economic and religious fundamentalists prevailing in the United States, faith in schools as democratic public spheres and as centers of critical thought must be reclaimed and fought for. This demand from Giroux and others means to become part of a larger critical social movement for the defense of public welfare, public goods and democratic values. This, however, is countered by a growing threat of authoritarian structures, or what could be called totalitarianism with elections in a representative system (electoral democracy). Politics itself has been changed to a system of rationalism supported by big data and far less space is given to philosophical argument and value decisions. In this way elections are nowadays a magical defense and justification for an authoritarian project. They serve to depoliticize the public with the aim of defending massive injustices in the distribution of power, wealth and capital accumulation and its devaluation of social, critical action and critical thought. It is an attempt to consolidate power in the hands of a predominantly corporate elite and Harvey (2007) argues that it signals a return to former glory days of social class privilege.

52 Situational factors to be considered

Knowledge is increasingly instrumentalized by the rationalized logic of quantification, standardization and measurement that, as a result, limits the culture of school education and controls efficiency, productivity and consumption behavior on a larger scale and shapes society (Lynch, 2014). As testing, especially in the United States, becomes an end in itself, "teaching-to-the-test", limits the possibility of critical thinking and affordances for teachers to bring about a creative and critical pedagogical commitment. These forms of devalued pedagogy, which receive impulses from a market-oriented corporate culture, regard teachers as low-wage workers and prevent the learning of complex ideas in public schools. With the increasing subordination of public schools to enterprise, teachers are curtailed in their independence and students become less educated (McLaren, 2016).

Giroux fears that teachers will be de-qualified by curtailing their self-reliance and creativity. Teachers are degraded to technicians whose only goal appears to impose annoying instrumental rationality, in which "teaching to test" preparation or a discourse of formative assessment for predetermined learning outcomes becomes the main and only allowable model of teaching and learning. Biesta (2012) calls this reductionism of schooling to "learnification" an "empty discourse of learning" that no longer needs a "teacher" and no longer has a "why". Zeichner (2010) similarly sees the depreciation of teachers as servants for the pursuit of performance rather than acting for the stimulus of authentic learning:

> In many teacher education programs across the country, a clash has been created by current accountability demands between authenticity (doing what one knows in the best interest of learning of one's students) and performativity (doing what one needs to do) to meet accountability demands even when one knows it is not in the best interest of one's students.
>
> (p. 1548)

As a counter-measure to the ethical suppression of teachers' moral agency within neoliberal tendencies, a new understanding of the public-school system as a vibrant democratic institution and the supporting role of teachers in such a project is needed (Zipin & Brennan, 2003). For teaching and teacher education, Zeichner (2010) proposes new and more collaborative and egalitarian forms of interaction and boundary-crossing alliances as hybrid spaces between universities, schools and communities:

> More democratic forms of professionalism in teaching and teacher education must lead to more democratization of knowledge in teacher education programs. . . . There may be a need to develop new hybrid spaces where more egalitarian forms of interaction in teacher education are possible.
>
> (p. 89)

To this end, Giroux proposed the idea of *teachers as intellectuals* who regard education as a moral and political activity, which always requires special interpretation concerning the democratization of knowledge, values, citizenship, forms of understanding and future perspectives. Instead of positioning teachers as disinterested technicians, they need to be positioned as committed intellectuals and cultural workers. Teachers as intellectuals, in this sense, are not just knowledge mediators, but, together with students, are interpreting themselves and their practice reflexively and mediating this with the world while trying to reach a common understanding and evaluation beyond existing knowledge and knower dispositions. This requires creativity, imagination and critical judgment in a constantly changing world.

In other words, teaching is intended to be a guide to enable students to act responsibly and to offer a special understanding of the past, present and future. And even though schools, through their traditions and cultures, often unwittingly reproduce the ideological contours of the existing society, with teachers often acting as functionaries, schools and teachers need to be given the sophisticated toolkit of boundary-crossing partnerships to intellectualize practices and contribute to societal beneficence. Hargreaves (2003) reminds of the danger of teachers acting as the clones and drones of policymakers and politicians' anemic ambitions.

Teachers need to attain the status of a respected professional group in order to play their part in setting the conditions of democratic education for future generations. Teachers clearly need and deserve the respect, autonomy, power and dignity that demand such a task. This requires teachers to be supported in attempts to build the school conditions that provide the knowledge, skills, dispositions and culture needed for students to deal creatively and critically with the past, to question authority, to argue against existing power relationships and to act as active and committed citizens in exchange with local, national and global public sectors.

For an open pedagogy one expects that teachers are not only critical intellectuals, but also need democratic control over the conditions of their own educational work. Teachers need sufficient support and time to prepare lessons and investigations, to cooperate with others and to use valuable resources. School should be a place for reasoning, understanding and critical engagement for all teachers and learners, in which judgments and freedom of action are founded on the democratic imperatives of equality, freedom and justice. To regard public schools as a place of learning for democracy and teachers as critical intellectuals make it possible to understand education as a support and challenge to democracy (Browning, 2018).

Giroux's call for the restoration of the public school system as a democratic body in a society should be considered here in the context of partnership-based schooling, which goes beyond a call for joint action of all parties to the recovery of vibrant democratic ideals for a discourse of humanization and professionalization.

54 Situational factors to be considered

Deliberative partnership means symmetric activity in collaboration for shared meaning-making, founded on an existing school culture of common understandings and historical development, communities of practice (Wenger, 1998), social and communicative skills for consensus formation (Warren et al., 2016), for agreement beyond consensus (Biesta, 2013), or boundary crossing through boundary objects (Engeström, 2001). In doing so, approaches from multiple communities with different cultures and solidarity are required.

Of particular importance could be deliberative partnerships as a platform for teacher professionalization between schools and universities as hybrid space, based on the theoretical framework provided by CHAT. Knowledge-in-practice, reflection-in-practice and instruction, on the one hand, for a practice in dynamic motion at the school setting, and research, theorizing and publishing, on the other hand, cannot be easily combined in an authentic and democratic way and bear testament to the theory-practice contradictions inherent in good teaching and teacher learning. On the other hand, a higher-order understanding of educational practice (Sawyer et al., 2007; Terhart & Klieme, 2006; Steinert et al., 2006; OECD, 2008) and collaborative education with universities (Warren et al., 2016) is necessary and supports schools and teachers moving beyond the converging notion of static singular communities of practice.

In addition, dynamic partnership approaches require justification through public discourse in order to develop their own positions and implement them along the lines of an authentic and vibrant democracy. This justification of curriculum innovation in deliberative partnerships using the CHAT approach as an alternative to contemporary reform is the basis of Chapter 3.

Chapter 3

Deliberative partnership as a new way for reform

In the given situation of mainly prescribed educational content and structures in a neoliberal atmosphere of rigid goals and regulatory controls, school-based reforms with a deliberative start for new topics and alternative structures are an exciting and challenging venture.

School-based change is a contradictory process to the official rhetoric of reform (where the term reform is generally accepted in policy and the literature to mean national public policies) and is guided by different justifications and expectations. A school-based change appreciates the important role of teachers in the context of their school environment. In this book, we are arguing that education change needs proactive engagement and higher-order activities of teachers and other actors in a deliberative process for justification in public space.

Reforms which do not appreciate the role of teachers in the context of their schools must expect difficulties (Fullan & Hargreaves, 1992). They can primarily be achieved by an inner conviction of teachers' commitment, accompanied by additional supports and this implies more than mere training for a type of functional behavior change (Terhart, 1999). Without the additional infrastructure and appropriate intellectual supports, administrative constraints often lead to resistance and can all too readily be misconstrued as a failure of teachers.

But what are the conditions for an adequate role of teachers as active policy players in reform processes, for fulfilling dual roles as problem solvers and at the same time problem posers? Accepting innovative curricular planning as a prerequisite is to involve teachers in collaboration with other institutions, not so much in the reproduction of prescriptions. This involvement can be realized in partnership with discursive deliberation. But it must be clear what is meant by deliberation and how this is realized by higher-order cooperation and knowledge for a justified innovation, different from a narrow-prescribed curriculum.

Planning of curricular innovation through a partnership is a complex process of meaning-making between actors from multiple communities, which requires consideration of necessary conditions and complex epistemic resources for justification. The participation of teachers in a partnership approach allows a *discursive justification* of curriculum planning with a claim of ownership that is different from the legal claim of institutions and their derived rights. A legal claim for external control of change is *politically legitimated* by a representative system of politicians with the support of an administration, experts and legalized groups. Each claim, political or discursive, has its own specific warrants and depends not only on power structures and relations but on quality of arguments and convictions.

Figure 3.1 shows the connections between respective reform processes and different ways of teacher professionalization and curriculum innovation: one of the typical ways is the prescribed regulation of reforms, in which teachers are qualified for change, the other is a notion of school-based partnership activity, in which teachers are involved in the process of change and qualify themselves through an expansive learning process.

An example of prescribed reform was the introduction of "teacher-proof curricula" in the 1960s, which sought to exclude the influence of teachers through detailed specifications of materials and activities. Instead, the Curriculum Workshop (Lang et al., 2007) or constructs from activity theory such as the Boundary Crossing Laboratory (Engeström, 2001) can be considered as school-based partnership processes for teacher ownership and curriculum innovation.

An example of changing the pathway is the prescription of standards and their use for deliberative change in the Australian "Professional Learning Partners Program" (Bloomfield & Nguyen, 2015), described later in Chapter 6. However, the comparison of these pathways is of analytical value to judge the conditions for partnership-based planning.

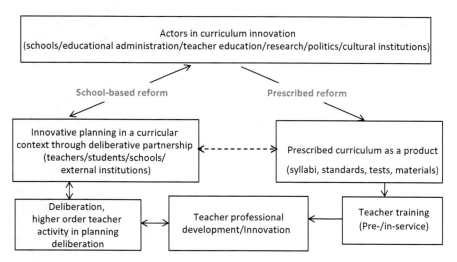

Figure 3.1 Paths of reform processes guided by curriculum innovation and teacher professional development

Deliberative partnership as a new way for reform 57

A *prescribed reform process* with finished products (e.g. syllabi, standards, competency grids, test evaluation, curriculum materials) is elaborated by planning groups, commissions or specialists outside schools, implemented in schools, legitimated by scientific arguments and controlled by tests, examinations or other modes of assessment data collection (e.g. data presented by teachers showing successful outcomes of assessment for each individual learner). The components are often developed independently and later compiled for a coherent curriculum. Teachers are generally introduced to these requirements in pre-service teacher education or in-service education and training courses. Correspondingly support for teacher professional development is primarily technical and is seen in the implementation of a curricular construct and the modes of evaluation. Cooperation in team teaching or supervision is aligned with predetermined goals or standards. Deviating curricular developments involving teachers' creative planning are limited to pilot projects in which teachers can also develop through reflexive work and indirectly influence the design of the curriculum product.

In the past two decades, prescribed reforms of a performative persuasion boomed as a result of comparative international studies (Cochran-Smith et al., 2017), the tyranny of metrics fixation and evidence (Muller, 2018) and the demands of a human capital argument such as found in TIMSS (Baumert et al., 2001) and PISA (OECD, 2010). The main focus was on the scientific, technical, mathematical and language competences of students. Accountable achievements and country rankings are nowadays used as the ultimate criteria for educational decisions of policy, experienced as a kind of shock by unexpected results in many countries. These political decisions were based on the assumption that science and technology are key elements of national competitiveness in a global economy (Harvey, 2018). Proposals are made for cost-effective training in terms of PISA points per dollar (Sjöberg, 2012) or standards in specified subjects, as well as assignments for training purposes.

In many countries, competence-based curricula and standards are developed to increase student performance independently of school context and without teachers' freedom and autonomy for localized professional judgments. In North America, OECD PISA results were received by policymakers – in much the same was the former Sputnik shock in the 1960s, when the Russians appeared to be willing the "space race" and which led to the search for rapid and unprecedented corrections for their own education system – and nowadays these are found by cherry-picking aspects from what appears as other more successful countries, such as, Singapore or Finland (Connelly, 2013; Hargreaves, 2010).

On the other hand, a *school-based reform process* is developed in the context of collaboration between teachers and partners from schools, universities or other educational institutions. The development is guided by requirements of the respective school context, problems or contradictions in a system, built on a tradition or school culture and aligned to new epistemic, social, moral and political requirements. Teachers and partners are involved in a discursive curricular process for mutual understanding and guided by critical reflexive practices.

58 Deliberative partnership as a new way for reform

A prerequisite for this deliberative partnership is an equal right of all and the suspension of rules and roles associated formally with each institutional culture. This requires the willingness of everyone to get to know one another differently using a new form of agreed ethics and discursive tonality, to invent a new messy narrative of change that reflects this new hybrid space. Developing the professionalism of teachers requires multiple epistemic resources, disciplinary knowledge, theoretical knowledge, pedagogical knowledge, personal reflexive knowledge and professional knowledge for competent action in the classroom. In addition, it also requires, in particular, political, communicative and pedagogical capabilities for vibrant collaborative and social processes. This process is not directed at curriculum as a product but is guided through processes of interaction between teachers, student teachers and other persons. The focus of attention is an innovative curriculum in daily use and its realization in practice. This curriculum is justified by discursive rules of common meaning-making in public space and supported by teachers' professionalization and participation.

The special feature of school-based partnership is not only a more intensive involvement of teachers, teacher educators and researchers in the design plan and realization of change, but requires feedback, indicated by double arrows in Figure 3.1. This makes use of the progressive professionalization of teachers and cooperating partners, e.g. teacher educators involved in an expansive learning process. Positive feedback from practice advances the process, directing all eyes on improvements sought for reforms. But this won't do, because reforms are more like experiments, controlled as well by significant negative feedback according to Olson (2002):

> Teachers can and will in the future provide the negative feedback most often ignored . . . Teachers are left out of the power process that leads to the 'roll-out' of policy . . . What teachers can provide are insights into reform initiatives seen as experiments which probe for the way forward.
>
> (p. 133)

The way in which a curriculum innovation is initiated depends on many educational, cultural and political conditions, relational, epistemic and structural resources and the inner commitment and willingness of those involved. In recent times policy planning is understood as a sovereign task, determined and enforced by laws, ordinances, syllabi, standards, prescriptions, budgets, personnel keys or regulations of political decision-makers and administrations. To a limited extent, schools are granted autonomy of decisions but this is tightly restricted by disciplinary regulations imposed by political and statutory decisions. Mooney Simmie, Moles and O'Grady (2019) argue that this model represents a tyranny of metrics and politics and colonization of the field of education by the economy that can only be met with a democratic ethics of care and productive pedagogy for an alternative framework that somehow successfully challenges *Human Capital Theory* as the predominant explanatory framework for contemporary education activities, as a public good rather than a private good for the competitive individual (Tan, 2014).

However, there are always discursive spaces in schools that need to be claimed by teachers for justified decisions in partnerships albeit within an uneven playing field (Apple, 2012). Partnerships involve participation in multiple competent communities. They can be used to support the justifications of decisions taken. At the same time, however, they face many challenges, as the respective culture of each community requires boundary-crossing movements. It presupposes the presence of communicative cultures and the willingness of all participants to engage at this level of dialogical intensity and interdependence. Nevertheless, partnerships beyond the boundaries of individual schools can be considered for innovative action, as they have the capability to generate new insights through discursive deliberation. For teachers, this means a new development of their professionalism beyond competent teaching toward sociocultural deliberation and justification of curricular innovation.

The deliberative practice of curricular innovation

Roth and Lee (2007) illustrate the possibilities and constraints of deliberative practices in two examples. In the first example, Katherina plans to teach about electric circuits in the fifth grade. She recognizes that instructions in the syllabus are inefficient, not motivating for the pupils and hardly understandable by the specialist language. Nevertheless, she feels tied to the requirements as performance checks and timetable limit her scope. She recognizes that learning objectives are achieved but student motivation has been lost. Roth and Lee, therefore, perceive the need to defend practical activities as deliberation in professional life at school, and to promote motivation in the classroom through comprehensive activities within the framework of the proposed *Cultural-Historical Activity Theory*.

In a second example, Roth and Lee show a positive case of deliberative practice on environmental education, a context-dependent approach of two teachers with positive effects on student behavior. As a starting point for teaching with diverse student activities, a newspaper article about a polluted stream in the municipality is used as the resource material. Through a number of activities, the students learn scientific and responsible action in the community in the context of their environment. As a result, their knowledge is not just scientific vocabulary but is shared knowledge in the community. The joint approach of the two teachers is embedded in a discursive process of understanding among themselves and with the pupils, parents, scientists and persons from the wider community.

As demonstrated in the first example, a prescribed curriculum poses the danger of standardized and decontextualized students' learning, preventing an adequate strategy for instruction and incentives for student motivation that depends on the specific context and situation in the classroom. This kind of

60 Deliberative partnership as a new way for reform

curriculum obeys rules of technical rationality (Au, 2014), predefined by means-end argumentations for the acquisition of subject learning and school structure, neglecting social or environmental particularities. This is different in the second example, where various activities for deliberation allow students to develop their interests and apply them in a local environment with social exchange. Embedding learning in such a context does not exclude traditional subject matter learning but integrates isolated parts of disciplinary content in a meaningful and more interesting topic.

Connelly (2013) draws attention to the fact that curricula and teaching methods are now decontextualized within the formal argument that they can be calculated and compared:

> There has been a shift from a debate over subject matter versus life-adjustment curriculum for children to questions of accountability and achievement. Like the focus of the curriculum theorists, educational reformers have, to use Schwab's language, taken flight from the field as they now worry about accountability and achievement.
>
> (p. 362)

A deliberative approach of curricular practice was elaborated in the earlier work of Schwab, which has recently been discussed by various authors (Deng, 2013). These authors examine the relevance and importance of Schwab's reflections on the role of deliberation in an idiosyncratic practice for curriculum theories, policy and development of standards and rationality in the current context.

Deliberative partnership in teacher professional development is an intellectually and morally responsive political practice that requires "the formation of a new public and new means of communication among its constituent members" (Schwab, 1970, p. 36). Deliberation understood as the "arts of the practical" is a complex and arduous task (Schwab, 1970):

> Deliberation is complex and arduous. It treats both ends and means and must treat them as mutually determining one another. It must try to identify, with respect to both, what facts may be relevant. It must try to ascertain the relevant facts in the concrete case . . . it must weigh alternatives . . . and choose, not the right alternative, for there is no such thing, but the best one.
>
> (p. 36)

Deliberation in curriculum theory aims to achieve justified decisions by joint communicating participants in a discourse (Au, 2014; Englund, 2016). Teaching is seen as an intelligent and morally justified political action, the decisions of which are negotiated in public space, taking into account communicative rules with members accepting equal rights for participants. These decisions are, according to Schwab, eclectic for practical purposes and not necessarily academically theorized or empirically stated. The legitimation of eclecticism lies in the complex dynamic situation with many uncertainties, the dependency on a particular context and value decisions. Deliberation, therefore, requires intellectual and moral reasoning power to make appropriate decisions and justified professional judgments in the respective context. It is not a matter of the technical principle of "what works" but a democratic principle of normative, philosophical co-inquiry and political decisions in public space (Biesta, 2013).

Pereira (1992) argues that deliberation is a grounded decision in a practical context:

> To deliberate, in the sense in which Schwab used the term, is to examine, within a specific context, the complex interplay of means and ends in order to choose wisely and responsibly amongst competing goods... The object of curriculum decision is to reach a warranted decision about what to do in a particular context. Although the decision needs to be justified, the grounds for justification are seldom clear at the outset.
>
> (p. 4)

A deliberative discourse about curriculum innovation in school practice is based on deficiencies in a specific teaching context, discussed and justified by a number of stakeholders in a common meaning-making process. Justification is found in a negotiated discourse and put into discussion in the public space (Pinar, 2008):

> In public space . . . various discourses and practices intersect and diverge, reflecting and creating a political location. Political struggle is discursive; it involves different patterns of thought which cannot finally, be separated dualistically.
>
> (p. 309)

In doing so, general theories or formal rules of ethical engagement can only be applied secondarily, taking into account the practical context. In the given context, a decision is often a balancing of cultural or ethical norms or means and purposes. From teachers, the deliberation demands professional arguments and discursive rules of equality and autonomy.

According to the authors Connelly, Westbury, Takayama, Biesta and Künzli (Deng, 2013), Schwab's conception of practice can contribute significantly to the promotion of school-based education. Policy impulses for an eclectic change of practice without "escape from the field" take into account the lived experience of the real-world setting and cultural and social contexts. This context always interrupts attempts at one-sided curricular constructs of political or scientific elites and requires public consultation and meaning-making of partners with equal rights as democratic deliberation (Biesta, 2013). Schwab defines this public dimension as a community of learners from multiple institutions. Similarly, Lave and Wenger (1991) define a community as a closely related group in practice with common resources, common action and understanding of knowledge, who deal with a common task in social co-participation. In systems theory, communities are separate subsystems that have the potential of boundary crossing for innovative developments, taking into account traditions, social and cultural developments, sociopolitical perspectives and environments.

Deliberation is related to a search for solutions within an identified problem of contradictions in a practical context. In her article "Curriculum in and out of Context", Cornbleth (1988) distinguishes a product approach of specialists without context and a context-dependent curriculum approach as a process of moral and social activities. The context explicitly takes into account critical philosophical, social and political questions and evaluations of what is taught, how, why and for whom. This translates into a number of consequences for curriculum innovation: changes are not just a result of technical planning but an understanding in the sociocultural and everyday context: "Curriculum is not a tangible product but the actual, day-to-day interactions of students, teachers, knowledge, and milieu" (p. 89).

Different rationalities for an expansive understanding of knowledge and capabilities from teacher groups and schools as well as from research results and theoretical foundations, teacher education and politics must be combined in a new alchemy in order to cope with and to identify problems of a rapidly changing world. Education reform needs to balance local educational needs and national and international policy requirements (Fullan & Stiegelbauer, 1991; Olson, 2002; Valli et al., 2002). Currently the balance between official (policy and political) discourses and pedagogical (recontextualizing) discourses is strongly distorted by the epistemic dominance of a performativity discourses relayed by constant comparison, such as OECD PISA and TALIS and supported by a global policy impulse to introduce standards for the assessment of predictable performance metrics (Ball, 2017; Biesta, 2012).

A deliberative curricular innovation in partnership requires meaning-making between multiple communities in a sociocultural context. The professional development of teachers in a collaborative environment is of crucial importance. Klieme et al. (2010, p. 23) state: "There is a lot of evidence that the professionalism of the teaching staff is the decisive resource for quality development in education". Hattie (2009) comes to a similar conclusion in his meta-analysis on more than 800 studies on teacher influence. Hargreaves and Fullan (2012, xii) state that:

> There is widespread agreement now that of all the factors inside the school that effect children's learning and achievement, the most important is the teacher – not standards, assessments, resources, or even the school leadership, but the quality of the teacher. Teachers really matter.

However, in this book, we are arguing for caution in an education system of subsystems that currently seeks to set up the professional teacher as a compliant neoliberal subject, a dysfunctional blame game that allows other policy actors assume narrow impersonal roles as judges and evaluators – e.g. educational researchers and state inspectors.

According to Hiebert, Gallimore and Stigler (2002), teachers can be regarded as significant political actors in curriculum innovation, if they go beyond their traditional role as subject matter specialists. For this purpose, their professional knowledge base needs to be expanded by collaboration across boundaries. This involves teachers crossing boundaries between their school and the public space, involving institutions such as universities, research institutes and/or political bodies. This capability to cross boundaries will result in new constellations for deliberation with the possibility of reaching new understandings.

Deliberative practice is a complex relational and epistemic puzzle that needs to be based not only on technical or scientific rationality but take into account other ways of knowing and the opinions and reflexive understandings of the participating partners, the identification of relevant problems, rules, values, prerequisites, practical applications, building trust based on mutuality as opposed to functionality and reductionist feedback (Mooney Simmie, Moles & O'Grady, 2019). Since participants come from multiple communities, meaning-making across boundaries is possible only through the development of a new culture over a longer time period and shared meaning-making across boundaries (Engeström, 2001).

Deliberation about school-based innovation requires discursive rules to enable boundary crossing communication. These rules are concerned with the equality of all participants for an understanding without exercising differential power relations or enforcing majority decisions. The results have a special justification in a deliberative democracy (Mawhinney, 2004).

The model of deliberative democracy seems to be a special case of classification that does not fit usual distinctions of direct or participatory democracy on the one side and liberal or representative democracy on the other (Held, 2006). It is a variant that seeks to justify political decisions in a process that involves free and equal citizens in deliberations. Special features are that the quality of decision-making is at the center of public debate, that political rationality is inseparable from the idea of justification to others and the strengthening of discursive rationality is vital to the search for substantive solutions to collective problems. In case of deliberative curriculum innovation, a model of deliberative democracy does not necessarily intend to substitute an existing political system but searches for deliberative public spaces, such as discussion forums or round tables, that provide for rich, critical, self-reflexive, tolerant and sustained citizen engagement with equal rights for all.

Examples of deliberative spaces are the Curriculum Workshop for innovative planning (Lang, 2007b), the Boundary Crossing Lab (Engeström, 2000), the Professional Learning Partners Program (Bloomfield & Nguyen, 2015) or the Learning Studio (Lambert, 2003). These are all discussed in later chapters.

Higher-order teacher deliberation

Deliberation in the curriculum is a complex, relational and epistemic process between partners for shared meaning-making. It requires deliberative efforts for creative and critical thoughts and solutions that cannot be realized by informal communication about singular problems but needs higher-order knowledge and cooperation with careful preparation and agreement.

OECD TALIS Report (2013) confirms that teachers cooperate for the most part on a lower-order level, using informal discussions or exchange of teaching material. Cooperation with colleagues on a higher epistemic level in a pedagogical discourse is an exception. A similar conclusion is made in the literature by Asay and Orgill (2010), Terhart and Klieme (2006), Sawyer et al. (2007) and Steinert et al. (2006).

Steiner et al. (2006) underline this lack of school-based teacher cooperation with statistical arguments: only 2 percent of teachers relate to each other at a high level in professional learning communities by talking about teaching and making arguments transparent through the use of mutual visits in classrooms using a quorum as a social resource, which integrates organizational, personal and teaching tasks and practices and coordinates action.

In communication among colleagues teaching science subjects, they found few explanatory attempts with adequate justification or profound pedagogical reasoning. Collaboration among colleagues, justification of selections for classroom practices and problem-solving is only found irregularly and informally on the initiative of individual teachers. It appears that higher-order discussion by agreed rules and protocol writing, the formation of curriculum design teams or working groups are the exception rather than the norm.

In general, spontaneous conversations in breaks or on corridors are more usual (Hargreaves, 1994), mostly between teachers at the same school, about individual students, or for preparation of teaching, requests for materials or planning aids. There are rarely "open enough" spaces for "intellectual quality" generated for teacher talk about pedagogy matters, teaching methods, goals, evaluation or spatial settings in classrooms (Gore et al., 2017). However, some teachers have an awareness that intensive and formalized communication can initiate change, reduce uncertainty in decision-making and/or promote a positive school climate. The specialist knowledge base and attitudes of teachers are no longer based on the individual but include a collective understanding of the school as a community system. However, this communal-orientation cannot be realized easily because of school barriers, individual restraint and the historically and culturally rooted power relations with vested interests (e.g. Churches, Corporations) and with higher education institutes (Mooney Simmie & Edling, 2016, 2018). Furthermore, the historic isolation of teachers has been well described by Lortie (1975) and appears to continue today through many forms of contrived collegiality (Hargreaves, 2000). Deliberative boundary crossing offers new possibilities and insights into more imaginative and innovative ways to circumscribe traditional social and power relations between schools and higher education institutions.

Teaching as a deliberation requires more than the realization of planning of subject matter knowledge and methodological strategies for the achievement of assigned goals. In addition, higher-order practical activities in a sociocultural context and boundary crossing discourse need to be taken into account and are not generally taken into consideration in traditional teacher education or policy guidelines.

Murray (2005, 2014) characterizes the knowledge-base of teachers as a first- and second-order knowledge, based on training or deliberative practice. She notes that in teacher education, the focus is on first-order knowledge to impart disciplinary knowledge to students. Teachers' work as a complex sociocultural task is not only an individual activity in the classroom behind closed doors but a collaborative practice with other participants inside and outside the school. Professional learning is a sociocultural process of working in partnership with multiple communities, such as those in the school itself, universities, training institutions, research institutions or communities. Access to and communication with these communities is often difficult as cultural, structural and language boundaries must be overcome. Teacher education needs to focus on the transition from first-order knowledge to second-order knowledge. In this way a valuable connection can be made between the *What* (teaching content), the *How* (educational methods and mode) and *Why* (legitimation) of teaching (Loughran, 2006). Teacher learning is thereby broadened by norms and moral reasoning and philosophical co-inquiry that cannot only be applied but understood as an important inspiration for future practice. Standards for testing of performances and disciplinary regulation need to be replaced by new frameworks for pedagogical practices.

Young et al. (2015) call for teacher education with new triadic partnerships between student teachers, cooperating teachers as mentor teachers and university tutors. Up to now, partnerships between university and schools have usually been shaped in a formal, hierarchical manner according to expert-novice models of apprenticeship and not by second-order knowledge for higher-order cooperation. By involving cooperating teachers as a significant partner in a critical "third space" between institutions, opportunities for new educational processes such as teamwork, Productive Mentoring (Mooney Simmie & Moles, 2011) and professional development are opened outward for reconceptualization and interpretation (Gore et al., 2017; Opfer & Pedder, 2011). Democratic deliberation with the agreement of equal partnership, however, requires dialogue and reflexivity and a dedicated timeline to gain ambitious communication on educational problems, and support for education, in order to build trust and negotiate fairly and openly.

The problems of higher-order deliberation as a prerequisite for partnership innovation in a boundary-crossing discourse, mentioned here, are not readily solved but must be carefully planned in adequate settings such as the Curriculum Workshop, which will be discussed in Chapter 6. In such a setting complex structures for boundary crossing need to be considered, as suggested in

CHAT (Engeström, 2001) with the attempt of multiple communities to get to a justified public procedure of meaning-making about contradictory objects, agreeing on rules, mediating artifacts and division of labor.

Such a complex setting with a careful arrangement of people and agreements on a procedure for a justified outcome and a communication assuming equal rights for all participants and justice is challenging and goes beyond the usual requirements of everyday communication in schools and beyond the everyday logical place of rational argumentation in universities. It needs an intellectually and morally responsive political practice with new requirements for teachers to communicate in public space, as pointed out by Schwab (1970). For this, an especially critical point is the agreement on rules for justification that is not sufficiently elaborated in Engeström's CHAT model.

Such ethical rules of agreement go beyond material rules and conventions or institutional requirements, regulating interactions for meaning-making between subjects, as described by Engeström's (2001) activity theory. More than that, additional rules for communication need to be considered for a public justification of selections, as specified in the Curriculum Workshop. These additional rules are realized in an ethical discourse for justice, fairness, humanitarian values and deliberative democracy.

Chapter 4

Prospects for an innovative curriculum process

In this book, we have viewed curriculum innovation using the framework of school-based deliberation across boundaries in a specific context and public space. However, the existing situation of a tightly fixated system using high control structures of policy enforcement makes it difficult for schools to claim the necessary discursive spaces for teacher autonomy and situated professional judgment to overcome contextual constraints and limitations for reforms by means of an innovative curriculum process. As discussed in the previous chapter, a promising approach is a curricular innovation through discursive partnership with legitimate ethical values of deliberative democracy.

According to Mawhinney (2004) and Habermas (1996), deliberative meaning-making is a prerequisite for a deliberative democracy or, according to Pinar et al. (2008), the political place in public space in which discourses are overlapping. A curricular concept of deliberation, based on Engeström's (2001) system of boundary crossing among multiple communities in activity theory and on discursive justification, is elaborated in Chapters 5 and 6.

Starting points for curricular innovation have been identified in Chapter 2, in particular, problems of prescribed content and reproductive structures of an education system, accompanied by systems of policy management. It was especially pointed out, that disciplinary knowledge dominates classroom lessons with standardization and public accountability measures for comparison of student competencies. Standardization and accountability are instruments to defend prescribed learning with quantifiable measures and to neglect cultural context, individual interests of dedicated students and other complexity.

Due to the cellular structures in schools, teachers and students are generally excluded from collaboration beyond classrooms. In this rather confined environment, boundary crossing in relation to identified dilemmas and contradictions is a concept for an innovative dynamic to interrogate existing problems.

To overcome constraints, there is a need to critically counter the consequences of established structures and learning content and the contemporary neoliberal narrowing of democratic conditions in innovative curricular processes. This may be realized as boundary crossing in an environment of school-based

68 Prospects for an innovative curriculum process

collaboration, context-specific curricular processes and reconstruction of public spaces. These aspects are now explained in more detail.

Collaboration in the context of school practice

The assumption of the curriculum as a *process* places the development of innovation in its course and its conditions in the foreground. This process is viewed as collaboration for the purpose of interrogating problems of teaching and learning and contradictions between teachers, students, institutions, educationally interested persons and others in an open enough system of schooling. Stenhouse (1975, pp. 4–5) defines this curriculum process as "an attempt to communicate the essential principles and features of an educational purpose in such a form that it is open to critical scrutiny and capable of effective translation into practice". This conception is in sharp contrast to the concept of the curriculum as a *product* with the principle of the technical implementation for subject learning according to prefabricated curricula, as suggested by Tyler (1950).

Collaboration in a curriculum process is based on the assumption that teachers' voices are valid in the debate about reforms (Clandinin & Connelly, 1992; Barab & Duffy, 2000). Collaboration means that teachers' actions extend beyond classroom teaching and allow partnership-based curricular design and planning in public space with other colleagues, teacher educators, educational researchers and other persons. In this process, teachers' voices need to be given a stronger weight than usual in order to be adequately heard in the discussion with other actors from science, business and politics. In a democratic discourse collaboration is a basis for an innovative curriculum process, in which teachers develop an agreed understanding with others about questions of educational change and professional development (Schwab, 1983; Conle, 2000).

For the planning of school-based reforms, teachers as professionals become collaborative curriculum designers and developers (Carlgren, 1999). Curriculum design characterizes teachers as policy actors and enactors and not simply as implementers of given curricula.

Sometimes innovative approaches in schools are isolated efforts of individual teachers without sustainability (Hargreaves, 2003). To change this, teachers need to develop a shared understanding to bring coherence into curricular planning by finding a common basis for the selection and justification of all aspects of their practices. There is, at the same time, a moral imperative need to ensure that difference is celebrated and respected as we live in an era where the concept of "shared vision and values" can all too readily be used as a governance tool for hegemonic closure and silence of contrarian views (Watson, 2014). One important way to secure this outward-looking purpose is to ensure that good teaching and teacher education are not fully defined as a problem-solving exercise. As an equally important problem-posing exercise the wider moral, social and political aspects of education are included. In this regard, teachers are not only expected to mediate with the interrogation of themselves and their practices but are in a continual mediation with the wider world. It is this latter aspect that is currently missing from a neoliberal imaginary of schooling.

As a consequence of Schwab's (2013, reprint) warning about the flight from the field of practice, there were various efforts to involve teachers in a collaborative curriculum process. Schwab himself proposed the process of deliberation for curriculum revision. By this, a team of teachers and other persons try to change school practice with active partners accepting equal rights of participants such as specialists from universities, subject specialists and moderators. Schön (1983) also gave teachers a special role in school change with his proposal of the reflexive practitioner. Furthermore, Altrichter, Posch and Somekh (1993) proposed a method of self-reflection in action research, Conle (2000) a narrative method of collaborative storytelling, Clandinin and Connelly (1992) the concept of teacher as a curriculum developer and Carlgren (1999) the concept of teacher as a curriculum designer.

These collaborative approaches for curriculum innovation have led especially in science subjects to partnerships between teachers, teacher educators and researchers from different sciences and educational disciplines.

For science curricula, a wide range of materials have been developed in collaboration of teachers with teacher educators and researchers beyond the respective boundaries of subjects. For example, in the PING project, teaching units with different topics and for all levels of education were developed, evaluated and used in schools with broad support from schools, ministries, teacher education institutions, the IPN (Leibniz Institute for Science and Mathematics Education) and universities (Lauterbach, 1992; Lang, 1997; Riquarts & Hansen, 1998).

Similar projects from 13 countries such as the SMTE from Australia or the Voyage of the Mimi from the United States are presented in the OECD study "Changing the Subject" which integrate natural sciences, mathematics and technological subjects (Black & Atkin, 1996; Olson, James & Lang, 1999). These projects reflect boundary crossing in the sciences in the context of everyday problems or practical issues and discuss implications for reforms and related changes for teacher professional development.

Posch (1993) noted that school-based environmental projects in environmental education put the transmission of knowledge into the background in favor of personal experiences, interdisciplinary learning, research, social interaction and collaboration. These projects created networks and flows for the exchange of experiences and the creation of new structures for teachers' professional development. Some networks included municipal policymakers, industry, families or environmental groups with similar objectives.

For teachers, such approaches are a particular challenge, as they overcome the understanding of their disciplinary training and they are challenged to discuss "real" questions with new categories of understanding (Roth, 2003).

In the discussion of reforms, the practical relevance of teachers' collaboration in schools is hardly disputed. Generally, the term collaboration is used with the meaning of cooperation as practical action or doing things together for job-related

70 Prospects for an innovative curriculum process

purposes in the particular context of a school (Kelchtermans, 2006). Within this context, collaborative action as joint work constitutes important working conditions for teachers and as such, they influence the professional development of teachers. Little (1990) distinguishes this kind of joint work as a prerequisite for change from storytelling and scanning for ideas, aid and assistance or sharing, which contributes a positive collaborative atmosphere of collegiality, friendship and support.

The difficulties of such collaborations have been summarized in the Journal of Pedagogy (Steinert et al., 2006) and an anthology of Huber, Ahlgrimm and Hader-Popp (2012). Several authors of these publications conclude that the intensity of collaboration in schools is rather limited, conceptually contradictory and of negative connotation such as contrived collegiality (Hargreaves, 2000). Despite its high value for curricular processes, results about the impact on student performance, school development or teacher professional development are controversial (Muijs, 2015). It was found that school-based collaboration develops gradually on the basis of a long tradition and culture for collective learning (Postholm, 2016) and differs according to school type or regions. The conditions for such collaboration were found to be complex, diverse and contradictory. Because of this Muijs (2015) suggests settings with mentoring and leadership support for the development of a clear set of shared goals, search for suitable partners, building trust and collective responsibility and staff development.

Various aspects and conditions of collaboration are illustrated in lists such as the one by Huber, Ahlgrimm and Hader-Popp (2012, pp. 354–355). They distinguish institutional, personnel and organizational aspects. This listing albeit incomplete can help to become a starting point for differentiation in a collaborative partnership concept:

Table 4.1 **Central aspects of teacher collaboration in schools after Huber, Ahlgrimm and Hader-Popp (2012, p. 354–355; translated by the authors)**

Institutional aspects:

- Participation of the staff in decisions and design
- Team structures in the teaching staff for the development of the school such as class teams, teams of same grades and study groups
- A "real topic" for cooperation, which is concrete and accepted by all involved, with an interest of a successful mastering
- Perceived usefulness of cooperation
- Common and clear objectives
- Voluntary participation
- Responsibility for the success of the joint work processes and result
- Individual autonomy
- Liability, clear rules for cooperation
- Agreement about time

Institutional aspects:

- Suitable premises
- Open space
- Internal support and external advice
- Transparency of the procedure, supported by the cooperating group, a just division of labor within the cooperating group
- Regular feedback
- A reflective documentation and presentation of results
- Appreciation and recognition
- Relief in another place

Personal aspects:

- Competences for the topic of the cooperation
- Communicative and social competences
- Personal reflection
- Agreement about rules and rituals
- Experiencing satisfaction, effectiveness and efficiency
- Positive attitudes, initiative, courage and creativity
- Interest in exchange and improvement
- Recognition and respect for colleagues
- Self-discipline and reliability

Aspects of the organizational culture:

- Professionality
- A climate of support instead of competition
- Constructive interaction with staff
- A leadership culture of treasure hunting
- Fundamental values and objectives of cooperative work
- A constructive culture of collegiality with respect, recognition, mutual acceptance and tolerance
- A climate of the openness for innovations and the readiness to change

This list is the first overview and is limited to collaboration in schools not beyond their boundaries in a broader context. Thus, the often-mentioned necessity of participation and constructive work of colleagues under the premise of institutional and organizational aspects in larger schools is scarcely feasible for an entire teaching staff and is partially subject to the risk of becoming contrived or enforced by administrative control. There can hardly be an effective interaction, understanding of values or personal appreciation between all teachers across the entire school. A social intensity of this nature is only possible in manageable groups with common understandings. Group structures can take the form of teams that work together in grades, classes, work courses or "real subjects".

72 Prospects for an innovative curriculum process

For partnership-based collaboration, meaning-making across boundaries between and beyond schools in public space needs to be considered. Thus, the listed aspects of cooperation must be structurally differentiated for purposes of networks and be appropriately affiliated to boundary-crossing activities. Under these conditions, the institutional aspects as context, the personal aspects of higher-order cooperation, such as communicative and social competence, or the organizational culture as rules and work conditions, gain a collaborative character.

This listing, albeit atomized helps understand requirements for deliberative discourse, boundary crossing and the strengthening of teachers' voice for curriculum innovation.

Context-specific curricular processes

Curricula are often delivered as ready-to-use products, without considering the particular situational or cultural context of schooling. Documents or plans for the teaching of individual subjects are often published by educational administrations or elaborated by commissions. They can be general or detailed regulations about the teaching of subjects, use of worksheets, syllabi, learning objectives or a selection of textbooks, materials or tests. These planning and policy documents refer to prescribed situations of learning leaving no additional scope for context-specific conditions. The emergence of standardized curricula is assumed as politically neutral, rational and free of value according to scientific criteria. Objectives are assumed to be given and the necessary resources are substantiated by scientific arguments.

These curricula represent technocratic models, which are assumed to be objective without contextual reference. In practice, these are no more than planned intentions, which in the realization of lessons undergo many changes through the educative and pedagogical work of policy enactment, viewed by Ball, Maguire and Braun (2012) as the complex creative and critical work of recontextualization, reconceptualization, interpretation and translation of content, through social processes and knowledge-for, -in and -of practice (Cochran Smith & Lytle, 1999) and through background understandings (e.g. tacit knowledge, Polanyi, 1958; hidden curriculum, Jackson, 1968). The poor success of these curriculum reform projects suggests that they are unrelated to the practical as defined by teachers and schools and by Schwab and others.

As an alternative, generic school-based curriculum innovation can facilitate deliberation as the means of the practical. Deliberative curriculum processes respond to a practical problem that is contextually bounded. Each setting contains actors who have their own preconceptions of what should be taught, political realities that influence the process and personal practical knowledge and discursive positions. Curriculum innovation occurs in a specific site, whether that site is a school, a school department, a school board, a province or a nation.

According to Cornbleth (1990, p. 5), a curriculum refers to the course of classroom teaching: "an ongoing social process comprised of the interactions of students, teachers, knowledge and milieu". Curriculum as a social and context-based process in everyday use is significantly influenced by the respective school context and the interaction between students and teachers. It is not a prefabricated construct but a complex process, taking into account critical philosophical, cultural, social and political questions.

Teaching is not conducted without eclectic theorizing but is substantially a practical act in a specific classroom with individual students. Teachers use the touchstone of research and the literature and draw from theoretical frameworks and readings, but professional decisions about teaching are dependent on practical considerations, values and assumptions from a complex amalgam of past experiences and access to a complex, relational and epistemic puzzle that is "good teaching" (Mooney Simmie, Moles & O'Grady, 2019).

In addition, practical reflections are important in the context of alternatives, the often contradictory needs of students, colleagues and administration, material offers and school conditions, the legal situation and the municipality. Likewise, teaching content is not simply value-neutral, but a selection from culture and as such content encroaches on controversies, history, cultural peculiarities of the respective region and social environment.

This concept of the curriculum in context is not to be confused with subject content in the context, as it was elaborated e.g. in teaching units named *Chemistry in Context* (Gräsel et al., 2005). Here, the focus is on concepts based on relevant questions, applications or learning competences. Contexts, according to this conception, are real-life-world-related questions, within which meaningful contributions of a scientific discipline can be made visible. These are prefabricated curricular products whose context is related to the subject knowledge itself and not the social processes of curriculum development. It would, however, be possible to offer these subjects with already developed application contexts as learning opportunities for interaction in the social context of a curriculum process. In this way, the subject content offered would be tailored to specific conditions of teachers and learners.

According to Aikenhead (1996), the cultural identity of learners as a context plays a special role in successful teaching practice. In particular, this cultural identity is rarely consistent with the culture of natural sciences. Natural science is experienced as a transcultural experience, in which the boundaries of one's own culture and those of the natural sciences must be overcome. Aikenhead refers to four subcultures: 1. *Potential scientists* whose culture in the family is consistent with scientific thinking; 2. *Other children*, whose culture is quite different from scientific thinking; 3. *"I do not know"* learners with significant cultural differences; 4. *Outsiders* who may not have intellectual access to science learning.

Aikenhead proposes that teachers assume the role of a cultural mediator, to pick up learners from their location as tour guides and accompany them in new territories across boundaries. Here the question of context-related curricular

74 Prospects for an innovative curriculum process

innovation comes into play. According to Aikenhead, the possibility of boundary crossing between subcultures by the support of teacher mediators is only one of several possibilities. Cultural peculiarities can be understood as a component of a context, in addition to context dependencies of the teachers, the content and situational milieu (Cornbleth, 1990). Teachers are in a context of social interaction with colleagues, educators, researchers, students or parents, dealing with educational content in a context of cultural, epistemological, moral or other background and with school situations in structural, political, economic or life-world environments.

In order to cross boundaries in collaborative partnership, teachers can refer to *Cultural-Historical Activity Theory* to find an understanding with other communities, to negotiate contents as boundary objects or to recreate school situations by communicating with other teachers outside schools. Since the respective context is not an arbitrary construction but developed from a local tradition, this tradition cannot be neglected in an innovation. In particular, Olson (2002) points to the importance of traditions in school-related reforms involving teachers:

> These professional practices entail questions about human values, beliefs and moral considerations − questions about tradition. Teachers need to be able to bring such issues to the policy table in the context of systemic reform not so much to join in the 'roll out' as to offer feedback.
>
> (p. 133)

Traditions are a basis of knowledge, experiences, values and attitudes, on which new things can be built through deliberation, reflection and collaboration. They should not be removed as obstacles to progress but should be used positively for development.

Restoration of the public in curriculum innovation

With OECD PISA studies, standards for knowledge and skills for life in a globalized society were propagated on a grand scale (Klieme et al., 2010). These standards, independent of the cultural context of the schools, were designed to give learners access to conceptual and abstract knowledge and its application, based on disciplinary knowledge (Young, 2007).

This system, elaborated by experts of the OECD PISA commission in agreement with political institutions, was not without critique, because of their limited approach of learning and decision in public space. As an alternative task, a sociocultural approach was proposed with the aim of enabling learners as democratic citizens to deal critically with life and work in their society (Aronowitz & Giroux, 1991). This latter aim cannot be prescribed by experts or political decisions but must be negotiated and justified in a context in public space. Accordingly, innovation in education as a public matter of discourse has to be reconceptualized as a democratic process between teachers, learners, politicians and other partners, responsible for education.

Justification of curriculum in a public space can be realized in a deliberative setting for shared meaning-making with actors from schools, teacher education, academia, politics and daily life. Deliberative discourse is guided by normative agreements and reasoning between partners with equal rights. A normative agreement is justified in a process guided by ethical rules in social interaction. The basis for such a public discourse would be a model of deliberative democracy (Mawhinney, 2004; Habermas, 1990, 1996; Held, 2006), in which participants from multiple communities strive for agreed understandings while respecting discursive rules of the agreement.

Habermas (1990, 1996) argues for a communicative model of deliberative democracy, where decisions of a political system are to be tied to public opinions of civil society and a democratic procedure for justification. Habermas (1990) outlines a theory of the public as a communication space in which citizens meet under the conditions of an ideal speech situation with the possibility of equality and symmetry in order to formulate claims which can be criticized. He assumes that deliberation puts the quality of decision-making at the center of public debate, that justification becomes a part of political reasoning in public space and that affordances for the messy narrative of change between such diverse policy actors are vital to the search for substantive solutions.

Held (2006) discusses various options of deliberative democracy ranging from local fora for special issues to radical systems of participatory democracy. He regards deliberation in democracy "as a transformative mode of reasoning which can be drawn upon in diverse settings, from micro-fora and neighborhood associations to national parliaments and transnational settings" (p. 252). This deliberative variant of democracy seeks to justify decisions of free citizens but does not clarify its status as a new innovative model of democracy or as an addendum or a modification of representative democracy.

Held (2006) points to the importance of public culture for the development of reflective deliberative procedures. In educational systems, deliberative settings may have a double function, namely as an institutional subsystem to enrich or transform a democratic system and, in addition, to introduce learners as citizens into higher-order reflective deliberation for democratic participation. Respectively these two functions need first, an understanding of the discursive justification for decisions and second, reflective social reasoning from the point of view of others' or a reflection of one's own immediate reflexive positioning in critical relation to those of others.

The conditions of ethics for responsible communicative action are found in Kant's philosophy of practical reason. However, Kant's arguments refer to the moral attitude of the *individual* and not to discourse ethics of multiple communities, where every person offers points of view for common understanding. Habermas (1974, 1981) took this step towards discourse ethics in a social context. In order to communicate freely, an equal distribution of chances for the

76 Prospects for an innovative curriculum process

utterance of speech acts must be given to all parties involved. Conditions must be clear and agreed upon by all discourse partners and should not be violated during a communicative process. In doing so, ideal presuppositions for an equitable communicative exercise and an unrestricted public are made as "conditions of possibilities".

This ideal presupposition of communication is implicit in each speech act if we are concerned about truth, the ethical and logical correctness of meaning-making in society. An ideal speech act is defined as communication with equal chances and symmetry of dialogue for all participants, equal chances of reflection and quality about arguments, no exertion of power and no "fake news". It is a reflective process for meaning-making in a discourse of multiple communities and not a technique with rules, moral norms, means-ends relations or instrumental programs. This presupposition is part of democratic justification in public discourse. It is different from a strategic communication of instrumental rationality using the power of authorities, markets, neoliberal regulations, jurisdictions or post-truth reasoning.

Mawhinney (2004) argues that communication in a deliberative democracy of an immediate face-to-face community with local school-based interactions and personal relationships in communities is limited through local restriction and networking. For the legitimacy of higher-order education reform of a country or a whole state, supra-regional participation and interaction of additional communities would be necessary with increased difficulties of boundary crossing than found in local communities with a historically grown communication culture. However, it can be assumed, that local and transregional communities are able to link with voter feedback or deliberative polls and promote deliberative shared meaning-making through networking with electronic platforms in a policy process (Castell, 2000). To what extent this public space can be justified, however, remains open, since social media networking may involve problems of manipulation, control over websites and violation of privacy as a boundary crossing of a negative nature.

Communication in public space as an ethical discourse for justification is a basic requirement for deliberative democracy that implies dilemmas and constraints for meaning-making and understanding in a specific situation. Even if we assume the acceptance of the "conditions of possibilities" for an ideal speech act with equality and symmetry for all participants there are still differences of culture or language skills in different communities that obstruct substantial meaning-making beyond boundaries. Aronowitz and Giroux (1991) remind us about language barriers and cultural trenches to be overcome in the attempt to communicate with various communities. A particular example is the problem encountered in communication between teachers and university researchers with different language use, different relations to research literature and different interests. Teachers from disciplines such as natural sciences or languages are also developing in demarcated communities with their own values, language styles, working methods and traditions (Aikenhead, 2003). Specific rules are needed to overcome boundaries, recognition of equality and pedagogy for recognition of difference: "Educational theory has to begin with a language that links schooling to democratic public life, that defines teachers as engaged intellectuals and border crossers, and develops forms of pedagogy that incorporates forms of difference and plurality" (p. 187).

The principle of equality between usually asymmetric educational institutions (schools, universities and state agencies) with differential power relations and an uneven playing field of vested interests (Apple, 2012), is not without power and political issues. With or without the expertise of sophisticated brokerage and even expert-knowledge or goodwill to agree on common rules, it is not always possible to guarantee that boundary-crossing partnerships will not become the site of symbolic violence. In this regard, there is a moral imperative on all policy actors partaking in this boundary-crossing deliberation to fully reveal their reflexive positioning and their vested interest, thus revealing the "hidden hand of the powerful" in such interactions (Bourdieu, 1991).

Processes to deal with boundaries between multiple communities are described by *Cultural-Historical Activity Theory* (Engeström, 1999, 2001). This approach relates to a complex dynamic between communities in given situations.

Boundaries between different communities of teachers in schools or between teachers, students, teacher educators and universities can be productive. For this, open questions between partners, wise experimentation with possibilities, reflection on prerequisites and hidden assumptions and close networking are necessary. By overcoming boundaries and opening a public space, new cultural forms of dialogue and new modes of knowledge of action are generated (Akkerman & Bakker, 2011; Cochran-Smith & Lytle, 1999).

Through conditions of communication, an understanding is linked with social legitimation in public space. A discourse is only legitimated if ethical rules for pragmatic communication are respected. Here, communication is not only a matter of talking together, but communication acts as a political text (Pinar et al., 2008) with normative implications for the development of a society. From a philosophical standpoint, normative positions are not absolute truths or ontological values but arise from discursive ethics in social systems (Jank & Meyer, 1991; Habermas, 1981). As noted by Richmon (2003):

> The debate surrounding ethics and particularly professional ethics, continues. Yet more recently, notions of professional reflection have offered an alternative approach to addressing this debate (Schön, 1990). A process-oriented focus on values contemplation seems to be gaining momentum. And in some ways provides a far more promising direction for the future, than calls for the objectification of values through rational, arbitrary criteria.
>
> (p. 44)

Such a discursive process provides an approach to curricular planning in which teachers meet with partners from other institutions and agree on rules of procedural ethics (Löwisch, 2000).

The Curriculum Workshop is one such setting enabling a public discourse between equal partners for educational planning with ethical justification (Lang, 2007b), and this will be presented in detail in Chapter 6. It involves curricular planning in cooperation with teachers, teacher educators, researchers and other education protagonists with the aim to select and justify an innovative curriculum document for educational practice.

Chapter 5

A framework for partnership-based curricular innovation

Partnership as productive collaboration

A partnership approach for curricular innovation of school practice requires a cross-institutional infrastructure to link experiences and epistemic resources from multiple communities of practice. For example, institutional links are often defined between schools, universities and higher education institutions. The boundaries between institutions are relatively rigid in terms of space, knowledge, values and culture, and this can often provide invisible forms of restriction on a partnership-based collaboration for curricular innovation.

Lillejord and Borte (2016) note, that efforts to improve partnerships in teacher education are not always understood. They refer to Zeichner (2010) who argues that the paradigm of high-school teacher education while regarded as an authoritative source needs to change in favor of a non-hierarchical interplay involving boundary crossing between academic, practical and municipal expertise. Zeichner suggests the metaphor of "third space" for collaboration between schools and university, a new place of a third player in which partners can communicate, avoiding or at least deliberately lowering hierarchical positions. This proposal corresponds to a partnership approach, based on Engeström's (2001) CHAT model with multiple communities or the Curriculum Workshop and is explained in detail in Chapter 6.

Lillejord and Borte compiled a mapping of results on school-based partnerships and found that this area is hardly ever explored and shows few productive approaches of partnership. In most of the 25 significant studies from a total set of 97 references, there were tensions and contradictions in collaboration between student teachers, experienced teachers, mentors and supervisors due to conflicts of loyalty, differing understandings and expectations, differences in differential power relations or authority claims. As a result, knowledge, values and experience from multiple communities does not readily combine for expansive learning.

For a productive partnership, they propose a model of partnership in which the learning of students is at the center of so-called boundary brokers, actors who have first-hand experiential knowledge of both activity systems and have

80 A framework for partnership-based innovation

the capabilities to play a mediating role. Wenger (1998) describes the task of a boundary broker as complex processes of translation, alignment, coordination, mediation, support for joint action and negotiation:

> The job of brokering is complex. It involves processes of translation, co-ordination and alignment between perspectives. It requires enough legitimacy to influence the development of a practice, mobilize attention and address conflicting interests. It also requires the ability to link practices by facilitating transactions between them, and to cause learning by introducing into a practice element of another. Toward this end, brokering provides a participative connection – not because reification is not involved, but because what brokers press into service to connect practices is their experience of multi-membership and the possibilities for negotiation inherent in participation.
>
> (p. 109)

This model of partnership takes contradictions and dilemmas into account and requires the building of open and trusting relationships that can develop with common goals over an extended period of time. These aspects of common goals and trusting relationships in partnership for school-improvement were confirmed in an empirical study by Muijs (2015). In addition, they found that partnership in schools is dependent on mutual benefits and a procedure of developmental phases. However, successive partnerships need intensive interventions focused on teaching, learning and leadership.

To this end, projects are of special interest, where partnership structures can be developed and results of cooperation and professionalization achieved. *Professional Development Schools* (PDS) in the United States connect schools with universities (Pepper et al., 2016).

Traditions as long-term agreements and relationships can be of central importance for a collaborative partnership in curriculum innovation (Olson, 2002). While they are rooted in culturally regulated daily activities, they offer continuity for teacher learning and professional knowledge. In policy and educational research, they are often interpreted as teachers' unwillingness to change (Carlgren, 1999). These traditions, however, should be understood as part of collective wisdom that is not negligible due to its stability (Tyack & Cuban 1995). The question here is how these traditions are tackled and how they influence the design.

In any case, these are not individual solutions, but constructions through which partnerships can reach an agreement through mutual understandings and inclusive of tensions or contradictions. Lillejord and Borte (2016) point at problems where differences between partners on the basis of loyalty conflicts, differing paradigms, principles, purposes and expectations, differences in power or authority need to be processed in new relationships. In this regard, tensions

A framework for partnership-based innovation 81

and contradictions in teaching practices are taken as a point of departure and as a useful starting point for co-inquiry and change as boundary crossing.

Partnership as a collaboration of multiple communities with conditions of long-term relationships, traditions, leadership, mutual agreement or boundary crossing on the one side and tensions through social conflicts and power or contradictions can best be subsumed under *Cultural-Historical Activity Theory* (CHAT, Engeström, 2001). It is the intention here to adapt the systematic view of CHAT to conceptualize deliberative partnership as a platform for curriculum innovation and teacher professionalization. CHAT offers a broad concept for social and cultural relationships to be developed, prospects of contradictions and social interactions as boundary crossing, related to communities, rules, tools and division of labor.

A curricular perspective of networked collaboration in multiple communities extends the focus of a reflexive system for designing communities. Collaboration encompasses personal and social media, exchanges in networks, for teacher-centered and student-centered learning. The possibilities of linking in a network are manifold: interactions between teachers and learners, institutional relations between school administration and universities, integration of content between subject areas, topics and outside-school areas, multicultural relations between different countries and cultures.

The orientation of such linkages is open and allows reflective references in discourses and developments of innovative practice. Innovation and changes in this collaborative curriculum design depend on partners in the activity system engaging mutually in discursive spaces and being willing to undergo change and not simply a narrow view of teachers' change process.

Such collaborative networks can be face-to-face or virtual. Laferriére (2018) presents the extraordinary chances of virtual networks of an enduring school-university partnership about active learning as boundary crossing, using Engeström's CHAT model for analysis. She used papers written for conferences over a period of 20 years for active learning and exchange in a network using VitualU or Knowledge Forum as interactive ICT platforms. Central to the work in the collaborative partnership were contradictions at different levels of the CHAT model: contradictions within the same component, between components, between an established activity system and between the new and neighboring activity systems. These contradictions were analyzed for each component of the CHAT model: partners' roles, rules and tools in different communities of the university and schools. As a result, she found, that the collaborative platform supported active learning and initiated innovation through boundary crossing in classrooms, but technology seemed to add to, rather than diminish complexity. This might lead to the conclusion that ICT is making things complicated, but in a digital age, it is necessary to include virtual communication. This can be part of a blended learning platform, where face-to-face interaction is understood as the key deliberative component and where an online teacher learning platform is an additional aid used to supplement this boundary-crossing deliberation. Other more expedient views of teacher learning signal the possibility of replacement of intensive relational modes of face-to-face interaction, found in boundary crossing work, with remote online teacher learning in MOOCs for a new managerial view of teacher learning and development (Livingston, 2018).

Networking in teaching and teacher education enables the development of key qualifications of networked and interdisciplinary thinking, interactive learning, cooperative work and responsive action. Interaction and social networking in multiple activity systems require new communicative and epistemic supports, resources and structures.

In multiple activity systems, partners make joint decisions in an atmosphere of professional autonomy and a decentralized discourse about meaning-making with boundary objects. This allows a common position as it is sufficiently plastic to take into account the needs and limitations of participants. But in discourse the question remains about what needs and limitations exist and how teachers and experts with different backgrounds can come to a new understanding and move beyond simplistic modes of agreement or worse again some form of conformity and groupthink (Strike, 1994):

> In public discourse the attempt must be made to construct an overlapping consensus such that it can be agreed upon by people with diverse and incommensurable outlooks without posing unresolvable issue of conscience for them. The question to be answered is: "What can we agree on, given ample time for debate, that allows us to meet in the commons and that does not require us to abandon those background convictions on which we differ?"
>
> (p. 5)

Strike talks about aspects of restructuring what is really important in education, which must be discussed in a public forum. The participants in such a forum come together with different values which need to be brought to the discourse. Joint decisions by participants of different communities are to be expected, brought to a final outcome by discursive leadership. This process needs to be critically examined lest it becomes merely an exercise in "cruel optimism" as mentioned in recent work of Cochran-Smith et al. (2017).

Depending on the theoretical approaches taken to the partnerships reported in this book, it was found that teachers, teacher educators and researchers could try planning for changes in school practice, or act as reflexive practitioners, through self-reflection, collaborative storytelling or as curriculum designers. What is common to these approaches is that in a deliberative process a common understanding is reached in a public forum of real problems and issues. For this, various skills, rules, settings and value orientations are required, such as respectful interaction and communicative competence, avoiding hierarchies, access to knowledge or recognition of discursive ethics and responsibility.

Traditionally, at universities, research and teaching are conducted separately from school practice. Teacher educators and researchers in higher education usually demonstrate their status as experts in rational argumentation, in using and generating knowledge claims in the international peer-reviewed literature. Values and passions from the real-life world of schools are often expected to remain separate from "objective" sciences and publications. This is particularly the case in relation to post-positivistic research and is less so in relation to interpretivist, poststructuralist and feminist research for emancipatory teaching and research (Creswell, 2003; McLaren, 2016; Giroux, 2015). Post-positivistic researcher values for evidence-based clinical practice are in sharp contradiction to the rules of deliberative collaboration discussed in the previous paragraphs and difficult to combine with the practice of subjective care and practical deliberation in the classroom and school. Such an effort at a deliberative discourse, such as, between the practical philosophical reasoning of high-school teachers in a practice setting and argumentation with evidence conducted by specialist academic personnel engaged in logical rationality will inevitably and invariably always result in a win: lose situation and the ethical suppression of the moral agency of teachers' voices (Zipin & Brennan, 2003).

It is, therefore, necessary to create prerequisites for collective reflexive understandings through collaboration in higher education institutions, in the same way as for schools (Mooney Simmie & Moles, 2011; Young et al., 2015). Approaches such as the Community-Engaged Scholars (Warren et al., 2016; UMASS, 2014) and the Cross-Professional Collaboration may be useful in this regard (Schenke et al., 2016).

In the analysis of the Cross-Professional Collaboration of the University of Amsterdam, it was found that employees from schools, colleges and advisory bodies in the course of boundary crossing collaboration, proposed by Engeström (2001), were able to familiarize themselves with the other communities: teachers developed approaches for research in the school sector or made decisions on change based on research results; researchers were increasingly concerned with the complexity of practice and focused their decisions on wider issues. However, this mutual understanding was partially subject to a one-sided influence, depending on the assignment of tasks to schools, universities or both. Through the planned establishment of a publicly financed institution, the collaboration between school and university could achieve a better balance of partnership interests.

The *Community-Engaged Scholars* program in the United States refers to university education for doctoral students. It promotes collaboration with schools, families and communities. The work with partners from schools and communities is done jointly in contrast to the traditional exclusion of committed practitioners.

The program identifies four areas for community-engaged scholars:

1   To articulate personal values and stories about themselves: through personal stories and values, a relationship with others should be established and the work evaluated and interpreted accordingly.

84 A framework for partnership-based innovation

2 Establish horizontal collaborative relationships: research should not be undertaken on, but with other communities under the same conditions and mutual respect.
3 To relate the researcher's personality to different groups: the diversity of the communities involved should serve as a basis for different aspects and standpoints as far as possible.
4 Identify as a community-engaged scholar: by identifying with persons of different backgrounds, gender, income, health or appearance, there is a better possibility of personal intervention for social change.

Hierarchies in higher education can hardly be avoided because of the system of certification, promotion and responsibility for research. Nevertheless, the opportunity is seen through boundary-crossing partnership projects to promote a new willingness to compromise and lower differential power relations and to develop a higher level of risk tolerance and a new generation of community-oriented persons for teacher professional development.

In *Cultural-Historical Activity Theory* (Engeström, 2001), boundary crossing as shared meaning-making about boundary objects allows for a common understanding in practice when dealing flexibly with differing opinions or reduced consensus. It is the special function of a boundary object as a flexible concept with a common identity at different standpoints that allows collaborative partnership for a common understanding. Of particular importance are demands for an agreement on rules in a discourse without power claims, autonomy, decentralization and distributed leadership as described in various models of activity theory and in the Curriculum Workshop.

These demands are not always fully realized in practice but are supported by Habermas' (1996) notion of an ideal speech situation, with the claim of the "conditions of the possibility", assuming free action without dominance. However, as Bourdieu, Giroux, McLaren and other critical theorists remind us, good intentions, while necessary, are not sufficient to assure no ethical suppression or colonization by the contemporary unquestioned official language of teaching and teacher learning as evidence-based learner-centered practices.

The processes of meaning-making get increasingly difficult in multiple activity systems with several standpoints from different communities. It requires discursive collaboration with shared understandings of content, values and agreed rules for communication and possibility to discuss beyond agreement, as will now be described in the following section.

Curriculum innovation as a deliberative partnership in multiple communities

As described in Chapter 3, Murray and Male (2005) and Murray (2014) distinguish teachers' practices on the basis of first and second-order knowledge. First-order knowledge is carried out as transmission according to given content

A framework for partnership-based innovation **85**

and rules. Second-order knowledge is based on well-founded communication with discursive rules, a complex undertaking that involves teachers in a collaborative approach of boundary crossing for curriculum innovation.

Boundary crossing in a system is a concept for describing system boundaries and their challenge to work on contradictions. These can be overcome as problems in professional practice in teaching through transformations in an expansive learning process (Engeström, 2000) or through collaboration in a curricular process (Roth & Lee, 2007).

Here the main focus of boundary crossing in partnership is on several communities in networked activity systems trying to get to a common agreement about boundary objects in public space (Engeström, 2001; Akkermann & Bakker, 2011; Bloomfield & Nguyen, 2015). Within this space of activity systems, understandings of components in each activity system and their interacting dynamic can arise as a productive partnership.

Engeström (2000) describes this process of boundary crossing as a transformation in an expansive learning process as follows:

> Activity systems are in constant movement and internally contradictory. Their systemic contradictions, manifested in disturbances and mundane innovations, offer possibilities for expansive developmental transformations. Such transformations proceed through stepwise cycles of expansive learning which begin with actions of questioning the existing standard practice, then proceed to actions of analyzing its contradictions and behaviour a vision for its zone of proximal development, then to actions of examining and implementing the model in practice. New forms of work organization increasingly require negotiated 'knotworking' across boundaries.
>
> (p. 960)

A triggering moment of expansive learning is a conflict or contradiction on different levels, initiating a process of transformation of common practice. Engeström (1987) distinguishes four types of contradictions on different levels in activity systems:

1   Primary inconsistencies *within a component* of an activity system (subject, object, rules, mediating artifacts, communities and division of labor);
2   Secondary contradictions *between components* of a central activity system;
3   Tertiary contradictions between objects of different *neighboring central activity systems*;
4   Quaternary contradictions *between other arbitrary components* of different neighboring central atypical systems.

If we refer to curriculum innovation in education with cooperating teachers and university teachers, for example, activity theory offers an approach for the analysis of deliberative boundary crossing between different activity systems through tensions and contradictions. For this purpose, Xing, Wadholm and Goggins (2014) offer an example with a problem about the effect of different working methods on the outcome of learning strategies. University teachers carry out a study to investigate teaching practice, and teachers review their practices and gain a systematic understanding. In a discourse, university lecturers and teachers can define and construct a common object as a germ cell. One goal could be to improve classroom management by developing different methods for various learning strategies and appropriate communication. During the communication about a common object, the lecturers can introduce artifacts such as a lecture.

Curriculum innovation is a process of shared meaning-making through a collaborative partnership between systems (e.g. school and university) about the purposes or objects of importance and an agreement about a common boundary object. In terms of this model, Bloomfield and Nguyen (2015) specify different system levels of contradictions for the outcome of a boundary object as a collaboratively constructed Object 3 in Figure 5.1. It is a physical, practical or conceptual entity that implies shared meaning-making and significance across the interacting systems.

Referring to Bloomfield and Nguyen (2015), a starting point of this partnership between the sketched systems of school and university may be collaborative pre-service teacher education. At a university, student teachers with high-quality requirements are prepared as "critical reflective practitioners" (object 1) and in schools "teachers with classroom-ready competence" are expected (object 2). In collaborative partnership these two different expectations require considerations for agreements about secondary contradictions

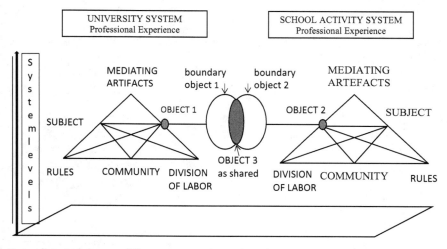

Figure 5.1 Activity on different system levels based on a partnership between school and university

within each system and about tertiary contradictions between the two systems: within the system of "school" pre-service teachers are not directly dependent on a singular object of competencies, because they agree on different perspectives presented by other communities like experienced teachers from different departments as colleagues, mentors, the principal or parents. Within the system of "university", they are not restricted to a specific qualification of a "critical reflective practitioner", because communities in other disciplines or research centers have a modified view. These contradictions need to be specified and discussed for an agreement and be put forward for discourse about tertiary contradictions between the two systems.

A central tertiary contradiction can be expected about the aspect of learning content as a pedagogical or disciplinary subject. In the system "school" the pedagogical subject for student development in life is not necessarily identical with the subject defined by disciplines at the university. But here a quaternary contradiction comes into play between "school" and "university" on the one side and educational policy as a third system. A political system with another perspective of subject learning may define standards for economy, international competition or social flexibility. This will have some influence on the other views of education in schools or universities.

In this case expectations and purposes are not identical at universities and schools and are always modified by changes in public policy, but there are overlapping conceptions (Object 3 as boundary object). The identification of these overlapping boundary objects can form the basis for co-inquiry and offer some solutions to overcome contradictions.

An adjustment requires compromises or innovations of the subsystems to overcome problems. In this regard, there is a need to clarify existing processes of communication taking place in each activity system with different interrelationships of components. Different rules, communities, instruments and division of labor play a role. These can make it challenging to reach agreement on the education of young teachers in Initial Teacher Education. To overcome this, a partnership for boundary crossing is required, a jointly organized setting with facilitating conditions and participants with higher-order communicative competencies.

In the example of boundary crossing between schools and universities in preservice teacher education Bloomfield and Nguyen use a setting similar to the Boundary Crossing Laboratory of Engeström (2001), called "Professional Learning Partners Program". This and other settings like the Learning Studio or Curriculum Workshop are described in the next section.

The related activity systems indicate symmetric relations between various components. The effects of tensions or inconsistencies between or within these components on curricular innovations are specified by Postholm (2015):

> Tensions and contradictions as foundations for change and contradictions within and between factors in the activity system and between activity systems are the foundation for development and change. . . . Change and development

are thus accentuated by continuous transitions and transformations within and between the factors in the activity system and between activity systems.

(p. 46)

This kind of deliberative partnership in multiple communities offers a complex system with the central elements of CHAT as a powerful explanatory framework for this work: a cultural-historical approach for a new epistemology in educational thinking, contradictions as starting points for curriculum innovation and professional learning – with different components within and between activity systems for a systematic analysis of innovative processes. These aspects become a foundation for the search and development of deliberative partnership platforms in curriculum innovation and teacher professionalization in the following chapter.

Chapter 6

Models for innovative planning based on partnership

As discussed so far, a deliberative partnership requires mutual, high trust and discursive collaboration in public space, and this is provided by Engeström's framework of *Cultural-Historical Activity Theory* (CHAT) for boundary crossing and justification. This is a sophisticated demand where all elements need to be taken into account in an interrelated system. If the kind of partnership, the process of boundary crossing or the prerequisites for justification are not adequate, the partnership will not satisfy moral standards of decent human life and deliberative democracy, differing from a neoliberal approach of controlled, measurable quality assurance and publicly accountable relationships (Bloomfield & Nguyen, 2015). In Chapters 6 and 7 we will present some models to analyze their claim in this respect.

First, we interrogate models based on CHAT, developed by the working group around Engeström in Helsinki. These are the Boundary Crossing Laboratory (Engeström, 2001) and the Learning Studio (Lambert, 2003) for the practical planning of change in schools, businesses and medical facilities. The basis for these models is the joint communication of participants from different communities about objects that contain problems for an upcoming solution. On this basis, according to specified rules, negotiation of a problem with certain divisions of labor and mediating artifacts in the sense of CHAT (see Figure 5.1) is conducted in a setting of a round table.

These models are invariably complex. In the examples presented about the working groups, successful changes result from contradictions and contrarian views from different communities. However, the round table settings of these groups are not well defined for higher-order discourses about change. Therefore, more specific models need to be found.

Next, the Curriculum Workshop is presented as a pragmatic approach with specific organizational and discursive rules, related to CHAT for the special situation in the planning of curricular innovation through deliberation. These rules take into account that teachers may have little or no experience with discursive deliberation on pedagogical issues (Sawyer & Rimms-Kaufman, 2007; Terhart & Klieme, 2006; Steinert et al., 2006; OECD, 2008) and at this point, the Curriculum Workshop provides special support. This is to ensure that curricular innovation is not only documented in planning but that this innovation has discursive legitimacy in public spaces and thus becomes politically significant.

The Curriculum Workshop puts an emphasis on justification procedures but does not go into details for elements of CHAT and boundary crossing, the basis of Engeström's model above. As a consequence, the Curriculum Workshop became a boundary crossing system that was applied and critically analyzed in the CROSSNET project. With this extended model, we combined the structural elements of the CHAT and a procedure of curricular justification.

The models have their own significance, but a greater degree of effectiveness in curricular planning may well be achieved through a stronger transfer of elements from the models.

Boundary Crossing Laboratory and Learning Studio as activity systems

The Boundary Crossing Laboratory (Engeström, 2001) and Learning Studio (Lambert, 2003) are applications for business, hospitals or schools that have emerged from Engeström's work on activity theory.

The *Boundary Crossing Laboratory* is, according to Engeström, a setting for the modification of complex organizations such as medical facilities or schools. Originally, it has been introduced for the treatment of patients with multiple disease symptoms requiring a practical collaboration of several specialists beyond the limitations of individual departments.

Usually, these patients are treated in a hospital according to traditional rules by a physician. The division of labor provides for a doctor designing an individual plan of treatment and, if necessary, to transfer the patient to another doctor, but not to seek practical cooperation in accordance with a joint plan of treatment.

In the Boundary Crossing Laboratory, physicians come together with various specializations, nursing staff and other employees to discuss the patient's case. In these meetings, contradictory positions are negotiated in various discussion sessions and recorded in a treatment plan. The joint activities question existing standards of treatment and look for new solutions in so-called expansive action cycles and enable new learning experiences.

The Boundary Crossing Laboratory was used as a conceptual basis for the development of the "Professional Learning Partners Program" at the University of Sidney (Bloomfield & Nguyen, 2015). It is a program that aims to develop a partnership between school and university through the provision of a structured workshop as dialogic spaces about professional teaching standards. This workshop uses the elements of CHAT for boundary crossing between the two-activity systems school and university. It provides the opportunity of expansive learning through presentations from teachers and academics in an atmosphere of mutual understanding, openness and trust through the negotiation of priorities, hierarchies, resource constraints, role attributions or institutional imperatives.

Boundary crossing tools were defined as professional standards documents. Objects from schools and university were negotiated with an agreement of a boundary object as "sustaining quality teacher learning". In this program, CHAT is acknowledged as a useful way to enhance the quality of university and school partnership practices, where actors cross their organizational and conceptual boundaries in a common identity of purpose. It is an attempt to realize a productive partnership in negotiation between practical require- ments of schools and top-down political requirements about standards against the background of a "performative" neoliberal policy imaginary.

The official system of standards was an object for boundary crossing to overcome contradictions between CHAT subsystems, but was transformed into a boundary object of shared meaning-making in the project (Bloomfield & Nguyen, 2015):

> The Professional Teaching Standards for the Graduate Teacher as a fra- mework and practice has emerged as a key *boundary object,* to be critically interrogated and reflected against mentoring practices. As a *boundary object* the Standards have sufficient common identity of purpose to link the work of schools and universities.
>
> (p. 39)

The Boundary Crossing Laboratory and its adaptation by Bloomfield and Nguyen (2015) is a more technical application of CHAT, neglecting curri- cular demands of specific teacher professionality, localized autonomy and justification of selections. There are no instruments used to verify the agreement on contradictory positions about standards in ethical or rational terms, as in the Curriculum Workshop. This may be a result of Engeström's original medical application. In the medical arena, the acknowledgment of professionality is different from the educational area as explained in Chapter 2. The criterion of the correctness of decisions and actions for the well- being of students is not as clear as for doctors who can point to tangible consequences in the recovery of ill patients. Therefore, normative aspects of decisions in messy narratives play a far bigger role in education and need to be taken into account.

The *Learning Studio* (Lambert, 2003) is a partnership-oriented approach with boundary crossing participation of different communities. As an example, participants in an initial teacher education program are students, teachers, social workers, nurses, a teacher educator and a headmaster. As an object, a student teacher is presenting a project, which is discussed by all participants taking into account discursive rules.

Lambert defines the discussion in the *Learning Studio* as part of an object- oriented activity. The object is a task or a problem that the participants in the

92 Models for innovative planning based on partnership

discussion are dealing or working with and that is developing and changing. It is challenging a search for a common understanding of it and the construction of a shared object as boundary crossing. Object-oriented activities are mediated by cultural artifacts. These include tools and signs, such as external implements and internal representations as mental models. With the help of these tools, people can obtain knowledge from the object of activity, interpret and evaluate the state of the object and modify the object so that a purposeful result can emerge.

For a *Learning Studio* at a primary school, Engeström, Engeström and Kärkkäinen (1995) give the following example. In this example, two teams are discussing course selection at their school:

Teachers with five participants each formed teams A and B. The aim of both teams was to plan and execute a curriculum design in cooperation. A group of teacher educators and researchers accompanied the two teams for a period of about two months. During this time, Team B planned and implemented a new curriculum unit with the aim of getting to know the community. The course of the problem began with the initial search for an agreement and continued in a phase of planning up to the implementation of unity in the classrooms.

Two teachers in team A collaborated closely over several years. At the beginning of the school year, they presented their model of curriculum design to the team. Team B spent their two first meetings exchanging ideas for interesting themes for collaborative curriculum units, not settling for a specific model.

The next meeting was conducted jointly with the two teams. Team A wanted to present their model to team B. Team B was not willing to emulate team A, but was open to an exchange of ideas. In the discussion, the division of students into groups becomes the trigger issue.

Team A's model was based on elective courses given to selected students during each of the six periods of the school year. These elective courses were taught in small groups, with 10 students in a group. Together with their parents, students had to select one of two alternative courses offered to them. Teacher B5 questioned the rationale of the model. For her, it offered forced alternatives, not a genuine choice:

TEACHER B3: So then you divide your students, you divide them into groups of appropriate size . . . ?

TEACHER A1: We give them two alternatives. You, two alternatives, which can be for instance video and soccer. They are together because both have the objective of strengthening social skills. And now they got a slip which says that we have selected for your child this and this course, and for some of them, there is video or soccer from which . . .

TEACHER A5: Fill the selection slip.

TEACHER B5: So, they select at home one or the other.

TEACHER A4: Then they select one or the other.

TEACHER B5: But what is the ideology here, since the basic idea would be to increase the child's right to choose according to his or her own interests and to progress in the direction of his or her own choice? And now, however. it's like "take this or this, but this is what you'll take".

TEACHER A2: Our point of departure is . . .

TEACHER A1: These elective courses are not for that purpose.

TEACHER A2: Yes, they are not electives in that sense. They must be in line with the objectives. They have to serve the objectives, and the selection must be based on the teacher's familiarity with the student and on educational work done together with the parents.

Team B held its own meeting after the joint meeting of the two teams. In their meeting, members of team B settled for a model of their own, based on groups of 30 students, with each group having a different theme within a shared curriculum unit. The discussion within team B continued the argument with team A's ideas, although team A was no longer present.

The discussion led to a formulation of team B's own model as distinct from that of team A. This model meant that students could choose between five different themes within the shared broader topic of a curriculum unit. Members of team B called their model "theme teaching".

Here, the joint meeting of the two teams was a form of boundary crossing. It did not lead to a shared concept or action plan between the teams. To the contrary, it sharpened the differences between the views held by the two teams. Teacher B5 used the argumentative question ("But what is the ideology here?") as a key discursive tool to sharpen the differences. This argumentative sharpening of differences was decisively important for the evolution of team B's model. Team B formulated and subsequently successfully implemented in practice the theoretical notion of "theme teaching".

Argumentation is not helpful if there is no common point of reference. In this case, the question of dividing the students into groups functioned as a temporary boundary object or "springboard" that enabled the teams to compare and contrast views. It led to the formulation of questions of ideology and choice, of individualism and social interaction and then back to the pros and cons of working in groups of 30. Such stepwise movement between theoretical principles and practical strategies seems typical in creative concept formation.

The Curriculum Workshop as a process approach for deliberative curricular innovation

The Curriculum Workshop was originally developed in the European project EUDIST (Lang et al., 2007), conducted from 2002 to 2005 for curricular

94   Models for innovative planning based on partnership

innovation in teacher education. It presupposes a school-based curriculum development in which teachers are the central person in collaboration with other persons in education, such as colleagues, teacher educators, researchers or education policymakers. The Curriculum Workshop is a pragmatic approach to school practice with concrete action for curriculum innovation through discursive understandings. This justifies school-based research and at the same time serves as a theoretical advancement within the framework of boundary crossing.

The pragmatic model of discursive communication in the Curriculum Workshop is based on the work of Frey (1975). A uniform theory, e.g. activity theory of Engeström (2001) did not initially exist and was only conceived as part of the later development of EUDIST and realized through the introduction of the Boundary Crossing concept in the CROSSNET project. The Curriculum Workshop was initially a method of school-based collaboration in a partnership that, in various case studies, explored the possibilities of curricular innovation under national reform conditions. In case studies, the demonstration of successful Curriculum Workshops for the planning of curricular innovations could be provided in part by intensive preparations and multiple supports. This was particularly noteworthy because, in school practices, the limits of cooperation had to be presupposed by lack of autonomy in schools through political prescriptions such as educational standards and the lack of advanced communicative competence for a discursive pedagogy and discursive ethics. Here, the embedding of national case studies into long-term background projects with personal experiences from the past can provide a statement for successful cooperation but must also take into account necessary compromises on political guidelines and cooperation.

For the conduct of a Curriculum Workshop, it is easy to see that the constraints for school change are strongly influenced by policy guidelines concerning teaching content and teaching methods. In the period from 1970 to 1990, these constraints were modified in a positive climate of educational reform in many European countries, where new educational concepts were presented, and teachers' groups were committed to new school curricula. Thus, Kayser and Fuhr (1983) characterize the work of many teachers and politically engaged actors in German education as an attempt to change teaching in the classroom by means of jointly developed concepts and to influence didactic requirements in preservice teacher education and in-service teacher education by means of productive feedback from practice.

However, this approach to teacher professional development came to a standstill because of a lack of evidence in a new era of metrics, yielding the policy context of the study reported in EUDIST (Olson, 2007):

This focus on the teachers' role came to an end in the 1990 with the institutionalization and standardization of curriculum by the educational bureaucracy in Germany. Today the professional role of teachers is partially reaffirmed but controlled by standards as more school autonomy is sought. This is the context of the EUDIST project at least in Germany but to varying degrees in the other countries as well.

(p. 193)

Experienced teachers were influenced by this period of autonomy, and they continued to do so after 2000, although teacher autonomy has since been severely restricted by international constant comparative methods and the introduction of educational standards and hierarchical modes of public accountability, in preference to democratic and intelligent accountability worthy of an advanced professional practice (Cochran-Smith et al., 2017; Harvey, 2018). Although some autonomy in the development of school curricula for the achievement of given learning competencies was given, the output itself could not be questioned and was regularly assessed and compared. It was during this phase of the increasingly restricted autonomy, that the EUDIST project was undertaken and subsequent projects CROSSNET and GIMMS. In this regard discourse on curricular innovation, related explicitly or covertly to ways of realizing learner-centered teaching standards, was not in all cases related to teacher localized autonomous decision-making for emancipatory purposes.

Thus, in the Rhineland-Palatinate case study, a procedure for the development of competence matrices was developed, for which teachers could choose suitable topics to reach predefined competence requirements efficiently. This is illustrated by a sketch of professional work in teacher education (Figures 6.1 and 6.2; Bayer, 2009). In a Curriculum Workshop, standard-related competencies of students are first presented, in which topics are used as a vehicle for the attainment of competences for knowledge and action.

Curriculum Workshop

General question:

What kind of competencies should students develop, working for the topic "Energy supply for the future"?

1. Educational standards need to be structured and specified.
2. Competencies need to be defined for the topic (competency matrix).
3. Lesson planning.

Figure 6.1 Sketch of a work plan for the development of a competency matrix of given standards (translated).

96 Models for innovative planning based on partnership

For example, electricity in the house can be developed using the cell of the competence of everyday knowledge for the gain of knowledge in Figure 6.2. This topic ranges from electrical hazards to handling electrical equipment. It must include an educational standard.

A competency grid is created by filling the empty cells with appropriate topics or contents in the following table (Figure 6.2).

Activity Knowledge	gain knowledge	apply knowledge	communicate knowledge	judge (with) knowledge
everyday knowledge	e.g. electricity in the house			
practical-technical knowledge				
disciplinary knowledge				
meta-knowledge				

Figure 6.2 Competence grid for the completion of topics (translated).

The appearance of free choice enabled teachers to concentrate on creativity in the design of lessons, but at the same time reduced their practices to the realization of measurable competencies. There was a risk in a tight focus on the achievement of good test results, the so-called "teaching to the test" or what has become teaching to reproducible learning outcomes. Complex topics for open discussions with moral considerations, weakly structured topics of students from their life-world, personal or cultural themes with a strong emphasis on values fall out of this narrow framework, since they cannot be oriented to measurable results.

In the Curriculum Workshop, these limits of political prescriptions were not questioned in order to develop curricular innovations beyond these prescriptions, but the work was done in accordance with prescriptions in favor of teachers' practices. The possibility of crossing boundaries of political objectives was made possible by the theoretical introduction of boundary crossing, defining communities and objects as components of activity theory for discussion as alternatives in curriculum innovation.

Consideration of multiple communities as discourse partners opens the school system for new points of view, which can open unforeseen aspects. The component of objects differs from the narrow view of the measurable competencies by emphasizing problems with different solutions and aims at opening performances in learning.

In addition to the limitation of the Curriculum Workshop by policy guidelines, the lack of communicative competence in pedagogical matters in school-based discourses, as stated in Chapter 3, has to be considered. These restrictions may have objective reasons for spatial separation or lack of time, subjective reasons, habits or cultural and structural reasons for the group structures in schools. Terhart and Klieme (2006) offer the following explanatory pattern:

> The present analysis on the causes of wholly lacking or only slight cooperation in the teacher's profession is characterized by a relatively hermetic picture: The organizational conditions favor a targeted cooperation side by side, the central workplace classroom is characterized by an internal process structure, giving teaching a kind of private character, in the face of which every making public must appear as a threat to the person, and because of personal dispositions, many teachers are only too happy to accept these basic conditions, confirm individualism of teachers and seek protection in a formal principle of collegiality, which essentially consists of an unspoken, if you leave me alone, I will leave you alone. Rejecting this offer is considered to be non-collegial, is negatively sanctioned, and can lead to exclusion processes.
>
> (p. 165, translated)

In addition to the limitation of teachers engaging in higher-order cooperation, it must be taken into account that the described topic refers to imminent preservation of school quality and not to more advanced perspectives of school changes, as originally intended in the Curriculum Workshop. As a consequence, therefore, it must be taken into account for higher-order cooperation in the Curriculum Workshop that the prerequisites for this need to be created.

Participants need to agree on common discursive rules and processes, develop corresponding professionalism or form learning communities as outlined by Bonsen and Rolff (2006). In schools, these competencies developed only for individual teachers involved in the projects. There was no existing infrastructure or epistemic or social support in schools and no respective border-crossing teacher education as a prerequisite for broader reform.

The results of a Curriculum Workshop can be used to find a codified curriculum in teacher education, but only in accordance with policy guidelines. However, for a wider change on the basis of discursive democracy, the support for schools for discursive deliberation in learning communities is lacking in order to achieve a common understanding of change.

Corresponding problems can be identified in the case studies in Schleswig-Holstein for integrated science education (PING) and Rhineland-Palatinate for the development of competence grids. In these cases, the results have been accepted by the ministries to be used for teacher education, syllabi and work in conferences. Teachers' advanced communicative skills for discursive meaning-making about reforms were not encouraged.

The Curriculum Workshop was developed from theories of curriculum deliberation of Schwab (1970), communicative competence of Habermas (1974) and discursive justification of Frey (1983). Additional considerations were given by Schön (1983) on reflexive practice, Oser (1992) on procedural ethics, Engeström (1999) on activity theory and Toulmin (1958) on the structured argumentation of problem-solving. These theories have a common basis with regard to collaboration for the purpose of innovation and change in practice settings. They emphasize partnership-based reflection, evaluation and justification for practical improvements, professional learning and development of teachers and teaching.

The importance of teachers as equal partners in school-based curriculum construction was taken up by a pragmatic approach of Frey's Curriculum Conference and carried out and evaluated in various projects (Frei et al., 1984). In this work, the basic idea was elaborated, that rules of argumentation and legitimation supported the planning process of the Curriculum Conference and generated an innovative effect. A criticism, however, remained that the Curriculum Conference was carried out in academic institutions and not at schools and as a consequence did not sufficiently align with the original idea of deliberation of Schwab and boundary crossing of different communities e.g. schools and universities. Therefore, a school-based Curriculum Workshop was developed and extended with the concept of partnered boundary crossing according to Engestöm (Lang et al., 2007).

A central element of the Curriculum Workshop is a deliberative discourse of participants in order to develop and justify curricular innovation. A deliberation consists of formal reasoning and normative discourses. In this way, results are justified logically, scientifically and technically as well as according to cultural values and norms.

A normative argumentation deals with values, beliefs, morals or ethics of practice. In the school sector, this is described by Jackson, Boostrom and Hansen's (1998) book "The Moral Life of Schools". This illustrates the ubiquitous presence of the more or less obvious normative influence in pedagogical practice. A philosophical background is a conceptual distinction between Kant's practical reason and pure reason.

A normative argument is determined by discursive ethics, in which all participants accept normative rules and accept themselves as equal partners with equal rights. It is not just about making decisions for successful work or by rules. Discursive decisions require constant effort, responsible interaction with others and consideration of consequences.

This type of deliberative discourse troubles some authors who perceive that a discourse is an unusual procedure, dominated by a tight academic language of argumentation in preference to the everyday language of the school community, shows whose (abstract) knowledge ultimately matters and becomes a governance tool to "silence" and bring hegemonic closure to other ways of knowing, including elision of experiential knowledge-in-practice and knowledge-of- practice (Watson, 2014). In this way, any effort at generating "open enough" spaces for teachers, teacher educators and researchers to discourse across boundaries fails to achieve epistemic justice and can readily do symbolic harm (Nixon, 2004).

This problem of epistemic justice is a genuine problem worth further troubling. It is especially compounded if the university or higher education personnel are unwilling or unable to move into the critically reflexive "hybrid" spaces opened in a boundary-crossing deliberative partnership that understands good teaching not as a perfect technology (where one "partner" has all the answers and predetermined outcomes and the other "partner" is laden with deficiencies), but rather understands the inextricable links between different ways of knowing for a wholesome view of humanity and discursive ethics, for good teaching and teacher learning to encompass the beautiful risk of education (Biesta, 2013).

In this way, if the deliberative discourse between teacher educators and researchers from the academy of teacher education and school-based teachers is based on a logical rationalism of evidence-based practices then it will be no match for the messy narrative, nuanced, philosophical reasoning, critical literacy and complexity required for what Schwab understood as an idiosyncratic practice (Schwab, 1970).

If this happens, the partnership will collapse into the epistemic dominance of the scientific community and will not become a deliberative partnership of equals (Galvin & Mooney Simmie, 2017). Instead, rather than an emancipatory boundary-crossing discourse the teacher will at some point experience loss of moral agency and ethical suppression of voice (Santoro, 2017; Zipin & Brennan, 2003).

In the European teacher education projects reported here this problem was sought to be overcome by a method of "elementary speech act", seeking to talk, listen and respond in everyday language about the multiple paradoxes, dilemmas, tensions and living contradictions involved in the clash between policy, practice, theory, experience and research and to proactively broker the messy narrative of change in deliberative meaning-making ways (Mooney Simmie, 2007; Mooney Simmie, Moles & O'Grady, 2016; Nixon, 2004).

In a Curriculum Workshop, a coordinator invites teachers from different schools, parents, educational administrators, teachers, politicians and academics to discuss the professional development of teachers, teachers' needs, improving the school or other innovation.

The discourse is based on well-defined elements of the Curriculum Workshop: the selection of participants, work plan and invitation, discourse rules, an information brochure, a key question and a curriculum document (Figure 6.3):

100   Models for innovative planning based on partnership

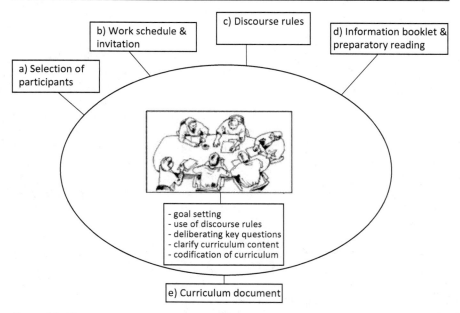

Figure 6.3 Elements of a Curriculum Workshop

The elements of the Curriculum Workshop are defined as follows:

(a) Selection of participants

A coordinator as the initiator of the workshop determines the participants from schools, teacher education facilities and research facilities as discourse partners and sends them invitations and a work schedule and timetable. The invitation contains the theme of the workshop, the agenda and the necessary preparations by means of an information brochure. The selection of the participants follows the general goal of the school-oriented curriculum development with requirements for school-practical experiences, a background of collaborative cooperation and a "good company" of persons with sound judgment (Arendt, 2006).

In addition to these discourse partners, knowledgeable persons are invited as resources of information which, on-demand, can support the discourse competently and credibly. Discourse partners and persons as resources of information should allow self-determination of all parties, partnership-based cooperation, the representativeness of different social forces and a strengthening of the personality of each individual in a nonhierarchical deliberation. Of general importance is a pedagogic commitment in the respective educational institutions and communicative competences of the participants.

Models for innovative planning based on partnership 101

In addition, the participants need to have a broad knowledge, a sense of justice and fairness and capability for critical reflexivity (Pillow, 2003). As stated previously, a dominance of education experts as one-sided knowledge mediators counteracts a common understanding process.

Resource persons are not directly involved as discourse participants in the processes of curriculum planning, but are available on request with special knowledge, techniques or knowledge and observe compliance with criteria of the discourse as reasoning and normative argumentation.

The various roles of the participants are reflected in the communicative design of the spatial arrangement: the discourse partners and the coordinating person form a narrower circle for the promotion of reciprocal communication. Resource persons are located outside this circle in good accessibility.

(b) Work schedule and timetable

A detailed work schedule and schedule for the Curriculum Workshop determines the order of the activities. It consists of the following parts: learning to know one another, searching for a key question, presenting an information brochure and conducting the discourse for the planning of a curriculum as a final document.

(c) Discourse rules

A discourse for a curricular innovation is a process of partnership-based understanding of a problem with normative and rational reasoning. For successful conduct with an innovative result, certain rules of argumentation must be observed. For the Curriculum Workshop, an agreement to common rules is needed between the parties.

Two lists of rules are proposed (Lang, 2007, p. 18).

The following rules are available for *normative argumentation*:

1 Be your own chairperson, responsible for your own situation and environment. Each participant has his/her own value and is equally entitled as a partner.
2 Disorders of social interaction must be given priority.
3 All participants are familiar with a common language and have basic knowledge about the subject. Unusual expressions must be explained according to an elementary logic.
4 Assumptions must be justified.
5 Arguments of a partner are not rejected in advance.
6 Convictions are critically examined for prejudices.
7 Arguments are not dominated by the exercise of power, status or sanctions such as rewards or penalties.
8 General prejudices must be critically analyzed and rejected.

9 Intuitively developed arguments must be accepted by all participants and critically exposed to trans-subjective validity.
10 Participants must be competent in the area under discussion, be willing and open to all arguments, be honest and be willing to accept the normative rules of the argument.
11 Norms must be well-grounded and publicly accepted.
12 Participants must take account of the consequences of decisions and possible impacts.

A rational argumentation consists of logical, technical, experience-based, experiential and scientific arguments. Rules for argumentation follow the scheme of Toulmin (1958; Figure 6.4), beginning with a fact as a problem definition and suggestions for solutions through justifications, rejections and various forms of evidence:

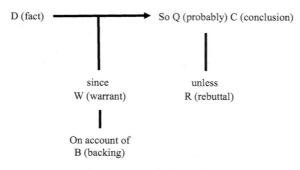

Figure 6.4 Argumentation scheme of Toulmin (1958, p. 97)

(d) Information brochure

The information brochure is intended to bring together the current state of knowledge about the subject of the key question of the workshop. It contains a commented literature compilation or presentations of project partners on topics such as professional development of teachers, curriculum innovation, current political topics such as standards or evaluation and presentations of various elements of the Curriculum Workshop (discourse rules, communicative competence, theme-centered interaction). The brochure is intended to provide specific knowledge on all areas of the Curriculum Workshop in order to provide participants with information for preparation and argumentation.

(e) The curriculum document as a result

The result of the Curriculum Workshop is usually a curriculum document about a key issue of an education problem, which serves for teacher learning and teacher professional development for some aspect of school-based curricular innovation and change.

The final document was used for feedback to participating schools and administration to be evaluated and revised. This was realized by partner countries in various ways: in Austria and Germany specific CWs in schools were designed on the basis of a national CW; in Sweden educational administrators were involved in the national CWs for feedback to educational change and schools did some planning about transition; in Spain the CW output was a set of recommendations for support of envisioned innovations as information feedback to schools without specific practical implications; in Ireland the CW output was a policy document for further discussion of innovation and reflection in a summer school.

The discourse between Curriculum Workshop participants about a problem of innovation was guided by a leader. This person can be regarded as a "broker" operating with the first-hand experience of each of the different cultural worlds in each community. In post-positivistic research, this person is mostly viewed as a neutral and objective chairperson (Stenhouse, 1975). In this latter positioning, the chairperson does not influence other discourse participants by revealing her/his reflexive positioning. However, in other fields of education research (Creswell, 2012), for example, found in the GIMMS project discussed in Chapter 7, the chairperson acts as a "broker" between worlds and reveals their critical reflexive positioning and invites others to do likewise (Pillow, 2003). This reflexive work is done using a shared desire with other participants to be "open enough" for listening with other perspectives in an effort to respect a diversity of viewpoints and to reach agreement beyond consensus.

At the center of the discourse is the problem viewed as the issue under interrogation, to be grounded through evidence from different materials and perspectives. The task of a chairperson is to offer materials covering the different positions in this controversy.

In the Curriculum Workshop, these materials were distributed in advance as information booklets and differential positions in controversy could be completed by participants or elaborated by asking external experts for additional information. In addition, the chairperson did not have the right to interfere with the discursive process by advising participants about the use of discursive rules. For this an elected participant was responsible.

In more recent publications, this concept of a chairperson is further discussed as a democratic situational approach such as distributed leadership (Spillane, 2015), emphasizing the interaction of leaders and followers in a social structure of a flat hierarchy. However, this rather reduced concept of leadership does not cover all aspects of Engeström's cultural-historic activity theory (Ho, Chen & Ng, 2015), such as the exchange of different activity systems for boundary crossing, taking tools, rules and division of labor into account. For this, an

104 Models for innovative planning based on partnership

extended view is developed here in the Curriculum Workshop and is combined with activity theory.

Applications of the Curriculum Workshop in teacher education projects

In the EUDIST project (Lang et al., 2007), the Curriculum Workshop was carried out in five case studies in Austria, Spain, Ireland, Sweden and Germany with different thematic priorities. In the beginning, issues were formulated as key issues by national working groups. In Austria, this was based on the education of teachers in natural sciences, in Spain, on the advantages of school-based professional development for curricular innovation, in Ireland on mentoring in teacher learning for an outcome of pedagogical innovation, in Sweden on teacher competence for autonomous work and in Germany on the development of a competence matrix for given educational standards.

The discursive orientation of the Curriculum Workshop offered a degree of openness for the planning of curricular innovation in teacher education for the case studies. This openness, however, was restricted to a greater or lesser degree by the context of national policy:

In the case of Austria, schools were seen as a learning organization with great freedom against the backdrop of a state monitoring system. On the other hand, national coordinators of Sweden, Germany and Spain identified a stronger restriction on the basis of state requirements by standards, demands on teachers for more measurable performance or national curricula. As an example of a restriction by preselection, the development of a competence grid in Rhineland-Palatinate can be considered. The key question of the Curriculum Workshop was the development of a competence matrix for predefined educational standards, which should be achieved by appropriate selection of topics. The aim was to find suitable content in the form of competences and to develop meaningful learning paths. This is illustrated by a sketch of professional work on teacher education in Calw (Figure 6.1 and 6.2).

In Ireland, this issue remained "open enough" as the Curriculum Workshop invited policy representatives as well as teachers and teacher educators who were involved in the process and became jointly responsible for policy enactment, curriculum planning and development.

Perspectives for the use of the Curriculum Workshop in school innovation

The Curriculum Workshop and its elements supported the collaboration of school-based communities with representatives of school authorities and experts for curriculum innovation. This collaboration demonstrates a productive partnership which involves crossing boundaries between traditional practice and different activities of colleagues, other schools, research groups and political institutions. It has the potential to impact school policy through the analysis of curriculum documents, school-based research, shared meaning-making and deliberative discourse among equal partners for the justification of curricular innovation.

This deliberative discourse is at the heart of the Curriculum Workshop. It was based on the following assumptions that were never totally met in practice but were tried with full negotiation and agreement: full disposal about knowledge concerning the common issue, absence of coercive power among the participants and willingness to keep to discursive rules.

While discursive rules had been accepted, it was sometimes not explicitly practiced. The better the participants knew each other, the less they were willing to accept these formal rules, claiming a strong enculturation to a democratic tradition that makes the formal registration of these rules needless. At a minimum, however, discourse rules were accepted and applied as a prerequisite of justification for curriculum innovation.

Collaboration in a Curriculum Workshop enables teachers to play an active role in a school-based discourse and to contribute to changes with their experiences, goals and justifications. The Curriculum Workshop implies the idea of deliberative democracy, which emphasizes discursive decisions in local communities alongside policy sovereignty. What and how teachers learn is characterized by equality, autonomy and reciprocity in a deliberative process.

On a local level, the Curriculum Workshop supports teacher discourse with other teachers, teacher educators and educational researchers. The Curriculum Workshop provides teachers with information they need to engage in school improvement through local action. On a systemic level, it supports school-based professional development as a dynamic process in schools as part of school development and educational reform.

In the discourses about knowledge progression, a tension exists between different demands of change: learning goals and standards defined in terms of subject matter knowledge and the cognitive and emotional development of students with student interest as a point of departure. Thus, some teachers seek to entice students' knowledge to emerge as they experience real-world phenomena while others look at the formal requirements of the school system.

The EUDIST project (Lang et al., 2007) was used for the first time in various case studies and then later in other projects to determine the possible ways in which opportunities and conditions can be enacted in practice. It considered cultural and contextual layers of conditions, where teachers' voices were given appropriate attention in a joint search for key questions about problems of innovative needs, the compilation of information for an information brochure and the discursive conduct in Curriculum Workshops. This was the case because participants from multiple institutions were able to develop cultural and educational ideas and find agreement in meaning-making of curriculum innovation.

The systematic conduct of cooperation in the Curriculum Workshop is an opportunity for reflection and feedback and exceeds usual routines in a typical school day. The final curriculum document was provided to the participating schools and school administrations for feedback and revision. This was initiated by partner countries in various ways through recommendations for the administration and local Curriculum Workshops at schools, policy documents for discussion of curriculum innovation and reflection, the continuation of work on concepts of school-based teacher education and development of teaching units.

Part of the professional activity of teachers is to take risks for exploring unknown terrain at the boundaries between routines and the unknown and where solutions are not yet visible. This risk of boundary crossing is not necessarily voluntarily chosen but can be part of a common action of multiple communities. This extended cooperation in a complex boundary-crossing situation for innovative design is a major challenge for a sustainable process.

Specifying partnership as collaborative boundary crossing in an extended Curriculum Workshop

The Curriculum Workshop approach is a procedure of actions for the planning of justified curricular innovation, based on different theories of deliberation, communicative competence and discursive justification. These theories serve as a pragmatic framework of action but do not provide a uniform theoretical construct for curricular reasoning. For this purpose, the *Cultural-Historical Activity Theory* (CHAT) of Engeström (2001) with the concept of boundary crossing was combined with the Curriculum Workshop. By this, the policy aspect of curriculum justification in the Curriculum Workshop and the more theoretically grounded aspect of boundary crossing for contradictory objects in the CHAT model are unified.

This is possible because the components of the Curriculum Workshop are directly comparable to activity theory, as shown in the following Table 6.1.

Comparing the components in each line, an extension of the Curriculum Workshop for boundary crossing according to the CHAT model is possible if the conditions of the CHAT model are fulfilled. This means for the first component in the first line, that *participants* need to be defined in terms of *subjects* of a *community*. These *subjects* in the Curriculum Workshop were partially persons from different educational communities but as well as persons with special roles, such as experts from other communities as advisors. In the Curriculum Workshop *communities* were defined in a narrow sense of institutions. As a consequence, the participants were required to view participants in a broader sense as members of a community, which was not easy in each case and had to be discussed in the project.

The components in the other lines in the table need to be specified for the extended Curriculum Workshop in a corresponding way: as *mediating artifacts*

Models for innovative planning based on partnership 107

Table 6.1 Comparison of components in activity theory (Engeström, 2001) and the Curriculum Workshop

Curriculum Workshop	Activity theory (CHAT)
Participants: Teachers, teacher educators, scientists, experts as advisory participants of the Curriculum Workshops	*Subjects of a community*: Teachers, teacher educators, scientists, politicians, other stakeholders in educational policy
Information input: Information booklet for the preparations of participants, key questions	*Mediating artifacts*: Teaching material, videos, key questions, physical or mental representations
Institutions: Schools, special departments, research projects, universities, in-service education departments	*Communities*: Persons with a common culture at or outside school, distinguished by boundaries inside and outside school
Constellation: Round table with discourse partners and an outer circle of available experts	*Division of labor*: Collaborative composition within or between different communities
Discursive and ethical rules: Specifications for the communication between participants	*Rules*: Cultural, social, discursive rules of collaboration and communication
Curriculum document as an output of a discourse	*Objects, boundary objects*: Curricular concepts and problems of different communities for meaning-making about a curricular innovation as an object

for the Curriculum Workshop the introductory information booklet needs to be considered, *division of labor* needs to be represented in the round table discourse, *rules* must be specified especially for an ethical discourse, a central theme for the discourse about a *boundary object* is the agreement on a curriculum document as outcome.

Thus, a construct was available which, by means of a system of related components, provided contradictions as dynamic elements for explaining curricular processes and partnership actions as a concept of boundary crossing for curriculum justification. Integration e.g. of physical and chemical content knowledge did not have to search primarily for a curricular connection of scientific knowledge but started with boundary crossing for shared meaning-making between communities from physics and chemistry teaching. In these subject-related communities, competent experiences and knowledge could be expected, combined into an integrated topic in meaning-making.

At the center of boundary-crossing for shared meaning-making in the CHAT model is the negotiation of a mutually agreed boundary object (see Figure 1.1), originating from related objects brought to the table for a discourse by participants as subjects from different activity systems. These relations of subjects and objects are central to the CHAT model but not sufficient. For a complete picture the following components are missing:

108 Models for innovative planning based on partnership

- Communities,
- Mediating artifacts,
- Rules,
- Division of labor.

With these additional components, many questions arise that need to be discussed within the theoretical framework for boundary crossing innovation.

If we talk about *subjects* as participants of a discourse the question arises, where these persons come from with what justification. This is important in a curricular process approach, because the process depends on the kind of persons representing different communities. The selection of subjects in practice does not guarantee a complete picture of opinions or interests about different aspects of a problem or controversy to be discussed. Often a pragmatic solution is preferred, asking persons with specific competencies from a variety of distinct communities and an extended influence in their communication to share the outcomes as distributed leaders with their partners. In the Curriculum Workshop, this task was undertaken by the project leader, preparing a detailed list of participants to be asked as project members for collaborative discourse and to be engaged to introduce the outcomes of the project to the respective school communities in a setting such as a local Curriculum Workshop.

Mediating artifacts are more than language expressions in a discourse about objects of controversies or problems. In many cases, documents for basic information, scientific or governmental publications, position papers or news can be used as artifacts with different realizations such as print, multimedia or personal message. In the Curriculum Workshop a variety of artifacts were introduced such as information booklets for introduction into a topic, papers, presentations or experts as resources. This variety of artifacts was a basis for an equal level of information supply as well as support for progress in the discussion.

Rules were guiding subjects in the process of deliberative discourse. They are important as social agreement about communicative acts, social and cultural interchange and values and as a prerequisite for justification of an outcome. In the Curriculum Workshop, these rules were presented in written form and mediated during the discourse through a nominated participant, critically observing the adequate use of rules and interfering, when rules were violated.

Division of labor was a neglected component in the Curriculum Workshop. It only distinguished discourse participants, a neutral chairperson and external experts, but did not specify subjects with different specialization or roles in their communities or artifacts for special purposes in more detail. Another aspect would be the leadership role. Gronn (2000) argues that it is an important but neglected concept in activity theory, central to the definition of subjects from communities and their activity in communities.

Crossing Boundaries in Science Teacher Education CROSSNET

In the European Comenius teacher education and training project CROSS-NET (*Crossing Boundaries in Science Teacher Education*) case studies for curriculum innovation were conducted and analyzed with this extended model of Curriculum Workshop on the basis of *Cultural-Historical Activity Theory* for boundary crossing (Hansen et al., 2012).

National coordinators, teacher educators and teachers in seven countries were challenged to apply this new perspective on boundary crossing as a curricular process in several meetings and applications in schools. The procedure and outcomes of this project are discussed here in order to give some insight into the feasibility and perspectives of the framework.

The CROSSNET project was conducted in 2006–2009 with ten partners from seven European countries, based on the concept of boundary crossing in *Cultural-Historical Activity Theory* (Engeström, 2001). It was coordinated by the Institute for Pedagogy of Natural Sciences and Mathematics in Kiel (IPN). In this project, boundary crossing for curricular innovation and justification was applied and its value analyzed in case studies. Boundary crossing was determined by partnership-based deliberative communication on problems of curricular innovation in regional case studies between teachers, researchers and teacher educators. The case studies were part of larger projects in which partnership work could be developed by agreement on rules and concepts without external constraints or competition.

The case studies were based on different topics and curricular contexts of teaching. As a result, strict experimental designs were not possible for the direct comparability of the results, but only feasibility studies for the realization of planned boundary-crossing situations. The creation of situational conditions in schools for boundary crossing and the systematic monitoring of the school procedures in the case studies allowed comparisons to be made for different questions between the case studies. This allowed transfer to similar cases in practice with corresponding expectations for curricular innovation. E.g. a case study on boundary crossing of different subject areas such as Physics, Mathematics and English with the aim of integrating subject matter and language with the starting conditions of a partnership-based culture for collaborative understanding between university and school can reveal new paths of interest to other schools and similar conditions can be realized.

Here such transfer conditions must be treated with caution since the detailed planning and preparation in the CROSSNET project cannot be carried out in the same way in schools outside the project and the necessary epistemic and relational resources and support mechanisms may not be available. However, the case studies can give suggestions for partial aspects of boundary crossing in schools.

As preparatory work, the concept of deliberative teacher education, based on the Curriculum Workshop and boundary crossing, was further developed and presented in a reader (Lang, 2007a) and a book publication (Lang, 2007b). Through this information, all participants in the project agreed on a common basis and developed concepts for their case studies. At the end of the CROSSNET project the results were published (Hansen et al., 2012).

The national coordinators were involved in one or more ongoing projects on curriculum innovation in teacher education, in which they completed a case study using the CROSSNET approach.

Each participant in the project developed a concept of discursive boundary crossing as an innovative curricular approach for the professional development of teachers in selected schools. The selection of each national coordinator of three teachers from four schools for the participation and planning of case studies was made on the basis of willingness to work with existing projects. A teacher in each partner school was asked to provide data from questionnaires and interviews to the coordinator and, together with selected colleagues, to write a report on the school's innovative activities and discuss them in a local Curriculum Workshop with regard to the theoretical concept of boundary crossing in CROSSNET.

Each national project had its own focus. However, this should be subordinated to the overall plan of the collaborative project with colleagues from different schools, teacher educators, researchers and other persons about innovative teacher education in a Curriculum Workshop.

In the CROSSNET project, the national case studies were analyzed by each of the national coordinators and compiled into a report and a book chapter. In addition to these specific results on case studies, cross-country interviews and questionnaire interviews were conducted with 44 schools and 132 teachers.

The first data collection tool was a telephone interview at an early stage of the project. The intention was to obtain baseline data on the background projects in the individual countries and to elaborate on the relevant aspects of the concept of boundary crossing in activity theory. These aspects were defined by the theoretical framework of boundary crossing: communities and members involved in the case studies, perceived boundaries for boundary crossing, identified boundary objects as problems of innovation, forms of boundary crossing and settings for discursive collaboration.

The second instrument was a questionnaire on the professional practice of teachers with rating scales about cooperation in school and about the school environment. The questions were taken from a standardized questionnaire about the collaboration of a study by Sawyer and Rimm-Kaufmann (2007). This study examined features of formal or informal teachers' cooperation with different actors and the corresponding barriers as well as characteristics of the collaborative context such as collegiality, support, participation, shared values and school culture. The analysis of these variables determined predictors of teachers' professional cooperation. These predictors provided a basis for the analysis of teachers' cooperation and related barriers, boundary crossings and the potential for innovative effects. One of the key findings of the study was that teachers involved sought positive cooperation, particularly in searching for educational goals and values, participation in school decisions and collegiality. Barriers were determined in terms of time deficit, lack of willingness or support from colleagues or administration and fixed routines.

For the CROSSNET project, these results were a reason to identify predictors of barriers and characteristics of cooperation that provide evidence of boundary crossing. The national case studies used settings of boundary crossing for innovative conduct for teacher professional development. Therefore, predictors cannot be traced back to single curriculum design, but require a qualitative analysis of complex contexts in addition to quantitative methods.

Boundary crossing is not an innovation per se but has to be related to a curricular process through an innovative key question for discourse in a Curriculum Workshop. In CROSSNET boundary crossing in the case studies was understood as overcoming traditional knowledge transfer in the classroom, overcoming of isolated subject teaching and non-networked subject departments in schools, unrelated disciplinary courses in teacher education at universities and opening of schools for real life-world projects.

In the interviews, it became apparent that boundary crossing was primarily used in a colloquial sense without a theoretical background, and the importance of the concept of the community within the school was often neglected. Boundaries were mainly perceived as physical or ideological barriers in schools. Boundary crossing was mainly understood as the teamwork of a teacher group or in collaboration with researchers, not as an understanding of an object for problem-solving of different communities. The social aspect of the different communities and the structures of the different settings for boundary crossing were only considered at a later stage in the case studies and referred to curriculum innovation. Initially, the idea of curriculum innovation was related only to the theme of the background project.

Boundary crossing was specific in the case studies between subjects of science, mathematics or languages, between teaching routines as a transfer of expertise or active learning, between teachers of different subject departments, between experienced teachers and beginning teachers, between different schools, universities and educational policy institutions.

The case studies showed that the settings of boundary crossing and curriculum innovation were partly successful in teacher education. In schools, a cooperative climate had developed as a prerequisite for educational changes through partnership. Teachers regularly met with colleagues and principals. Researchers, teacher educators and teachers cooperated regularly, and in some cases, they attracted colleagues from other schools. Only a few teachers cooperated with policymakers and educational administrators. According to an Irish participant, teachers increasingly came into contact with colleagues in order to develop higher-order curricular planning that transcended daily survival:

Dialogue has certainly increased between us. Before, we were isolationists. Now we are not only planning from day to day but for a longer time and reflect this. And at the end of the year we can see that we achieved this and that. So, the dialogue brings more planning, reflection and learning. We are more close together as a group of science teachers, more than in other departments.

But there was also awareness about the socioeconomic context, which could have a profound impact on deliberative innovation at school. This was experienced as pressure due to the PISA results on education policy and its response to the introduction of national standards for reading, sciences and mathematics. Especially in the German case studies, but also in the Irish case study, this pressure was an explicit part of the reflection by the respective project team.

The cooperation among teachers had similar effects as in the study mentioned by Sawyer and Rimms-Kaufmann (2007). It was particularly important for the design of school norms, values and activity with colleagues, mutual support and active planning at the school.

Despite the positive view of the cooperation, barriers for boundary crossing were observed, in particular, the constraints of finding designated time for this activity and an intensive workload, but also organizational problems and divergent norms. However, these barriers have not prevented boundary crossing for curricular innovation in the CROSSNET approach. More than 50 percent of the teachers involved confirmed that communication with colleagues had improved, that variety of teaching methods had evolved and that cooperation for planning an integrated science curriculum had improved.

The many benefits of curricular innovation in the field of education have been experienced simultaneously with constraints and limitations from barriers and constraints in each group. As an example, this was identified in a Curriculum Workshop with participants from schools and the university in the Irish case study (Mooney Simmie & Power, 2012):

> Cultural dissonance between the world of the school and university was most evident in the early start-up phase of the project. Part of this early phase involved visiting schools, talking with teachers and explaining what the project involved. The clash of cultures was more acute in schools that remained unconvinced of the value of the project based on innovation and collaboration. Science teachers had busy and stressful lives in school and some were dismayed at the suggestion of becoming involved in a project that might increase their existing workload: The impression was given that this project would lead to more work and so was greeted with negativity straight away from all concerned . . . I felt that the teachers thought perhaps that we were questioning their ability to teach by asking them to take part in the project.

Models for innovative planning based on partnership 113

But the barriers to higher-order curricular innovation through professional collaboration and restructuring programs in schools are also maintained through comfort zones of safe routines and through traditional approaches to memorizing and learning for the state examination. Therefore, a curricular innovation is not only about overcoming barriers, but also about the overcoming and courage to leave the safe zones of proximal development found in boundary crossing. The process of innovation and change requires new competences and roles for teachers, teacher educators and other educational stakeholders, which are beyond the level of the usual classroom and involve boundary-crossing cooperation with multiple communities.

Curricular innovation requires boundary crossing in discursive collaboration between multiple communities in public space to select and justify practices. A driving factor, in any case, is the interaction of committed teachers at schools and teacher educators and researchers at universities or research institutes. This view of cooperating communities offers new paths for curricular innovation through shared meaning-making. Changes are not primarily a consequence of technical planning, but a consequence of the sociocultural dynamics in the school context. This context expands the scope of schools to engage with sociocultural and policy questions and values about what is taught, how and for whom (Cornbleth, 1990).

In the CROSSNET case studies, however, it became clear that boundary crossing between communities from schools and universities encounters difficulties from cultural differences. Teacher educators and researchers from higher education present ideas that overlap with those of teachers, but also conflict with established practices. This leads to dissonance and challenges for the schools, which can trigger an innovative practice as productive tension between the communities. Olson and Hansen (2012) point to positive cooperation:

> This process progresses as an emergence from abstract ideas to those that are more concrete. Those concrete ideas as they are tested in practice give rise to an elaboration and development of theoretical views in turn. CROSSNET projects illustrate how such a cycle works as school people and researchers interact in the process of innovation.
>
> (p. 27)

The extended Curriculum Workshop in CROSSNET supports this kind of interprofessional cooperation for meaning-making. However, the situational design of these constructs can only be successful in a sufficiently supportive framework of school culture with values and practices of collegiality, cooperation, mutual support and participatory planning. This culture grows and develops in a tradition which does not have the usual barriers and fragmented structures, as Lortie (1975) describes.

A curricular innovation based on boundary-crossing deliberative discourse and "hybrid settings" requires broad fiscal supports and epistemic resources, including access to "intellectual" and "critical literacy" toolkits, at the local level and in an extended network.

In CROSSNET, a culture of collaboration existed from the outset, the European Commission in this Comenius project of teacher education and training supported the design and enactment of each of these case study projects with structural, epistemic and relational supports and many background projects were already underway in each case study country. This greatly assisted the specialized and reflexive work of deliberative practices between teachers, teacher educators, administrators and researchers as a deliberative platform for curriculum innovation and teacher professionalization.

In the next chapter, we discuss the design, enactment and insights emerging from the European Comenius GIMMS project for the development of pedagogical innovation with the support of boundary-crossing mentoring relationships and inclusion of gender-awareness in science and mathematics classrooms.

Chapter 7

Putting into action deliberative partnership-based curricular innovation

The two projects discussed in this chapter offer some fresh insights into teacher education practices introducing theoretical aspects of boundary crossing and curricular settings for innovation that were previously discussed. They give insights about the eclectic conceptual use and limits in educational practice, defined by practical constraints and professional views, different from theoretical interventions of the CROSSNET research design, presented earlier.

The first project was a European Comenius teacher education and training project *Gender Innovation and Mentoring in Mathematics and Science* (GIMMS) coordinated at the School of Education in the Faculty of Education and Health Sciences at the University of Limerick, Ireland. This six-country project aimed to develop pedagogical innovation with experienced science and mathematics teachers and student teachers, with a particular focus on "productive mentoring" and developing awareness of gender for an emancipatory practice (Mooney Simmie & Lang, 2012, 2015, 2017, 2018; Mooney Simmie & Power, 2012; Power, 2012).

National coordinators from Ireland, Spain, Germany, Austria, Denmark and the Czech Republic became informed about the concepts of innovation as boundary crossing and discursive deliberation from the Curriculum Workshop through annotated literature, presentations and discussions of former European projects. In addition, and from the outset, the project team, including the project coordinator, agreed to share their reflexive positioning through a process of reflective writings (Pillow, 2003) and to adopt a Productive Mentoring framework (Mooney Simmie & Moles, 2011) for an emancipatory practice of care, agency and critical thinking, interpreted as a messy narrative of co-inquiry-in-context.

Critical thinking involved going beyond reductionist notions of thinking scientifically and instead was concerned with capability to critically reflect on personal experiences, to do the uncomfortable work of reflexivity (Pillow, 2003) and to mediate pedagogical practices with the world for an emancipatory and societal function of gender-awareness and authentic inclusion in a vibrant democratic society (Erickson & Erickson, 2018, p. 2).

116 Putting into action deliberative partnership

With these concepts as background, the GIMMS teacher educator team developed case studies with experienced teachers and student teachers in selected schools, representing different educational contexts. Depending on these practical contexts the planning of case studies resulted in a variety of innovative approaches with modified interpretations of boundary crossing as critical co-inquiry, partnership, deliberative collaboration and innovation.

In a second small scale local project, *Partnership in Learning between University and School* (PLUS), a spin-off project arising from outcomes from GIMMS, faculty members at the School of Education, University of Limerick – fourteen teacher educators and researchers – designed a new model of school-university partnership in four case studies schools. This project was brokered by four masters' in education students who acted as Researcher-in-Residence at each case study school (Young et al., 2015; Costello, 2017). The spin-offs from GIMMS offered into the design phase of the PLUS project included concepts of innovation as boundary crossing and discursive deliberation for school-university planning in the practicum.

In each project, partnership was developed as a policy incentive for deliberative democracy in school systems which were becoming increasingly dominated by a new neoliberal policy imaginary – rapidly supported by an existing strong tradition of conservative consensus – whereby a performative discourse of good teaching and teacher learning was becoming mainstreamed as standards of regulation, public accountability measurements and comparative constraints for individual competitiveness and a national policy imperative for success in international league tables (Ball, 2016; Mooney Simmie, 2009, 2012, 2014; Skerritt, 2018). In this context, the construct of partnership needs to be unsettled and critically evaluated not necessarily as ideologically neutral and some innocent type of public good but instead as possibly part of a power play, providing new "governance tools" for a performative rather than an emancipatory discourse (Bloomfield & Nguyen, 2015; Galvin & Mooney Simmie, 2017; Watson, 2014).

Partnership as boundary crossing in the European project GIMMS

In GIMMS, deliberative partnership-based innovation was conceptualized as a network for boundary crossing in public space in a collaborative framework, using aspects of Engeström's (2001) *Cultural-Historical Activity Theory* for shared meaning-making between teachers, teacher educators, researchers, mentors and significant others on multiple system levels (Figure 5.1).

In the first instance, GIMMS was established as an emancipatory research and development project where each national partner interpreted the deliberatively negotiated key principles to suit their own particularities, contexts and cultures. This supported local curriculum designs in the case study schools and showed tensions and living contradictions between how each national coordinator and their local teams of teacher educators, teachers and researchers interpreted the problem of changing teachers' practices to more active, innovative, gender-aware and engaged pedagogies. The critical insights gained from the project read like the real world "struggle for pedagogies" reported already in the existing literature (Gore, 2012).

The settings for boundary crossing did not in all case studies use principles of the Curriculum Workshop. However, case studies from Ireland, Spain and Denmark explicitly mentioned its use. While these case studies introduced the Curriculum Workshop for a limited time at the beginning or the end of the project, they did not use it consistently with all components as a basis for all activities. In this regard, the Curriculum Workshop is not fully integrated into the GIMMs framework and the effect is not due to this curriculum design.

In the case study in Ireland, a policy curriculum workshop was conducted at the end of the project for dissemination purposes and an opportunity for a national debate of important pedagogical issues with local and national policy-makers, teacher educators, researchers and teachers alike (Mooney Simmie & Lang, 2012, 2017; Mooney Simmie & Power, 2012; Power, 2012). In the case study in Denmark, experienced teachers and student teachers participated in a Curriculum Workshop with the intention of deliberative discourse. The Spanish project started with a Curriculum Workshop to initiate an atmosphere of equality and respect between student teachers, experienced teachers, teacher educators and researchers.

For the conduct of boundary crossing in a deliberative discourse ethical rules of agreement were at the center. They included co-inquiry, a lowering of differential social and power relations for equality understood as co-education (Lynch, 1999) and rules of communicative competency (Habermas, 1974) – for example, equal rights to talk and neglect of status. The broker for the GIMMS national team meetings had the first-hand experience of working within both cultures – as a former science and mathematics teacher in secondary schools and now as a teacher educator and researcher at the university. This brokerage aimed to maintain a social contract for epistemic justice of valuing multiple forms of knowledge and different ways of knowing from understandings of good teaching and teacher learning as messy narratives of change and as a worthwhile ethical principle (Mooney Simmie, Moles & O'Grady, 2019). In this way, ethical principles guided all decisions taken: how to offer and justify subject matter knowledge, to structure lessons, to set expectations and to answer questions. They are reflected in the way curriculum developers talk to others about colleagues or their school, respect traditions and engage in the processes of policy enactment (Ball, 2003, 2016). In GIMMS, the policy cycle was understood in a distinct way from a realist ontology of Process-Product policy implementation. Rather the policy cycle was considered as a complex critical epistemology of teacher education (Kincheloe, 2004) for policy enactment inclusive of a complex process of critical and creative thinking at schools.

In this way, the processes of policy enactment for new pedagogical strategies that are inclusive of gender-consciousness, require policy actors, such as teachers, teacher educators and researchers to engage in meaningful and careful ways that include "intellectual quality" and involve complex processes of translation, interpretation and transformation for "open enough" public spaces to make a difference in real-world contexts (Gore et al., 2017).

Furthermore, the policy lens of deliberating discourse for innovation focuses on the specific boundaries in a fragmented school system, diverse voices that open these boundaries for shared meaning-making, collaborative settings with different stakeholders, a diversity of "productive mentoring" relationships (Mooney Simmie & Moles, 2011), deliberation of hidden constraints and democratic attempts for equality and respect in an open "public space".

In GIMMS teachers were involved in multiple networks, at their schools and with others beyond the boundaries of their classrooms and schools, in order to generate pedagogical innovation and change. A framework for the project, agreed by the six participating countries at the outset, captured the multiplicity of "policy actors" and the complex relationships and interactions taking place for emancipatory and gender-awareness practices through Productive Mentoring (Mooney Simmie & Moles, 2011) and a structure of critical co-inquiry (Figure 7.1):

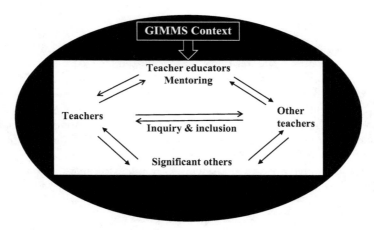

Figure 7.1 The GIMMS collaborative framework (Mooney Simmie & Lang, 2012, p. 17)

The relationships in this framework were realized as communication of equal partners from different communities with extended perspectives for curricular innovation and gender-awareness. This means that for mentor teachers and university teacher educators a collaborative partnership with other teachers, such as student teachers and beginning teachers was based on lowering of traditional hierarchical expert roles for co-inquiry and mutuality (Mooney Simmie

& Moles, 2011). Experienced teachers in the project collaborated with mentor teachers and teacher educators for the support of teacher professional development and curriculum innovation, communicating at different times with significant others such as researchers, politicians or parents. This multiplicity of policy actors for an extended professional development had previously been tried and tested at the national level using the construct of *Teacher Design Teams* for a favorable outcome of pedagogical innovation with biology teachers (Mooney Simmie, 2007).

Multiple interactions in the GIMMS project will now be elaborated in greater detail in the following account of the research report, using Engeström's *Cultural-Historical Activity Theory* (CHAT) for deliberation about problems within a system of subjects from communities, using artifacts, rules and division of labor and for boundary crossing in multiple communities. This allows us to analyze partnership as deliberative boundary crossing in interacting systems of schools and universities with contradictions and controversial issues as a starting point for change.

Within the GIMMS context, collaborative relationships were realized in project meetings with coordinators for discursive deliberation as well as activities for the involvement of teachers in the deliberative discourse of educational problems. However, work in this period from 2006 to 2009 did not quite free itself from the climate of policy imperatives for better performance through increased control by standards and new modes of public accountability.

GIMMS included seven partner projects from six European countries: Spain, Denmark, Czech Republic, Germany, Ireland and Austria. The partner projects were staged, planned and conducted by national coordinators in cooperation with selected case study schools and teachers. In transnational coordinator meetings, the planning was coordinated according to a time schedule and concept, and experiences and results were regularly exchanged. On this basis, a comparative analysis of the results was carried out.

The GIMMS curricular design aimed to bring about pedagogical innovation within a boundary crossing partnership of teachers working with teacher educators and researchers in "productive mentoring" relationships of teacher learning (Mooney Simmie & Moles, 2011) and within a social justice aspect for an outcome of gender-awareness (Mooney Simmie & Lang, 2012, 2017). *Productive Mentoring* was understood as a political and philosophical construct of co-inquiry and critical reflexivity that was contextually grounded and was different from the usual mainstream mode of reproductive teacher learning (Mooney Simmie & Moles, 2011), the latter seeking to inculcate teachers into technically efficient ways of teaching which were based for the most part on the "terrors of performativity" (Ball, 2003).

The aspect of partnership in a cooperative school-based process was particularly emphasized in models of inclusion and equal opportunities (Kreis, Wick & Labhart, 2016). The study sought to motivate and elicit science and mathematics teachers in case study schools to work with teacher educators, in activity

120 Putting into action deliberative partnership

systems based on boundary crossing for curricular innovation, such as, active pedagogies (learning methodologies) and reflective practices and, at the same time, carrying the "uneasy social conscience" of an educator by taking the diversity issue of gender awareness into account (Nussbaum, 2010). The selected diversity issue could have been ethnicity, race, etc. but for the purposes of this GIMMS project, it was identified as the gender construct. This was understood as "gender awareness" for critical consciousness, in keeping with research and teaching as emancipatory practices (Giroux, 1988).

Gender as a specific topic of inclusion in teaching is a controversial and contested construct in the literature (Horstkemper, 1999; Hoffmann, 2002; Scantlebury & Baker, 2007; Waitoller & Artiles, 2013; Döbert & Weisshaupt, 2013). It is more than just a question of competence in dealing with girls' and boys' deficits (Waitoller & Artiles, 2013) or stereotypes of gender-specific differences, often based on narrow technical approaches for selection (Osborne, Simon & Collins, 2003; Makarova & Herzog, 2015). Gender and inclusion are often viewed separately from the mainstream of education systems, increasingly defining individual learning for a successful entry into a competitive knowledge world, neglecting or subordinating issues of justice, equity and respect for all children (Thomas, 2013). In addition to the results of school-based research, more extensive impacts of gender attribution in society can be observed such as unequal pay for equal work and unequal distributions in professional responsibility and careers (Eurostat, 2015; Grummell, Devine & Lynch, 2009). These effects of gender-specific barriers are not readily altered by isolated symptom treatments but require a transformative and poststructuralist concept in education in a sociocultural context as proposed by a deliberative practice of boundary crossing in public spaces.

In the case study in Ireland, there was evidence of a deficit in consideration of the topic of gender and different curricular aspects were found in natural science lessons at the time of the GIMSS project. This became the identified "problem" under interrogation (Mooney Simmie & Power, 2012; Power, 2012). A key point was that at upper secondary level physics and chemistry were selected by a small number of students, and if so, were traditionally selected far more by boys than girls. This selective behavior must be seen in the context of traditionally restricted choices in schools and classrooms and was often socially and culturally bounded. In Ireland, there was a long historical cultural understanding of teaching as teacher-centered and "teaching to the test". Teachers often worked in isolation without sufficient cooperation, and innovation was only ever planned at the level of subject matter content and methods. Complex structures with higher-order cooperation, critical thinking, a rich interplay between theory, practice, experience and research, Productive Mentoring for co-inquiry, agency and care (Mooney Simmie & Moles, 2011), reflexive approaches or gender-awareness as an issue of diversity in schools were all under-developed and often neglected (Mooney Simmie, Moles & O'Grady, 2019). The low uptake of the physical sciences appeared pre-programmed and was often perceived as being not appealing for girls.

In the case study schools, similar tendencies of teacher-centered dissemination of essentialist knowledge or scientific competences were observed without adequate consideration of gender-awareness aspects in science education. Science and mathematics teachers perceived themselves for the most part as "purveyors of subject knowledge" and did not readily perceive themselves as teachers of young people taking into account diversity issues.

A particular problem of the gender-awareness construct was the official policy view of a gender gap – a deficit in the OECD PISA study in performance comparisons and not as a broader and more expansive sociocultural and poststructuralist fluid construct of gender.

The intention of the GIMMS project was to develop and apply Engeström's (2001) concept of boundary crossing in curricular innovation for an outcome of gender-awareness in teacher education for existential freedom and autonomy rather some new mode of performative self-evaluation (Brady, 2019b). Boundary crossing was understood as a meaning-making process for curricular innovation and gender awareness as discursive practices. It steps into a field of public justification by respecting discursive rules, not to exert power through a one-sided view of knowledge and evidence, communicative competence and honesty (Löwisch, 2000). In this context, there are overarching questions of social and epistemic justice, ethics and democracy beyond the hegemonic closure of culture and "governance tools" (Giroux, 1983).

Through a messy narrative of boundary-crossing deliberation, teachers and teacher educators moved beyond limited singular cultures and practices to seek alternatives for new and improved practices, such as gender-awareness in teaching and teacher education. We know, however, that teacher collaboration in schools is largely happening in informal contexts as a result of spontaneous conversations, which are rarely determined by discursive rules (Sawyer & Rimms-Kaufman, 2007). This kind of spontaneous talk is also evident in a statement by the Spanish project coordinator about the cooperation of the teachers (Mooney Simmie & Lang, 2012):

> In the school they discuss very little about pedagogy they discuss about content, what are we doing now or later, what is the best book we are going to use, most of the discussion is about formal things, like, when we start, when we finish, if we do a visit outside or things like that, it is not real cooperation for development, or development of materials.
>
> (p. 150)

For the duration of the GIMMS project from 2006 to 2009, participating teachers in case study schools cooperated with other teachers, mentor teachers, teacher educators, researchers and national coordinators at the university to select, develop and justify pedagogical innovations with an outcome of gender-awareness in a deliberative process. This work was supported by the national coordinators acting as teacher educators and brokers at case study schools using the framework of boundary crossing in activity theory.

At the project level, planning and results were reflexively developed in GIMMS coordinator meetings. Participating teachers at the project schools were not directly involved in the first level of the project design but were involved at the second level in boundary crossing meetings between teachers, teacher educators and national coordinators. This corresponds to the two-step plan of Postholm (2016).

GIMMS teachers and teacher educators sought to find a common understanding of a problem through dialogue and interpretation and were able to agree on a common goal of innovation in their practices. The work on this common goal can well lead, over time, to a culture of expansive learning in a trusting environment. The GIMMS national coordinators acted as CHAT "brokers", teacher educators and researchers and were for the most part directly involved in boundary crossing deliberations, first at the level of the evolving project design at GIMMS team meetings and second, in the messy narrative of pedagogical innovation and change in the case study schools with teachers, student teachers, beginning teachers and experienced teachers. Insights and findings are published in articles, books, a doctoral thesis and in seven case study reports (Mooney Simmie & Lang, 2012, 2015, 2017, 2018; Mooney Simmie & Power, 2012; Power, 2012).

Theory-practice contradictions confluence together and develop further when there is acknowledged lowering of differential social and power relations, avoiding an expedient escape route from the necessary uncomfortable hard work of reflexivity in the idiosyncratic field of real-world practice as described earlier by Schwab (1983). In this way, this construct of *expansive learning* for transformative potential applies to both schools and universities and requires interdependent processes and willingness to change among practitioners and researchers in both institutions (Engeström, 2001). It will not work if it is regarded as a one-sided process. It can offer no hiding place for positivistic researchers who are unwilling to engage in the reflexive work of positioning themselves (Mooney Simmie & Lang, 2017).

In a first coordinator meeting, a theoretical framework for innovative teacher education was developed with elements of boundary crossing and partnership cooperation as well as a concept of gender-awareness as critical consciousness, commensurate with an emancipatory framework (Creswell, 2003). This evolving framework was generally accepted for the project and allowed interpretation of the case studies in the sociopolitical context.

National coordinators introduced the problem of pedagogical innovation for an outcome of "gender awareness" at each of their four-team meetings. During the GIMMS meetings efforts were made to understand the problem of gender, how to think about the problem and to review the research literature. In this regard, progress in thinking about diversity issues occurred, starting from simple sex differences concerning gender traits, for a first wave, to a higher-order understanding of critical consciousness within a poststructuralist paradigm toward the end of the project (Mooney Simmie & Lang, 2017). The national coordinators presented this evolving framework to teachers for integration into practice and for evaluation. This allowed national coordinators to compile and analyze results in the project and evaluate the processes and contexts conducive for curriculum innovation.

GIMMS case studies focused on change in the area of gender-awareness through deliberative collaboration and notions of teacher learning and productive mentoring between teachers, mentors and teacher educators in secondary schools (Mooney Simmie & Moles, 2011; Mooney Simmie, Moles & O'Grady, 2019). In Austria, Spain, Denmark, Ireland, the Czech Republic and Germany, seven national case studies were conducted respectively at three schools each with different teaching subjects. An overview of the main areas of work undertaken in the case studies is found in Table 7.1:

Table 7.1 Main emphasis of the work in national case studies of the GIMSS project

Country	*Main emphases of the case studies*
Austria	Video analyses about teacher learning in physics lessons as action research between student teachers and teacher educators at the university. The examination of egalitarian, democratic and organic models of mentoring considering gender questions.
Czech Republic	New ways of motivating teamwork of students in teacher education according to a novice-expert model between teachers in case study schools and teacher educators at the university. Development of interactive teaching materials for physics, mathematics and computer technology.
Denmark	Developing models of egalitarian mentoring with spontaneous meetings, seminars and Internet platforms for reflexive and science-oriented teaching practice between student teachers and experienced teachers in case study schools and teacher educators at the university. Development of webpages and teaching materials about the topic of nuclear energy considering sex-specific prospects.
Germany	*Project I:* Comparison of different approaches about mentoring in two federal states. *Project II:* Development of an innovative approach and teaching materials for teacher-education in biology with main emphasis of ethical questions and gender inclusion.
Ireland	Use of democratic and reflective models of productive mentoring for the development of higher order cooperation between teachers of natural sciences and mathematics in case study schools and teacher educators at the university.
Spain	Development of a mentoring model for interaction between experienced teachers and preservice teachers in case study schools and teacher educators at the university.

The case studies at the schools were designed, organized and for the most part delivered by national coordinators, acting as CHAT "brokers" and teacher educators from the university. For GIMMS project meetings, the overall project coordinator at the University of Limerick invited each national coordinator to partake in transnational and European deliberations of the problems to be addressed, understood as pedagogical innovation in the science and mathematics classroom with an outcome of gender aware- ness and using productive models of mentoring and teacher learning through boundary crossing deliberations. In these meetings, an evolving conceptual framework for gender-awareness was developed as well as a case study design and agreed on procedures for the selection of schools, data collection and documentation.

Case study teachers at the schools developed with the respective national coordinator a concept of boundary crossing and gender awareness and dis- cussed an application. The setting for each case study included components for boundary crossing from Engeström's (2001) activity theory illustrated in Figure 1.1 (Chapter 1): A *subject* as a human actor in a pedagogical problem situation was understood as part of a *community* consisting of experienced teachers, student teachers, teacher educators, beginning teachers, researchers or other educators. Deliberation for mutual understanding between subjects was supported by *mediating artifacts* while adhering to agreed ethical *rules*. The *object* as a goal of an educational problem required agreement on an innova- tive pedagogical practice with a special interest in developing the concept of gender-awareness in teachers' reflective practices.

At the beginning of the project, the national coordinators were intro- duced to the concepts of interacting components and boundary crossing in activity theory. As the first step for case study planning, they were asked to use these components as a basis and later to rate the importance of the components in their own and the other case studies. For this, a ques- tionnaire was used relating these components of an activity system to ten statements about cooperation across boundaries, school-based planning, cooperation with mentors, innovation, school development, professional development, gender in teaching and teacher education, teaching technol- ogy and politics. The national coordinators gave judgment about the importance of each statement for the different case studies. The reason for this procedure was to get an overall estimate about the importance of the components from activity theory in each case study for the deliberation about pedagogical innovation and gender-awareness.

The specific procedure of questionnaire data analysis with statistical instru- ments such as comparisons of means and cluster analysis and comprehensive interpretation is already published in Mooney Simmie and Lang (2017). Here we present an overview. In the second step, the questionnaire results were related to contextual statements about gender awareness.

Questionnaire results

The question of the importance of gender in teaching and teacher education was answered with medium frequency. This means that national coordinators roughly attribute importance to gender in half of the cases. However, there were significant differences between the statements on gender in relation to other components for different countries:

In the case studies in Austria, Ireland and Germany 1 (with the focus on university teacher education), gender was regarded as a topic of importance in connection with the components of mentoring, innovation and school-related planning. In the countries Denmark, Czech Republic and Germany 2 (with the special focus on a Referendariat), this assessment was low.

This means that the gender aspects in connection with productive mentoring and an atmosphere of pedagogical innovation and school planning are of great importance in some countries. These components could be assigned to elements of activity theory. The components collaboration, information technology, school development and politics were not placed in relation to gender questions. Relating this to activity theory gender issues are assigned as "object" in relation to "community" and "rules". The issue of gender is, therefore, given a high priority if it is not discussed in isolation, but in communities, taking into account discursive rules. Cooperation, the use of information technologies, administrative questions of school development or political questions were not assumed to be important.

The low rating of cooperation for the work in the case studies and a missing component of the gender question also makes clear the low influence of cooperation in school practice. However, it also makes clear that the concept of boundary crossing through collaboration was only realized to a limited degree on the content level in the case studies.

According to Engeström (2001), Xing and Marcinknowski (2015) or Postholm (2015, 2016), the elements of activity theory are given a particular role in the process of change because they generate tensions that lead to attempts to solve a problem. This means that for the case studies in Austria, Ireland and Germany 1, curricular innovation can be expected with the appropriate interaction of the components. In the other case studies these components do not play any role and no pedagogical innovation regarding an outcome of gender awareness is to be expected.

In the following step, we take a closer look at the situational circumstances of the corresponding countries with high and low estimates of the gender component and their relationship to gender-specific goals and contextual understandings in teacher education.

In the Austrian case study with high significance rated for the gender question, the topic was promoted by a coordinator who was particularly active in gender research and who worked accordingly with students and other teachers by encouraging deliberative communication based on mutuality, trust and the ability to critique (Stadler & Newmann, 2012).

In the case study of the Czech Republic, gender awareness was reduced to the improvement of the motivation of *girls and boys*, in Spain to the neutral teaching material of *science in context* and in Germany 2 to a good understanding of *group dynamics*. In these case studies partial silence and hegemonic resistance to opening the question of gender were identified.

Case studies with high ratings of the gender component in connection with the components of mentoring, innovation and school-oriented planning as in Austria, Germany 1 and Ireland were conceived as a democratic project that required new methods and reflective/reflexive practices for teachers and teacher educators alike. For example, in Austria, the project was concerned with reflective practice in teacher education, supported by a virtual learning platform, video analysis and vignettes for teaching practice (Stadler & Newmann, 2012). There was an understanding of the inherent problem of teaching on gender issues and inclusion. In the case study in Germany 1, a deliberative discourse was developed between teachers in university education and teacher educators with the characteristics of a flat hierarchy, mutual respect and dialogical exchange. The case study in Ireland was a particular challenge as it involved experienced teachers rather than a mixture of student teachers and experienced teachers. The experienced teachers in the project, similar to experienced teachers in Ireland generally at that time, had little or no experience of engagement with multiple policy actors in public spaces for higher-order cooperation and the development of a common language and "intellectual quality" about their teaching (Gore et al., 2017). These teachers, however, took part in reflective diary writing and made efforts to advance innovative pedagogical practices in the classroom. However, interviews at the end of the project revealed a rather limited idea of gender-awareness depicted as sex differences despite deliberate communication with colleagues, teacher educators, researchers and other actors.

In summary, national coordinators were convinced that gender could be a topic of innovative education and school planning. Gender was primarily discussed as a sociocultural construct.

But there were also instances of silence and resistance to the issue of gender-awareness without conscious perception of gender boundaries in interactions with students. In the international literature, it is noted that teachers of mathematics and natural sciences often hold essentialist worldview as transmitters of knowledge, which is not commensurate with an outcome of gender-specific requirements (Castaño et al., 2015; Coronel & Gómez-Hurtado, 2015). This was evident in the concept of gender awareness adopted in case studies with low assessment of the gender component (the Czech Republic, Denmark and Germany 2).

Through new ways of active learning and pedagogical innovation, it was partially assumed that a boundary crossing discussion about gender was superfluous. For example, in the case study in the Czech Republic, new ways of teacher education were established using information technology, but according to a hierarchical expert-novice model with essentialist technical content in a strictly regulated and controlled context. Thus, boundary crossing collaboration in this case study was impossible. Accordingly, the topic of gender was understood as a formal problem of sex differences and motivations as outlined in earlier studies by Francis (2010). It was merely stated that boys are generally more active and better at learning by experience, while girls were generally better in tests and use of theory.

The case study in Denmark related gender awareness to a boundary crossing between experienced teachers, student teachers and teacher educators. However, in the case study teachers refused to open a discourse on gender awareness in teacher education and were only prepared to set up changes in seating order according to homogeneous groupings by gender. The national coordinators tried unsuccessfully to open discourses of pedagogical innovation for an outcome of gender awareness both at the schools and at the university with other teacher educators and reported their efforts thwarted in all cases. For Danish teacher educators, it was perceived that it was not gender awareness that was the issue but rather motivation or multicultural understandings, these latter topics as the only acceptable way this diversity discourse could be allowed for consideration.

The case study Germany 2, analyzed the professional development of teachers in the second phase of teacher education. The student teachers in the project personally experienced differences of treatment by gender during initial teacher education courses. But there was no possibility of cooperation for isolated group structures in which these differences could be discussed in school communities and deliberated using principles of CHAT.

In the case study in Spain, there was strong resistance and hegemonic silence in relation to opening the topic of gender awareness in teacher education – science teachers in the case study schools were unprepared for such a problematic discourse. There was fear expressed of stereotyping girls. This thinking was also expressed by the national coordinators and teacher educators at the university who argued that the applied approach of *science in context* was already proven in the literature as the optimal way for gender inclusion. Using this argument, the problem was shelved and the sociopolitical context was elided and excluded.

According to Engeström's (2001) *Cultural-Historical Activity Theory*, second- and third-order tensions and contradictions between components and activity systems are requirements for innovation and change in education systems (Chapter 5). In the present case studies, the *components* object, rules and community corresponded to pedagogical innovation in the study for an outcome of gender awareness, which led to curricular changes in certain case studies with deliberative collaboration. In other case studies, the component of gender as an object of discussion was limited to a traditional picture of gender gap without a willingness to open a new type of deliberative discourse for a critical reflexive approach of gender-awareness.

If we look to the aspect of *boundary crossing* between different activity systems, we can observe that some policy actors in teacher education, such as teacher educators, researchers, experienced teachers, student teachers and beginning teachers, were taking on new roles in curricular innovative practices with meaning-making across boundaries about the topic of pedagogical innovation with an outcome of gender awareness. The traditional expert-novice model of teacher learning and mentoring did not provide any impetus for change as there was no discursive space claimed for tensions and contradictions. These tensions are in-built in boundary crossing of multiple communities with rules of communication in public space. Such collaboration was realized among school-based teachers and university-based national coordinators, teacher educators and researchers in Curriculum Workshops in Ireland, Denmark and Spain and deliberative meetings in the case studies in other countries.

Overall, the results showed that the concept of teacher professional development with an outcome of gender awareness and innovation as deliberative boundary crossing was a promising approach. This was particularly evident in case studies when gender-awareness was accepted as a problem worthy to be opened outward for deliberation with a jointly developed culture of cooperation and critical reflexive practices to be agreed upon by all involved.

These results and insights arose with a small sample of teachers and teacher educators, who were particularly committed to the project ideals and willing to interpret the data within the agreed framework of deliberative boundary crossing. Thus, they cannot be generalized. However, it has been shown that certain settings can have a positive or negative effect on the development of pedagogical innovation for gender awareness. This limitation does not diminish the value of our framework and its results but opens up the prospect of making a more differentiated plan of boundary crossing, leading to a new, innovative dynamic.

To this end, the inclusion of other communities could be considered as a means of understanding gender-awareness problems as boundary objects. This would position the avoidance of the gender-awareness question in a discursive context and silence on gender could lead to a proactive debate at both the school and the university e.g. the gender aspects of a reduced view of biological gender differences and motivation and a cultural-historical view of different communities as boundary objects could be put on the deliberative platform for open discussion. An agreement to do this would be an agreement to practice despite differences and not necessarily to arrive at a compromise. This understanding to argue beyond consensus, in an agonistic way as previously asserted by Chantal Mouffe (Ruitenberg, 2009), could lead to a higher-order innovation due to contradictions between objects of different activity systems. It would go beyond contradictions within or between components of an activity system, as it was found in some cases in the understanding of the gender-awareness construct.

The perspectives and contextual understandings of GIMMS teachers in the case study schools reveal how the problem of pedagogical innovation for gender awareness with experienced and expert science and mathematics teachers, and teacher educators and researchers at the university, is intertwined with questions of power and politics and heteronormativity. It reveals the "invisible hand of the

Putting into action deliberative partnership   129

powerful" (Bourdieu, 1991) and the hidden curriculum of gender relations. This is particularly seen in the performative way the global policy imperative reduced the deliberation to narrow measurable competencies and standards. Recent studies confirm hegemonic resistance to open moral and political discourses and offer challenges for teacher education (Kedley, 2015; Sterling, 2014). These could lead to a limitation of the concept of the deliberative boundary crossing and require clear participation in teacher education in public forms of deliberative democracy with the challenge to justify curricular innovation in relation to gender awareness.

Partnership in Learning between School and University (PLUS)

The University of Limerick in Ireland has taken inspiration from the findings and critical insights gleaned from EUDIST, CROSSNET and GIMMS projects about deliberative innovation in teacher learning and professional development through boundary crossing partnerships between institutions of higher education and schools.

As a follow on from these European projects, and from an earlier study of *Teacher Design Teams* at the national level (Mooney Simmie, 2007), the Faculty of Education and Health Sciences of the University of Limerick developed an innovative school-university partnership model for the school-based practicum placement (Young et al., 2015). This was developed at the same time as a new national policy from the Teaching Council concerning practicum placement and an expressed need for new models of extended cooperation for teacher learning in the practicum placement, e.g. between student teachers, cooperating teachers at the school and university tutors (Teaching Council, 2011).

The *Partnership in Learning between University and School* (PLUS) project was designed by a team of interested teacher educators and researchers at the university in a boundary crossing deliberation staged by the School of Education and involving four faculties (teacher education, languages, physical education and science education). A suitable curricular design was intended to promote an understanding of deliberative democratic partnership models and their successful use in productive co-inquiry between schools and universities (Lang et al., 2007; Mooney Simmie & Lang, 2012; Mooney Simmie & Moles, 2011; Young et al., 2015). Through school visits, the availability of a researcher-in-residence during the timeline of the school placement and boundary crossing deliberations between student teachers, tutors and experienced cooperating teachers, an authentic democratic partnership was initiated and deepened for productive and deliberative co-inquiry (Young et al., 2015):

> The partnership was designed as an authentic structured partnership between the school and university, it was positioned within the requirements of the Teaching Council (2011a, 2011b, 2012, 2013), and sought to develop 'democratic professionalism' (Day & Sachs 2004, 10) with teachers working together.
>
> (p. 37)

130 Putting into action deliberative partnership

The PLUS partnership used appropriate rules of ethical engagement, agreed at the university and with school principals and teachers for boundary crossing "hybrid spaces" between diverse cultural contexts. The Teaching Council developed guidelines for school practice at that time (University of Limerick, 2013a) that introduced ideas and suggestions about the need for new partnership models for innovation of initial teacher education (ITE).

A School Placement manual (University of Limerick, 2013b) was available to document the activities and assessments of student teachers. The preparation and instruction planning, as well as their realization and evaluation, were listed in detail. The manual for the documentation was available to student teachers as well as cooperating teachers. In addition to the manual for the documentation, a folder was held, in which materials were compiled in six parts for each scheme of work and lesson design. On the basis of the documentation and folder entries, a mutual understanding and deliberation between student teachers and cooperating teachers were intended.

However, after the researcher-in-residence project indicated some positive and promising achievements (Young et al., 2015) the project was curtailed as it started to operate within a new governance policy of austerity economics (Ball, 2016; Mooney Simmie, 2012; Skerritt, 2018). The grant-aided funding model at the School of Education for master's students acting as Researchers-in-Residence in case study schools during the practicum was discontinued. At the same time a new workload model for faculty was introduced at the university which offered greater currency for teacher educators/researchers for high quartile research publications. This diverts faculty attention from the uncomfortable reflexive work of face-to-face democratic deliberations beyond agreement with teachers, schools and university tutors.

A prerequisite for the successful development of the PLUS-model was the epistemic, relational and fiscal support for schools and university. This is a particular requirement for a deliberative discourse rather than a managerial and technocratic discourse, since cooperation and communication of higher order in schools is underdeveloped and traditionally, teacher educators at university have steered away from giving of their time and energies in expansive learning work of deliberative co-inquiry at "eye level" with experienced teachers at school settings (Murray & Male, 2005, Murray, 2014; Smith, 2007; Lahelma, 2014).

Frequently, there is a lack of deliberation according to discursive rules for public justification, cooperation between student teachers, experienced teachers, teacher educators and tutors at the university. The interaction is not always defined by open communication with collaborative agreements and agreed "artifacts". The education system in Ireland is more familiar with the rules, roles and responsibilities that align with managerial discourses and traditionally holds strong hierarchical boundaries between schools and universities.

In this regard, the PLUS partnership in its first iteration was a new model of practicum placement with a Researcher-in-Residence at the school setting who

Putting into action deliberative partnership 131

agreed to act as "broker" in the hybrid spaces between two activity systems, school and university and partake in the messy narrative needed for a boundary crossing deliberation of teacher learning (Mooney Simmie, Moles & O'Grady, 2016; Mooney Simmie et al., 2017; Young et al., 2015).

The commitment of political and policy actors in higher education and the Irish state is clearly necessary for fiscal, structural, epistemic and relational supports for a PLUS partnership-based platform to be offered as a boundary crossing justification for teacher learning and productive mentoring. Nowadays, PLUS continues with a small cohort of interested teachers and schools and teacher educators but without systemic supports (Costello, 2017).

The PLUS model in Initial Teacher Education (ITE) assimilated the GIMMS deliberative framework of teacher education and was introduced to the Teaching Council (2011). According to Young et al. (2015), cultural constraints between different communities of the schools and university and traditional lower-order professional cooperation within the Irish case study schools existed as restrictive boundaries and continued to persist:

> There were a number of constraints and challenges identified in this study – the habitus of teachers who until now have not historically engaged in extended professional conversations in relation to pedagogy matters . . . There was equally concern that requirements from the university and school may be different.
>
> (p. 35)

For a partnership-based curricular innovation, it can be seen that the PLUS design for teacher education meets conditions for higher-order innovation (Young et al., 2015). In practice, however, there are limitations in the interactive boundary-crossing, communication about object-related problems and agreement on discursive rules. Limitations can be restricted by traditional cultures, a cultural-historical approach that is managerial, consensual and technocratic rather than dialogic and deliberative, higher education faculty with limited time resources while under pressure of international rankings.

To overcome limitations, a complementary understanding of participating communities has been offered in the PLUS, CROSSNET, EUDIST and CROSSNET projects and these alternative frameworks can be helpful to persuade policymakers and other interested policy actors to develop a more nuanced and sophisticated partnership-based culture for a complex critical epistemology of teacher education and with expansive learning for emancipatory practices and a democratic ethic of care and productive collaboration.

Chapter 8

Prospects for higher-order curriculum innovation and deliberative partnership

Curriculum innovation based on deliberative partnership is difficult to maintain in an environment of neoliberal trends to use *bigger, tighter* and *harder* mechanisms of regulatory control and hierarchical modes of public accountability in preference to "intelligent accountability" for a complex critical epistemology of teacher education (Hargreaves et al., 2010; Kincheloe, 2004; O'Neill, 2013). Through international comparative studies and external measures of standardization and competence requirements for comparisons of performances the direction of school innovation has become predetermined and predictable (Cochran-Smith et al., 2017). These top-down innovations are planned by state authorities with the support of a number of experts and researchers, restricting the influence of practitioners, such as teachers to a small number of feasibility pilot studies. Standards are mainly the result of large-scale studies such as OECD PISA and not addressed to a culturally appropriate context by means of school-based partnerships with universities and other higher education institutes. They were hardly justified in public space as objects of shared meaning-making among multiple communities with controversial issues and contradictions in a broader context. Such a justification clearly runs counterproductive to the current official mainstream quality management of state authorities using metrics fixation (Harvey, 2007).

Nevertheless, attempts are made here to offer alternative frameworks for teacher learning and development as deliberative partnership-based curricular concepts within the limits of today's social and political framing of schooling. Our framework allows "open enough" spaces to discuss contradictions for boundary crossing with higher-order activities between partners for discursive justification in public space. This is important for reclaiming the profession of teaching as an occupation where professional judgment and context matters and where theory-practice contradictions and tensions become the starting place for curriculum innovation and change (Cochran-Smith et al., 2017), while being aware of a perverted partnership in a competitive system as a political instrument of governance for control of outcomes (Bloomfield & Nguyen, 2015).

Prospects for higher-order curriculum innovation   133

Within the framework of Engeström's (2001) third generation *Cultural-Historical Activity Theory (CHAT)*, various components and a dynamic of productive partnership are described, which determine changes through contradictions of different orders in a network of activity systems and initiates a mutual understanding of problems and new goals through boundary crossing.

Contradictions in the school system are seen as problems or controversies in CHAT between subjects, objects, communities, tools, rules or division of labor, or between different activity systems of different institutions. These problems are systemic and may be resolved through a school-based deliberation of practice.

The dynamics of boundary crossing in such activity systems are expected to initiate change but need a more specific justification for curriculum innovation. This is a central point, where boundary crossing in CHAT is combined with a Curriculum Workshop setting for justification of initiated changes, as described in Chapter 6. The resulting collaborative boundary crossing in an extended Curriculum Workshop does not only lead to change, which might be important because of problems or contradictions in educational systems but introduces a value judgment for a change as a political justification in public space.

This political justification is of special importance for educational change as an agreement about a solution or controversy in CHAT. Not in every case do teachers, students or teacher educators agree on getting involved in solving a problem or contradiction for expansive learning or improvement of practice. The process of change in CHAT is a formal boundary crossing activity and does not distinguish between good or bad purposes. Therefore, in some cases, people might refuse to participate and prefer to live with a problem since they feel they may be exploited or alienated in a process that only changes for a better flow in the wrong direction. This has certainly been well documented by Santoro (2017) in studies where teachers expressed their sense of demoralization as a result of the moral good of their professional practices being compromised by a new business-like ethic of schooling as customer care. A perspective for justification, introduced in the Curriculum Workshop, gives change a normative value for an acknowledged purpose of co-inquiry. An extended Curriculum Workshop needs to take into account critical concerns about missing humanistic discourses and spaces for critical literacy as expressed by Gunter (2001).

Collaborative boundary crossing in an extended Curriculum Workshop was initiated and analyzed in the CROSSNET project, described earlier, with some basic structure and perspectives of feasibility in the restricted frame of project work. Taking into account a more complex educational system with collaborative relationships of multiple activity systems, additional aspects need to be considered in networked activities, as described by Yamazumi (2007) as hybrid activity or by Ho, Chen and Ng (2015) as distributed leadership. The networked activities emphasize boundary crossing with agencies from outside schools that position schools as societal change agents, a partnership of multiple communities. This aspect of leadership in networked activities offers the possibility of a systematic framework for the sustainability of change in complex situations of school systems.

A public justification of innovative practice can challenge discussion about today's externally determined accountability and quality management, which has arrived at a crossroads after almost two decades of international constant comparisons. According to Postholm (2016) in Norway and Shirley (2010) in Australia, one can recognize first steps turning back to school-related practical tasks in a community, which reverse a flight from the field (Schwab, 2013). Instead, theory-practice contradictions, triggered by community organizing for educational change (Shirley, 2010) with reciprocal understanding and expansive transformation of partners, could be applied as an important first step to reclaim the profession and return democracy, equity and situated professional judgment to teachers' educational rationale.

From considerations in this book, it can be concluded that higher-order partnership-based innovation within the framework of CHAT is a consequence of contradictions dedicated to authentic meaning-making and emancipation in a boundary crossing process with negotiated agreements on higher-order communication and discursive rules. In particular, the relationship between contradictions and boundary crossing in CHAT is to be clarified in order to specify the process of curricular innovation. However, deliberation is far more than collaboration and requires agreed discursive rules of engagement, shared experience and epistemic, relational and structural supports for the messy narrative that is good teaching and teacher professional learning (Kincheloe, 2004; Mooney Simmie, Moles & O'Grady, 2019).

Understood as collaborative relationships in CHAT (Yamazumi, 2007) a meaning-making process across boundaries takes place between multiple communities in a school-based socio-cultural context. Through boundary crossing, this context can extend across different schools, teacher education institutions, universities and other institutions. This involves severing all institutional boundaries of traditional understandings of knowledge and learning towards an advanced network. Teacher education institutions could strengthen this context through productive collaboration with teachers that include "open enough" spaces for intellectual quality and interruption of routinized practices (Gore et al., 2017). In the center of this deliberation, teachers play a decisive role as "transformative intellectuals" interrupting the cycle of reproduction and hegemonic closure (Giroux & McLaren, 1986). Teacher educators demand more critical teacher education, which not only teaches about democracy but promotes emancipatory practices in schools and among teachers (Mooney Simmie & Edling, 2018). This supports the expectation that an innovative and justified practice of education challenges the reproductive system of schooling (Angus, 2012).

However, through the development of quality management concepts compatible with Human Capital Theory, many teacher education institutions have been reorganized according to the principle of efficiency and a fixation on the tyranny of metrics (Muller, 2018). For example, isolated homogenous modules

Prospects for higher-order curriculum innovation 135

are often used in the induction of beginning teachers, favored for the purpose of efficient management at different locations, regardless of context.

This managerialist and technocratic system, however, does not promote a culture of co-inquiry, including welfare, trust and local deliberative democratic understandings where context and situated judgment matter. As a suitable alternative the Norwegian project of collaborative school-based teacher education (Postholm, 2016) or the PLUS model of teacher education in Chapter 7 would be appropriate alternatives worth considering (Mooney Simmie & Moles, 2011; Young et al., 2015), in which partnerships between schools and higher education institutions are fostered by deepening co-inquiry with the deliberative lowering of power relations, productive mentoring and high trust-modes of intelligent accountability.

Using the examples of CROSSNET and GIMMS it can be seen that individual schools in the local context act as nodes in a network with institutions in a higher-level context (Hansen et al., 2012; Mooney Simmie & Lang, 2012). This cooperation was particularly successful in an innovation if a partnership-based culture pre-existed as in the case of CROSSNET or was developed over a longer period, as in the GIMMS project or the Norwegian project for collaborative teacher education, described by Postholm (2016):

> The three schools in this study had worked on school-based development for almost two years, and at one school the principal clearly admitted that the culture for collective learning was not yet stable, but they were on their way from individual, traditional teaching. This means that it takes some time to create a collective new form of social activity.
>
> (p. 464)

The analysis of partnership-based school activities within the scope of CHAT in the presented projects CROSSNET and GIMMS clarified some connections in the complex process of curricular innovation through deeper boundary-crossing deliberation of contradictions and tensions. In view of the various contradictions within the components, between the components, between the objects of different central activities and other components of activities, a complete analysis of the entire system is hardly possible. It is only possible to use specific sections in the sense of a research question for an innovative process. They mainly refer to primary and secondary contradictions of individual components such as the object of pedagogical innovation for an outcome of gender awareness in GIMMS or a combination of contradictory components to gender as an object, communities as participants from schools and teacher education institutions, rules as discursive understandings.

The analysis of primary contradictions within components is carried out in other projects as a gap analysis. Nunez (2009) distinguishes e.g. mathematics in school from mathematics in the workplace. From the contradictions of this component, recommendations for an adaptation of school mathematics to requirements of a workplace can be made. However, if secondary contradictions between other components are not taken into account, there may be simplified interpretations that do not meet innovative practice at school. This can be seen in GIMMS where gender awareness was often understood as a simplistic gap of gender-specific characteristics as primary contradiction and not as a complex sociocultural poststructuralist phenomenon taking social constructions into account (Mooney Simmie & Lang, 2012, 2017).

As a result, other levels of contradictions in CHAT should be taken into account in addition to the primary contradictions. This leads to further questions such as:

- How can contradictions be registered in a complete system of all six components?
- How do objects of the activities of different activity systems develop as boundary objects for mutual understanding and boundary crossing?
- What contradictions arise in and between working groups at the lower level, institutions and a socio-cultural educational context?

The analysis of contradictions in CHAT reveals the possibilities of dialogue and deliberation in a curricular process but does not automatically offer a solution to the contradictions in school practice. For this, an active process of boundary crossing collaboration between schools, higher education institutes and other institutions is necessary.

Some contradictions may well prove themselves to be unsolvable in everyday situations despite boundary-crossing deliberative partnership efforts. In general, the tyranny of the markets, the dominance of a fixation of metrics and data analytics, the debasement of recognition of multiple ways of knowing, the sidelining of theoretical and disciplinary knowledge forms from the contemporary field of education in a utilitarian practice turn, the failure in lowering symbolic power relations all play their part in constraining democratic deliberation from a lived reality in relations between schools and higher education institutions (Bourdieu, 1991).

Examples of this can be found in the overview of partnership projects of Lillejord and Borte (2016). They found that projects regularly showed contradictions and tensions triggered by conflicts of loyalty, differing expectations or power demands. These tensions do not allow boundary crossing for an innovative process if appropriate settings do not allow questions of power, dependencies or willingness to agree on practical questions, which lead to an understanding by agreed discursive rules of engagement.

In everyday situations, the possibilities of these settings are often not obvious for the partners, since corresponding concepts with theoretical justifications presented here are not available. However, this problem can be highlighted by CHAT with corresponding rules of boundary crossing or constructs such as the Curriculum Workshop and can be solved in practice in a cooperative manner.

Questions of disturbed communication can be taken into account by agreeing rules of ethical discourse, or understandings of boundary objects for boundary crossing, despite differences of opinion. The peculiarities of these constructs for problem-solving are that contradictions can be discussed as "conditions of possibilities" for communication (Habermas, 1981).

Corresponding curricular concepts for resolving contradictions by boundary crossing in partnership between communities with different cultural understanding or between objects as problems of gender or integration of subjects have been given in the projects presented.

Boundaries are dynamic and may originate from historical, political or cultural sources and evolve over time through definition in communities and are not always clearly distinguishable. This is, for example, the case in the dynamic of disciplines and their socially constructed boundaries and as a consequence the construction of related educational subjects and didactics (Terhart, 2013). Thus, e.g. statistics developed as a separate subject in contrast to mathematics and created new perspectives for the teaching and learning of statistics. Nevertheless, mathematics and statistics have a common problem of measurement and variability. This results in flexible requirements for boundary crossing, in which different objects of defined fields of knowledge with a common core of a boundary object exist for common understanding.

Boundaries do not have to offer insuperable barriers but are an incentive for productive action to change through boundary crossing. Boundary objects are incentives for different communities to act together (Star & Griesemer, 1989). A lack of consensus can be diminished by a contextual reference of a problem or inclusion of other communities in third space. This allows a problem to be moved to a different level. This form of boundary crossing was realized in various context projects, e.g. *Chemistry in Context* (Gräsel, Nentwig & Parchmann, 2005) or *Mathematics in Context* (Wijers et al., 1998).

Deliberation as the "arts of the practical" is a complex and arduous task and requires "the formation of a new public and new means of communication among its constituent members" (Schwab, 1970, p. 36). According to Eisner (1984) deliberation is a process of high intellectual power, necessary for making decisions that suit changing contexts riddled with idiosyncrasies. It cannot be realized by informal communication about singular problems but needs higher-order knowledge and cooperation with efforts for creative and critical thoughts and solutions with careful preparation and ethical rules of agreement.

This is often difficult for teachers because they are not accustomed and not encouraged to higher-order activities of deliberation in public space. This is also difficult for some teacher educators and researchers in higher education institutes and universities who are more familiar with their role – in particular positivistic scientist researchers who claim neutrality and objectivity – and who may be unwilling/unable to engage in a deliberation closer to a messy narrative of change rather than the logical rationality of an evidence-based argument. This work of deliberation requires face-to-face settings and relational building,

138 Prospects for higher-order curriculum innovation

designated time and effort for the development of productive boundary-crossing partnerships.

This idea of an extended public space in education can already be seen in the early discussion about community education in England, the US, Canada and Germany (Kerensky & Logston, 1980; Zimmer & Niggemeyer, 1992). Schools collaborate with the municipality and act as a public forum for education, youth work, adult education or vocational training by offering support for cooperation including educational associations from outside.

In recent times, the idea of community education has gained more attention as stated by Wagner (2013) and Shirley (2010). Movements such as community-engaged scholars (Warren, Park & Tieken, 2016), teacher education involving neighboring schools (Catapano & Huismann, 2010), the Alliance Schools movement (Shirley, 2010) or the concept of Third Space for teacher education (Zeichner, 2010; Lewis, 2012) are bringing these concepts back. Third Space is an extended space of communities beside schools as First Space and universities as Second Space. The aim of this construction is to place the school-university partnership, which is in need of reform, on a new socially broadened foundation.

With the expansion of educational discourse in public space, knowledge from the neighborhood, from municipal institutions, libraries, churches, media producers or enterprises can be used to gain extended knowledge with academic knowledge of equal right from teacher education. The synergy resulting from this interplay of knowledge forms in multiple activity systems. Yamazumi (2007) expects schools in such a network to become a crucial site for social innovation and change.

Shirley (2010) argues that community development and school improvement are mutually supportive undertakings. She assumes that community organizing is increasingly focusing on educational change, estimating, that 500 out of 800 community organizing groups in the USA are working in school reform. This movement can impact neoliberal accountability, if communities are involved in an approach of *public* accountability allowing modalities of "empowering participatory governance", new cultures of "collaboration transparency" or community-initiated policy reforms in public space. If community organizers and educators deepen collaboration they will "slowly but surely transform schools from islands of bureaucracy to centers of civic engagement" (Shirley, 2010, p. 183). This optimism is not shared by all educators who argue that when schools operate as high-performance learning organizations for a bottom-line of performance outcomes they denigrate communal-orientation to a narrow exchange-value for instrumental outcomes (Fielding, 2007).

In the context of activity theory, however, this discussion of opening-up the school to a partnership-based curricular innovation would be of crucial importance in relation to teacher professional learning into the future. In addition to boundary crossing, particularly between teachers' communities, student teachers, teacher educators and universities, especially communities from political institutions or associations of private initiatives are important for an agreement about innovation. As a result, innovative processes such as those in the CROSSNET or GIMMS projects would be at a higher discourse level between different activity systems in a sociocultural context.

The practical realization of boundary crossing between open schools and institutions requires increased democratic action of those concerned inside and outside school. The special concern highlights the particular importance of processes for the realization of goals. Primarily the communicative processes for deliberation are relevant for this process. From the deliberation of communities, normative questions develop about desirable goals or avoidable crises. The change dynamic is therefore based on judgments about sociocultural processes, which can be expected from partners working with adequate supports, structures and suitable prerequisites.

For deliberation in the public sphere, it is important to support creative forces in the school and local environment to strengthen their capability to assert themselves against neoconservative forces through deliberative democratization (Mawhinney, 2004).

This support is important because the possibility of realization is restricted by different cultural-historical counter-movements. They are presented comprehensively for education by Giroux (2002) in his analyzes of neoliberalism and in various theories of economic reproduction (Bourdieu & Passeron, 1977) or the hegemonic reproduction of the state (Gramsci, 2012). These theories suggest that, increasingly, educational and economic structures correspond, that the economy has colonized the field of education and that concerns in relation to the economy have gained supremacy from the cultural, social and the political, which are all subordinated as externalities (Muller, 2018; Tan, 2014).

According to Giroux (2002), however, there are opportunities to break through and interrupt this reproductive cycle. There are places and spaces containing contradictions that initiate criticism and resistance to the reproductive function of school. These contradictions and tensions can be recognized and transformed with the involvement of communities for a productive change. Lumumba (2017) argues that in a non-progressive system at least spaces should be reserved for the constructive development of a common good:

> Some have argued that despite the fundamentally intractable nature of education as an institution set to reproduce the existing social structure, it is possible to envisage and engage in actions that deliberately aim at limiting conservative, non-progressive, and consensus-bound education. It is argued that even if it is not possible to completely create a new system out of the old, it is possible to create spaces for constructive subversion for the common good.
>
> (p. 18)

140 Prospects for higher-order curriculum innovation

As a source of consciousness formation, not only a reproductive formation but also a critical function must be attributed to education as part of the cultural sphere. Through education, processes of domination, oppression and destruction can be critically discussed and alternatives can be developed. These, however, cannot be expected through state-imposed reforms. Rather, a democratic base must develop at the breakpoints of the reproductive cycle, which can partly escape from economic or state constraints. Dewey (2004) thought to create democratic citizens through reform pedagogy within school. In his view, over 100 years ago, schools have the possibility to bring about social transformation as a democratic event. The question is how relevant is his work on democracy today, in the light of a persistent stream of fake news and the slow suffocation of democracy (Feldges, 2019).

Taking into account the diverse possibilities of state interventions, the democratization of schools appears to be particularly successful when schools expand the public space to the outside. According to Habermas (1996), deliberative democracy acts as a link between a peripheral civil society and a public political system. A democratic approach, intending to change something, has to expand contradictions and tensions in public space so that the state's presuppositions lead to discursive justification in controversy of an opposing movement. This is more likely with the support of forces outside the school. An opening up of the school is, therefore, an important prerequisite for change independent of reproductive development. This would correspond to Nunez's (2009) proposal to see innovation within the framework of activity theory in a broader institutional and cultural-historical context:

> I suggest that nesting the activity system within broader institutional and cultural-historical contexts provides an innovative view adept for the analysis of contradictions.
>
> (p. 7)

However, the partnership of schools with local communities requires a two-sided development with mutual undertakings. Recently, community education and the philosophical framework for activities gain more attention in the public sphere (Wagner, 2013). For the future Shirley (2010) predicts a renaissance of community organizing and proposes a more intense collaboration for innovation between schools and the community:

> In the years to come, it will be necessary to community organizers and educators to deepen their collaboration and to structure educational change in such a way that community development and school improvement are mutually supportive undertakings that are sustainable for the future. To do so, at a certain level, it will be necessary for community organizers to continue their crucial contribution by revitalizing democracy and expanding the public sphere. Educators in turn will need to find new ways to network not only with one another but also to reach out to community members to confront

common problems, to share expertise, and to slowly but surely transform schools from islands of bureaucracy to centers of civic engagement.

(p. 183)

The proposed theoretical framework for deliberative innovation and its application in the CROSSNET and GIMMS projects is not fully satisfactory since it leaves some questions open to take account of the complexity of good teaching and teacher professional learning and the need for the interplay of a multiplicity of communities and diversity of components. In the present context of reform strategies using *bigger, tighter* and *harder* mechanisms of control and hierarchical accountability (Hargreaves et al., 2010) only a few aspects could be analyzed in terms of partnership-based curriculum innovation. Central to these efforts would be changes in teaching content based on disciplinary knowledge and standards and structures of educational systems expanding traditional modes of teaching toward more integrated knowledge claims and context-specific activities between communities of practice through deliberative discourses across boundaries. Nevertheless, this provides an expansive framework for a critical analysis focusing on substructures imparting important insights into innovation that are becoming more important in the overall framework.

For deliberative innovation in teacher education, the search for appropriate substructures is necessary. For this purpose, modified cooperation between schools and universities could be used in teacher education with gradual involvement of other communities, such as research institutions or local neighborhoods. Deliberative partnership-based cooperation requires learning processes and changes on *all* sides: on the school side, a higher-order communication, and on the university side, the avoidance of authoritative claims as the ultimate source of knowledge for enabling stronger alliances for authentic deliberation.

Of particular importance would be an increased consideration of policy implications for the development of curricular innovations. In addition to teachers and teacher educators, a number of actors from policy communities may become involved. At present, the role of policymakers seems to be concentrated on ensuring public accountability through regulatory control and measurement of standards (Ball, 2012) and to engage in neoliberal market-based principles and reform prescriptions. However, deliberative participation is desirable within a deeper and more nuanced understanding of the problems of teacher education for productive curriculum innovation.

For this purpose, prerequisites could be created by self-organization, formation and networking of a new generation of deliberative practitioners in communities from schools, universities, regional municipalities or political bodies. A basis for the development of deliberative practitioners could be collaborative projects with the goal of developing a partnership-based culture as evoked by community-engaged movements. These projects could develop boundary crossing networking and would enable the professionalization of deliberative practitioners through solidarity and political discourse, which can justify curriculum innovation and open new spaces for "intellectual quality" and authentic deliberation in public space (Gore et al., 2017; Nussbaum, 2010).

For this development, boundaries are to be expected in a neoliberal climate through limits imposed by an overemphasis on legal mandates, competition, hierarchies or disciplinary sanctions. These limits, however, lose some of their justification in the willingness of practitioners to agree on contradictions and take risks in creating justice and equity. This supports the assertion of Biesta (2013) that spaces need to be "open enough" so that the beautiful risk of education as an encounter between humans, in preference to robots, is not lost and that educators, researchers and teachers alike continue to mediate between self, professional practice and the world for emancipatory practices of research and teaching. Only in this way will research move beyond the aim of providing "turnkey solutions" (Marcel, 2013) and take seriously the social, critical and heuristic functions of education.

In this book, we have argued that using *Cultural-Historical Activity Theory* for deliberative democracy, offers a real alternative to reclaim teaching and teacher professional learning as advanced professional practices, particularly at the current crossroads, brought about by a fixation on metrics and an audit rationality, dominated by human capital arguments (Tan, 2014), which reduce the purposes of education to the development of competitive individualism for the purposes of individual and national economic success.

This deliberative alternative does not offer fixed goals, because it is a process approach of meaning-making, open to views of others and open to future development. It offers perspectives for the arrangement of processes that support deliberative democracy: teacher professionalization for higher-order meaning-making, boundary-crossing partnerships of multiple communities for opening minds and expansive learning beyond boundaries, guided by the "forceless force of better arguments" (Habermas, 1981) as deliberation in democracy. Deliberative boundary crossing, that is sensitive to others, to the facts and future possibilities, is not an easy task and requires one's reflexive positioning in critical relation to those of others. It outlines a chance for reforms to be enacted and contested using new sophisticated understandings through deliberative partnership in public space for networks of local communities and the imaginative possibility for something new to break through beyond the contemporary hegemonic closure of data analytics, prediction, risk-management and high control.

References

Aikenhead, G. (1996). Science education: border crossing into the subculture of science. *Studies in Science Education*, 27, 1–52.

AikenheadG. S. (2003). Review of research on humanistic perspectives in science curricula. Paper presented at the European Science Education Research Association (ESERA) 2003 Conference, Noordwijkerhout, The Netherlands, August 19–23, 2003. Available at: www.usask.ca/education/people/aikenhead/ESERA_2.pdf

Akkerman, S. F. & Bakker, A. (2011). Boundary crossing and boundary objects. *Review of Educational Research*, 81(2), 132–169.

Altrichter, H., Posch, P. & Somekh, B. (1993). *Teachers investigate their work: introduction into the behavioral method of action research*. London: Routledge.

Angus, L. (2012). Teaching within and against the circle of privilege: reforming teachers, reforming schools. *Journal of Education Policy*, 27(2), 231–251.

Apple, M. W. (2012). *Education and power* (2nd ed.). New York: Routledge.

Arendt, H. (2001). *Ideology and terror: a novel form of government*. New York: Houghton Mifflin Harcourt.

Arendt, H. (2013). *The last interview and other conversations*. Brooklyn, NY: Melville House.

Aronowitz, S. & Giroux, H. A. (1991). *Postmodern education politics, culture and social criticism*. Minneapolis and London: University of Minnesota Press.

Asay, L. D. & Orgill, M. (2010). Analysis of essential features of inquiry found in articles published in The Science Teacher, 1998–2007. *Journal of Science Teacher Education*, 21, 57–79.

Atkin, J. M. (1998). The OECD study of innovations in science, mathematics and technology education. *Journal of Curriculum Studies*, 30(6), 647–660.

Atkin, J. M. & Black, P. (2003). *Inside science education*. New York: Teachers College Columbia University.

Au, W. (2014). *Critical curriculum studies education, consciousness and the politics of knowing*. New York: Routledge.

Ball, S. J. (2012). *Global Education Inc.: new policy networks and the neo-liberal imaginary*. Oxon and New York: Routledge.

Ball, S. J. (2016). Neoliberal education? Confronting the slouching beast. *Policy Futures in Education*, 14(8), 1046–1059. doi:10.1177/1478210316664259

Ball, S. J., Maguire, M. & Braun, A. (2012). *How schools do policy: policy enactments in secondary schools*. London: Routledge.

144 References

Barab, S. & Duffy, T. (2000). From practice fields to community of practice. In D. H. Jonassen & S. M. Land (Eds.), *Theoretical foundations of learning environments* (P. 15–56). London: Lawrence Erlbaum.

Bates, R. (2012). An anarchy of cultures: aesthetics and the changing school. *Critical Studies in Education*, 53(1), 59–70.

Baumert, J. et al. (2001). *PISA 2000, Basiskonzepte von Schülerinnen und Schülern im internationalen Vergleich*. Opladen: Leske & Budrich.

Bayer, R. (2009). Kompetenzorientierter Physikunterricht. Kompetenzmatrix als Beispiel für Fachschaftsarbeit. Calw. Available at: https://lehrerfortbildung-bwde/fa echer/physik/gym/.../modul1_kompetenzmatrix.ppt

Biesta, G. J. J. (2012). Becoming public: public pedagogy, citizenship and the public sphere. *Social and Cultural Geography*, 13(7), 683–697.

Biesta, G. J. J. (2013). *The beautiful risk of education*. London: Routledge.

Biesta, G. J. J. & Miedema, S. (2002). Instruction or pedagogy? The need for a transformative conception of education. *Teaching and Teacher Education*, 18, 173–181.

Biesta, G. J. J., Priestley, M. & Robinson, S. (2017). Talking about education: exploring the significance of teachers' talk for teacher agency. *Journal of Curriculum Studies*, 49(1), 38–54. doi:10.1080/00220272.2016.1205143

Black, P. & Atkin, J. M. (1996). *Changing the subject: innovations in science, mathematics and technology education*. London: Routledge/OECD.

Bleakley, A. (1999). From reflective practice to holistic reflexivity. *Studies in Higher Education*, 24(3), 315–330.

Bloomfield, D. (2009). Working within and against neoliberal accreditation agendas: opportunities for professional experience. *Asia-Pacific Journal of Teacher Education*, 37(1), 27–44.

Bloomfield, D. & Nguyen, H. T. M. (2015). Creating and sustaining professional learning partnerships: activity theory as an analytic tool. *Australian Journal of Teacher Education*, 40(11), 23–44.

Blömeke, S. (2007). The impact of global tendencies in the German teacher education system. In T. Tatto (Ed.), *Reforming teaching globally* (55–96). Oxford: Symposium Book.

BMBF (Bildungsministerium für Bildung und Forschung) (2016). *Neue Wege in der Lehrerbildung. Qualitätsoffensive Lehrerbildung*. Berlin: BMBF. Available at: www.bmbf. de/pub/Neue_Wege_in_der_Leh rerbildung.pdf

Bonsen, M. & Rolff, H. G. (2006). Professional learning communities of teachers. *Zeitschrift für Pädagogik*, 52(2), 167–184.

Bos, W., Wendt, H., Köller, O. & Seiter, C. (2012). *TIMSS 2011: Mathematische und naturwissenschaftliche Kompetenzen von Grundschulkindern in Deutschland im internationalen Vergleich*. Münster/New York/München/Berlin: Waxmann.

Bourdieu, P. (1991). *Language and symbolic power*. Cambridge: Polity Press.

Bourdieu, P. & Passeron, J. (1977) *Reproduction in education, society and culture*. London: SAGE.

Bourke, T., Lidstone, J., & Ryan, M. (2015). Schooling teachers: professionalism or disciplinary power? *Educational Philosophy and Theory: Incorporating ACCESS*, 47(1), 84–100. doi:10.1080/00131857.2013.839374

Brady, A. M. (2016). The regime of self-evaluation: self-conception for teachers and schools. *British Journal of Educational Studies*, 64(4), 523–541. doi:10.1080/ 00071005.2016.1164829

References   145

Brady, A. M. (2019a, January 24). Anxiety of performativity and anxiety of performance: self-evaluation as bad faith. *Oxford Review of Education*, doi:10.1080/03054985.2018.1556626

Brady, A. M. (2019b). The teacher-student relationship: an existential approach. In T. Feldges (Ed.), *Philosophy and the study of education: new perspectives on a complex relationship* (P. 104–117). Abingdon, Oxon: Routledge.

Browning, C. R. (2018). The suffocation of democracy. *New York Review of Books*, October 25, 65(16), 14–17.

Buchberger, F., Cimpos, B., Kailos, D. & Stephenson, J. (2000). High quality teacher education for high quality education and training. Green Paper on Teacher Education in Europe. Umea: TNTEE.

Cardini, A. (2006). An analysis of the rhetoric and practice of educational partnerships in the UK: an arena of complexities, tensions and power. *Journal of Educational Policy*, 21(4), 393–415.

Carlgren, I. (1999). Professionalism and teachers as designers. *Journal of Curriculum Studies*, 31(1), 43–56.

Castaño, R., Poy, R., Tomsa, R., Flores, N. & Jenaro, C. (2015). Pre-service teachers' performance from teachers' perspective and vice versa: behaviours, attitudes and other associated variables. *Teachers and Teaching: Theory and Practice*, 21(7) 894–907, doi:10.1080/13540602.2014.99548.

Castell, M. (2000). *The rise of the networked society*. New York: Wiley.

Catapano, S. & Huisman, S. (2010). Preparing teachers for urban schools: evaluation of a community based model. *Perspectives on Urban Education*, Summer, 80–90. Available at: http://files.eric.ed.gov/fulltext/EJ894470.pdf (27. 02. 2017).

Clandinin, D. J. & Connelly, F. M. (1987). Teachers' personal knowledge: what counts as "personal" in studies of the personal. *Journal of Curriculum Studies*, 19(6), 487–500.

Clandinin, D. J. & Connelly, F. M. (1992). Teacher as curriculum maker. In P. W. Jackson (Ed.), *Handbook of research on curriculum* (P. 363–401). New York: MacMillan.

Clarke, M. (2010). Educational reform in the 1960s: the introduction of comprehensive schools in the Republic of Ireland. *History of Education*, 39(3), 383–399.

Cochran-Smith, M. & Lytle, S. (1999). Relationships of knowledge and practice: teacher learning in communities. In A. Iran-Nejad & P. D. Pearson (Eds.), *Review of Research in Education* (P. 249–305). Washington, DC: AERA.

Conle, C. (2000). Narrative inquiry: research tool and medium for professional development. *European Journal of Teacher Education*, 23(1), 43–63.

Connell, R. (2016). Good teachers on dangerous grounds: towards a new view of teacher quality and professionalism. *Critical Studies in Education*, 50(3), 213–229.

Connelly, F. M. (2013). Joseph Schwab: curriculum studies and educational reform. *Journal of Curriculum Studies*, 45(5), 622–639.

Cornbleth, C. (1990). *Curriculum in context*. Basingstoke: Falmer Press.

Coronel, J. M. & Gömez-Hurtado, I. (2015). Nothing to do with me! Teachers' perceptions on cultural diversity in Spanish secondary schools. *Teachers and teaching: theory and practice*, 21(4), 400–420.

Costello, H. (2017). *The PLUS partnership approach to structured teachers' learning: teachers as transformative intellectuals?* Unpublished master's thesis in Education (Mentoring). Limerick: University of Limerick.

Creswell, J. W. (2003). *Research design qualitative, quantitative and mixed methods approaches* (2nd ed.). Los Angeles: SAGE.

146 References

Cuban, L. (2001). *Oversold and underused: computers in the classroom*. Cambridge, MA: Harvard University Press.

Dahrendorf, R. (1965). *Bildung ist Bürgerrecht: Plädoyer für eine aktive Bildungspolitik. Die Zeit Bücher*. Hamburg: Nannenverlag.

Darling-Hammond, L. (1987). Schools for tomorrow's teachers. In F. S. Soltis (Ed.), *Reforming teacher education: the impact of the holmes group report* (P. 44–48). New York: Teachers College Press.

Davis, B., & Sumara, D. (2007). Complexity Science and Education: Reconceptualizing the Teacher's Role in Learning. *Interchange*, 38 (1), 53–67.

Day, C. & Sachs, J. (2004). Professionalism, performativity and empowerment: discourse in the politics, policies and purposes of continuing professional development. In C. Day & J. Sachs (Eds.), *International handbook on the continuing professional development of teachers* (P. 3–32). Maidenhead: Open University Press.

Dedering, K. (2015). Stiftungen im Bildungsbereich und ihre Formen der Einflussnahme. *Pädagogik*, 7(11), 40–45.

Deng, Z. (2013). The practical, curriculum, theory and practice: an international dialogue on Schwab's the 'Practical 1' introduction. *Journal of Curriculum Studies*, 45(5), 583–590.

Deutscher Bildungsrat (1970). *Empfehlungen der Bildungskommission*. Bad Godesberg: Bildungsrat.

Dewey, J. (2004). *Democracy and education*. Mineola, NY: Dover Publications.

Donnelly, J. (2002). Instrumentality, hermeneutics and the place of science in the school curriculum. *Science and Education*, 11(2), 135–153.

Doyle, W. & Westbury, I. (1992). Die Rückbesinnung auf den Unterrichtsinhalt in der Curriculum und Bildungsforschung in den USA. *Bildung und Erziehung*, 45(2), 137–157.

Döbert, H. & Weishaupt, H. (2013). *Inklusive Bildung professionell gestaltet: Situationsanalyse und Handlungsempfehlungen*. Münster: Waxmann.

Drake, S. M. (1998). *Creating integrated curriculum*. Thousand Oaks, CA: Corwin.

Edwards, A. (2010). The role of common knowledge in achieving collaboration across practices. *Learning, Culture and Social Interaction*, 1(1), 22–32.

Edwards, A. (Ed.) (2017). *Working relationally in and across practices: a cultural-historical approach to collaboration*. Cambridge: Cambridge University Press.

Eijkelhof, H. M. C. & Lijnse, P. (1988). The role of research and development to improve STS education: experiences from the PLON project. *International Journal of Science Education*, 10, 464–474.

Eisner, E. (1984). No easy answers: Joseph Schwab's contributions to curri culum. *Curriculum Inquiry*, 14(2), 201–210.

Engeström, Y. (1994). Teachers as collaborative thinkers: activity-theoretical study of an innovative teacher team. In I. Calgren, G. Handal & S. Vaage (Eds.), *Teachers mind and actions: research on teacher thinking and practice* (P. 9–27). London: Falmer Press.

Engeström, Y. (1999). *Perspectives on activity theory*. Cambridge: Cambridge University Press.

Engeström, Y. (2000). Activity theory as a framework for analysing and redesigning work. *Ergonomics*, 43, 960–974.

Engeström, Y. (2001). Expansive learning at work: toward an activity theoretical reconceptualization. *Journal of Education and Work*, 14, 133–156.

Engeström, Y. Engeström, R. & Kärkkäinen, M. (1995). Polycontextuality and boundary crossing in expert cognition: learning and problem solving in complex work activities. *Learning and Instruction*, 5, 319–336.

References 147

Engeström, Y. & Sannino, A. (2010). Studies of expansive learning: foundations, findings and future challenges. *Educational Research Review*, 5(1), 1–24.

Englund, T. (2016). On moral education through deliberative communication. *Journal of Curriculum Studies*, 48(1), 58–76.

Erikson, M. & Erikson, M. (2018). Learning outcomes and critical thinking – good intentions in conflict. *Studies in Higher Education*. doi:10.1080/03075079.2018.1486813

European Commission. (2018). *European ideas for better learning: the governance of school education systems*. Brussels: European Commission.

Eurostat (2015). Eurostat statistics explained gender pay gap statistics. Available at: http://ec.europa.eu/eurostat/statisticsexplained/ (08. 03. 2015).

Feldges, T. (Ed.) (2019). *Philosophy and the study of education new perspectives on a complex relationship*. Abingdon, Oxon: Routledge.

Foster, W. (2002). The decline of the local: a challenge to educational leadership. Paper presented at the 7th Annual Conference on Values and Leadership. Toronto, ON: OISE, August 5, 2002.

Francis, B. (2010). Re/theorising gender: female masculinity and male femininity in the classroom? *Gender and Education*, 22(5), 477–490.

Frei, A., Frey, K., Lang, M. & Malliou, K. (1984). Die "Curriculum-Konferenz" als neuer Ansatz zur Entwicklung eines Mathematik-Curriculums in der technischen Ausbildung. *Lernzielorientierter Unterricht*, 3, 27–32.

Freire, P. (1970). *Pedagogy of the oppressed*. New York: Herder.

Frey, K. (1975). Rechtfertigung von Bildungsinhalten im elementaren Diskurs: Ein Entwurf für den Bereich der didaktischen Rekonstruktion. In R. Künzli (Ed.), *Curriculumentwicklung. Begründung und Legitimation* (P. 103–129). München: Kösel.

Frey, K. (1983). Kodifizierte Bestimmungsfaktoren curricularer Lernereignisse: Vorbemerkung. In U. Hameyer, K. Frey & H. Haft (Eds.), *Handbuch der Curriculumforschung* (P. 303). Weinheim: Beltz.

Fullan, M. & Hargreaves, A. (1992). *Teacher development and educational change*. London: Falmer.

Fullan, M. & Stiegelbauer, S. (1991). *The new meaning of educational change*. New York: Teachers College Press.

Furlong, J. (2013). *Education: an anatomy of the discipline rescuing the university project?* London and New York: Routledge.

Fuss, A., Gibat, G., Liebenberg, K. & Neumann, E. (1979) Laborschule Bielefeld – Die Entschulung der Schule im Kreuzfeuer der Bildungspolitik. In L. Landwehr & M. Lang (Eds.) *Alternative Formen schulischen Lernens*. Kiel: IPN. IPN-Arbeitsberichte 37.

Galvin, M. & Mooney Simmie, G. (2017). Theorizing participation in urban regeneration partnerships: an adult education perspective. *Journal of Education Policy*, 32(6), 809–831.

Gibson, I. (2005). Transforming education: linking technology, work, community and lifelong learning in a secondary college. 118–133. In S. Trinidad & J. Pearson (Eds.), *Using information and communication technologies in education: effective leadership change and models of best practice*. Singapore: Prentice-Hall.

Gillies, D. (2017) Developing the thoughtful practitioner. In M. A. Peters, B. Cowie & I. Menter (Eds.), *A companion to research in teacher education*. Singapore: Springer.

Giroux, H. A. (1988). *Teachers as intellectuals: toward a critical pedagogy of learning*. Westport, CT: Bergin and Garvey.

Giroux, H. A. (2002). Kritische Pädagogik und der Aufstieg des Neoliberalismus. *Das Argument 246*, 44(3), 325–332.

Giroux, H. A. (2005). *Border crossings*. New York: Routledge.

148 References

Giroux, H. A. (2015). *Education and the crisis of public values.* New York: Lang.

Giroux, H. A. & McLaren, P. (Eds.) (1994). *Between borders pedagogy and the politics of cultural studies.* London and New York: Routledge.

Gore, J. M. (2012). *The struggle for pedagogies.* Oxon: Routledge.

Gore, J. M., Lloyd, A., Smith, M., Bowe, J., Ellis, H. & Lubans, D. (2017). Effects of professional development on the quality of teaching: results from a randomised controlled trial of Quality Teaching Rounds. *Teaching and Teacher Education,* 68, 99–113.

Gramsci, A. (2012). *Gefängnishefte. Gesamtausgabe in 10 Bänden. (edited in 10 volumes).* In K. von Bochmann & W. F. Haug (Eds.), Hamburg: Argument-Verlag.

Gräsel, C., Nentwig, P. & Parchmann, I. (2005). Chemie im Kontext: curriculum development and evaluation strategies. In J. Bennett, J. Holman, R. Millar & D. Waddington (Eds.), *Making a difference: evaluation as tool for improving science education* (P. 53–66). Münster: Waxmann.

Green, J. & Luke, A. (2006). Introduction. Rethinking learning: what counts as learning and what learning counts. *Review of Research in Education,* 30, 11–14. doi:10.3102/0091732X030001011

Gronn, P. (2000). Distributed properties: a new architecture of leadership. *Educational Management Administration & Leadership,* 28, 317–338.

Grummell, B., Devine, D. & Lynch, K. (2009). The careless manager: gender, care and new management in higher education. *Gender and Education,* 21(2), 191–208.

Gunter, H. (2001). Critical approaches to leadership in education. *Journal of Educational Enquiry,* 2(2), 94–108.

Habermas, J. (1974). Vorbereitende Bemerkungen zu einer Theorie der kommunikativen Kompetenz. In J. Habermas & N. Luhmann (Eds.), *Theorie der Gesellschaft oder Sozialtechnologie* (P. 101–141). Frankfurt: Suhrkamp.

Habermas, J. (1981). *Theorie des kommunikativen Handelns.* Frankfurt: Suhrkamp.

Habermas, J. (1990). *Strukturwandel der Öffentlichkeit.* Frankfurt: Suhrkamp.

Habermas, J. (1996). *Die Einbeziehung des Anderen.* Frankfurt: Suhrkamp.

Hameyer, U. (1983a). Allgemeine Curriculumtheorien. In U. Hameyer, K. Frey & H. Haft (Eds.), *Handbuch der Curriculumforschung* (P. 29–51). Weinheim: Beltz.

Hameyer, U. (1983b). Systematisierung von Curriculumtheorien. In U. Hameyer, K. Frey & H. Haft (Eds.), *Handbuch der Curriculumforschung* (P. 53–100). Weinheim: Beltz.

Hameyer, U., Frey, K. & Haft, H. (1983). Einführung. In U.Hameyer, K. Frey & H. Haft (Eds.), *Handbuch der Curriculumforschung* (P. 11–22). Weinheim: Beltz.

Hammersley-Fletcher, L., Clarke, M. & McManus, V. (2018). Agonistic democracy and passionate professional development in teacher-leaders. *Cambridge Journal of Education,* 48(5), 591–606.

Hansen, K.-H., Gräber, W. & Lang, M. (Eds.) (2012). *Crossing boundaries in science teacher education.* Münster: Waxmann.

Hardy, I. (2018) Governing teacher learning: understanding teachers' compliance with critique of standardization. *Journal of Education Policy,* 33 (1) 1–12.

Hargreaves, A. (1994). *Changing teachers, changing times: teacher' work and culture in the postmodern age.* New York: Teachers College Press.

Hargreaves, A. (2000). Contrived collegiality: the micro politics of teacher collaboration. In S. J. Ball (Ed.), *Sociology of education* (Bd. III, P. 1480–1503). London: Routledge.

Hargreaves, A. (2003). *Teaching in the knowledge society.* New York: Teachers College Press.

References 149

Hargreaves, A. (2010). Change from without: lessons from other countries, systems and sectors. In A. Hargreaves, A. Liebermann, M. Fullan & D. Hopkins (Eds.), *Second international handbook of educational change*. New York: Springer.

Hargreaves, A. & Fullan, M. (2012). *Professional capital*. New York: Teacher College Press.

Hargreaves, A., Liebermann, A., Fullan, M. & Hopkins, D. (2010). Introduction: ten years of change. In A. Hargreaves, A. Liebermann, M. Fullan & D. Hopkins (Eds.), *Second international handbook of educational change* (P. 11–21). New York: Springer.

Harlen, W. (1999). The assessment of scientific literacy in the OECD/PISA project. In M. Komorek, H. Behrendt, H. Dahncke, R. Duit & W. Gräber (Eds.), *Research in science education: past, present, future* (Bd. II, P. 652–653). Kiel: IPN.

Harvey, D. (2007). *A brief history of neoliberalism*. Oxford: Oxford University Press.

Hattie, J. (2009). *Visible learning: a synthesis of over 800 meta-analyses relating to achievement.* London and New York: Routledge.

Held, D. (2006): *Models of democracy* (3rd ed.). Cambridge: Polity Press.

Hentig, H.von (1971) *Das Bielefelder Oberstufenkolleg*. Stuttgart: Klett.

Hesse, F., Grasoffsky, B. & Hron, A. (1995). Interface-Design für computerunterstütztes kooperatives Lernen. In L. Issing & P. Klimsa (Eds.), *Information und Lernen mit Multimedia* (P. 253–265). Weinheim: Beltz.

Hiebert, J., Gallimore, R. & Stigler, J. W. (2002). A knowledge base for the teaching profession: what would it look like and how can we get it? *Educational Researcher*, 31(5), 3–15.

Ho, J. P., Chen, D. V. & Ng, D. (2015). Distributed leadership through the lens of Activity Theory. *Educational Management Administration & Leadership*, 44(5), 814–836.

Hoffmann, L. (2002). Promoting girls' interest and achievement in physics classes for beginners. *Learning and Instruction*, 12, 447–465.

Holland-Letz, M. (2011). *Privatisierungsreport – 13. Private Stiftungen versus demokratischer Staat – wie der Neoliberalismus weltweit das öffentliche Bildungswesen untergräbt*. Frankfurt: GEW.

Hopmann, S. & Riquarts, K. (Eds.) (1995). Didaktik and/or curriculum. *Zeitschrift für Pädagogik*, 33, 9–34.

Horlacher, R. (2018). The same but different: the German Lehrplan and curriculum. *Journal of Curriculum Studies*, 50(1), 1–16.

Horstkemper, M. (1999). Gender and professionalism. In M. Lang, J. Olson, H. Hansen & W. Bünder (Eds.), *Changing schools/changing practices: perspectives on educational reform and teacher professionalism* (P. 55–64). Louven: Garant.

Huber, S. G., Ahlgrimm, F. & Hader-Popp, S. (2012). Kooperation in und zwischen Schulen sowie mit anderen Bildungseinrichtungen: Aktuelle Diskussionsstränge, Wirkungen und Gelingensbedingungen. In S. G. Huber & F. Ahlgrimm (Eds.), *Kooperation. Aktuelle Forschung zur Kooperation in und zwischen Schulen sowie mit anderen Partnern*. Münster: Waxmann.

Jackson, P. W. (1968). *Life in classrooms*. New York: Holt, Rinehart & Winston.

Jackson, P. W., Boostrom, R. E. & Hansen, D. T. (1998). *The moral life of schools*. San Francisco, CA: JosseyBass.

Jank, W. & Meyer, H. (1991). *Didaktische Modelle*. Berlin: Cornelsen.

Jenkins, E. (1972). The general science movements. In E. Jenkins (Ed.), *From Armstrong to Nuffield* (P. 27–86). London: John Murray.

Kayser, B. & Fuhr, R. (1983). Kompetenzen in Curriculumprozessen. In U. Hameyer, K. Frey & H. Haft (Eds.), *Handbuch der Curriculumforschung* (P. 275–265). Weinheim: Beltz.

150   References

Kedley, K. E. (2015). Queering the teacher as a text in the English language arts classroom: beyond books, identity work and teacher preparation. *Sex Education: Sexuality, Society and Learning*, 15, 364–377.

Kelchtermans, G. (2006). Teacher collaboration and collegiality as workplace conditions: a review. *Zeitschrift für Pädagogik*, 52(2) 220–237.

Kerensky, V. M. & Logston, J. D. (1980). A new foundation: perspectives on community. *Community Education Bulletin*, 59(394) 1–4.

Kincheloe, J. (2004). The knowledges of teacher education: developing a critical complex epistemology. *Teacher Education Quarterly*, Winter, 49–66.

Klieme, E., Artelt, C., Hartig, J., Jude, N., Koller, O., Prenzel, M., Schneider, W. & Stanat, P. (Eds.) (2010). *PISA 2009: Bilanz nach einem Jahrzehnt*. Münster: Waxmann.

Knab, D. (1969). Curriculumforschung und Lehrplanreform. *Neue Sammlung*, 1, 169–185.

Knab, D. (1983). Der Beitrag der Curriculumforschung zu Erziehungswissenschaft und Bildungstheorie: Versuch einer Zwischenbilanz. In U. Hameyer, K. Frey & H. Haft (Eds.), *Handbuch der Curriculumforschung* (S, 697–711). Weinheim: Beltz.

Krainer, K. & Kühnelt, H. (2002). *Lernen im Aufbruch: Mathematik und Naturwissenschaften. Pilotprojekt IMST²*. Innsbruck: Studienverlag.

Kreis, A., Wick, J. & Labhart, C. (Eds.) (2016). *Kooperation im Kontext schulischer Heterogenität*. Münster: Waxmann.

Krohn, W. & Küppers, G. (1990). *Selbstorganisation: aspekte einer wissenschaftlichen Revolution*. Wiesbaden: Vieweg.

Kultusminister-Konferenz. (2005). Vereinbarung über Bildungsstandards für den Mittleren Schulabschluss. *Friedrich Jahresheft*, 22(XXIII) 130–143.

Laferrière, T. (2018). Boundary crossings resulting in active learning in preservice teacher education: a CHAT analysis revealing the tensions and springboards between partners. *Frontiers in ICT*, 5(22) 1–9. doi:10.3389/fict.2018.00022

Lahelma, E. (2014). Troubling discourses on gender and education. *Educational Research*, 56(2), 171–183.

Lambert, P. (2003). Promoting developmental transfer in vocational teacher education. In T. Tuomi-Gröhn & I. Engeström (Eds.), *Between school and work: perspectives on transfer and boundary-crossing* (P. 233–256). Amsterdam: Pergamon/Earli.

Lang, M. (2007a). *Aspects of boundary crossing in education: summaries and sources of selected literature*. Kiel: IPN (unpublished).

Lang, M. (2007b). How to improve science teaching in Europe: focusing in teachers' voices in professional development. In M. Lang, D. Couso, D. Elster, U. Klinger, G. Mooney Simmie & P. Szybek (Eds.), *Professional development and school improvement: science teachers' voices in school-based reform* (P. 7–28). Innsbruck: Studienverlag.

Lang, M. (2012). Innovation in the Science Curriculum: The Intersection of School Practice and Research. In K.-H. Hansen, W. Gräber & M. Lang (Eds.), *Crossing Boundaries in Science Teacher Education* (P. 33~47)- Münster: Waxmann.

Lang, M., Couso, D., Elster, D., Klinger, U., Mooney Simmie, G. & Szybek, P. (Eds.) (2007). *Professional development and school improvement: science teachers' voices in school-based reform*. Innsbruck: Studienverlag.

Lauterbach, R. (1992). Praxis Integrierter Naturwissenschaftlicher Grundbildung (PING). In P. Häußler (Ed.), *Physikunterricht und Menschenbildung* (P. 251–274). Kiel: IPN.

Lave, J. & Wenger, E. (1991). *Situated learning: legitimate peripheral participation*. Cambridge: Cambridge University Press.

References 151

Lenzen, D. (2015, August 6). Warum Uni-Präsident Dieter Lenzen Angst vor TTIP hat. *Hamburger Abendblatt*.

Lewis, E. (2012). Locating the third space in initial teacher education. *Research in Teacher Education*, 2(2), 31–36.

Lillejord, S. & Borte, K. (2016). Partnership in teacher education: a research mapping. *European Journal of Teacher Education*, 39(3), 550–563.

Lim, L. (2014). Ideology, rationality and reproduction in education: a critical discourse analysis. *Discourse: Studies in the Cultural Politics of Education*, 35(1), 61–76.

Lingard, B., Sellar, S. & Savage, G. (2014). Rearticulating social justice as equity in school policy: the effects of testing and data infrastructures. *British Journal of Sociology of Education*, 35(5), 710–713.

Lipman, P. (2011). *The new political economy of urban education neoliberalism, race and the right to the city*. Routledge: New York and London.

Little, J. W. (1990). Teachers as colleagues. In A. Lieberman (Ed.), *Schools as collaborative cultures: creating the future now* (P. 165–193). New York: Falmer Press.

Livingston, K. (2018). Teachers' professional learning within learning systems. *European Journal of Teacher Education*, 41(4), 415–417. doi:10.1080/02619768.2018.1491379

Lortie, D. C. (1975). *School teacher: a sociological study*. Chicago, IL: University of Chicago Press.

Loughran, J. (2006). *Developing a pedagogy of teacher education: understanding teaching and learning about teaching*. London: Routledge.

Loughran, J. (2012). *Developing a pedagogy of teacher education*. London: Routledge.

Löwisch, D. J. (2000). Pädagogische Ethik und Normativität einer diskursiven Verantwortungsethik (Pedagogical ethics and the normativity of discursive responsible ethics). *Pädagogische Rundschau*, 54, 377–384.

Lumumba, N. T. (2017). The Ubuntu paradigm and comparative and international education: epistemological challenges and opportunities in our field. *Comparative Education Review*, 61(1), 1–18.

Lynch, K. (1999). *Equality in education*. Dublin: Gill and Macmillan Ltd.

Lynch, K. (2015). Control by numbers: new managerialism and ranking in higher education. *Critical Studies in Education*, 55(2), 190–207. doi:10.1080/17508487.2014.949811

Makarova, E. & Herzog, W. (2015). Trapped in the gender stereotype? The image of science among secondary school students and teachers. *Equality, Diversity and Inclusion: An International Journal*, 24(2), 106–123.

Marcel, J.-F. (2013). Critical approach to the contribution made by education research to the social construction of the value of teaching work. *Policy Futures in Education*, 1(3), 225–240.

Martin, M. O., Mullis, I. V. S., Foy, P. & StancoG. M. (2012). *TIMSS 2011: international results in science*. Chestnut Hill, MA: Boston College.

Mawhinney, H. B. (2004). Deliberative democracy in imagined communities: how the power geometry of globalization shapes local leadership praxis. *Educational Administration*

McLaren, P. (2016). *Pedagogy of insurrection*. New York: Peter Lang Publishers.

Mooney Simmie, G. (2007). Teacher Design Teams (TDTs) – building capacity for innovation, learning and curriculum implementation in the continuing professional development of in-career teachers. *Irish Educational Studies*, 26(2), 163–176. doi:10.1080/03323310701295914

Mooney Simmie, G. (2009). *The policy implementation process in the upper secondary education system (senior cycle) and videregående skolen in science and mathematics in the Republic of Ireland and the Kingdom of Norway from 1960–2005*. PhD thesis. Dublin: Trinity College Dublin.

152 References

Mooney Simmie, G. (2012). Democratic mentoring as a deliberative discourse for educational innovation and teacher continuing education. In G. Mooney Simmie & M. Lang (Eds.), *What's worth aiming for in educational innovation and change?* (P. 15–24). Münster: Waxmann.

Mooney Simmie, G. (2014). The neo-liberal turn in understanding teachers' and school leaders' work practices in curriculum innovation and change: a critical discourse analysis of a newly proposed reform policy in lower secondary education in the Republic of Ireland. *Citizenship, Social and Economics Education*, 13(3), 185–198. doi:10.2304/csee.2014.13.3.185

Mooney Simmie, G. & Edling, S. (2016). Ideological governing forms in education and teacher education: a comparative study between highly secular Sweden and highly non-secular Republic of Ireland. *Nordic Journal of Studies in Educational Policy*, 2 (32041), 1–12. doi:10.3402/nstep.v2.32041

Mooney Simmie, G. & Edling, S. (2018, March 12). Teachers' democratic assignment: a critical discourse analysis of teacher education policies in Ireland and Sweden. *Discourse Studies in the Cultural Politics of Education.* doi:10.1080/01596306.2018.1449733

Mooney Simmie, G. & Lang, M. (2012). *What's worth aiming for in educational innovation and change?* Münster: Waxmann.

Mooney Simmie, G. & Lang, M. (2015). Deliberative teacher education for inclusion of gender. Paper presented at the Toward justice culture, language and heritage in education research and praxis, American Educational Research Association, AERA Chicago 2015, Chicago, IL, April 16, 2015, Paper Session 14.027, p. 40.

Mooney Simmie, G. & Lang, M. (2017). Developing a framework for inter-professional deliberation of gender awareness and inclusion. Paper presented at the American Educational Research Association AERA 2017, San Antonio, Texas, April 27, 2017, Division B: curriculum studies, section 5 (Place and praxis – the places of curriculum), p. 52.

Mooney Simmie, G. & Lang, M. (2018). Deliberative teacher education beyond boundaries: discursive practices for eliciting gender awareness. *Teachers and Teaching Theory and Practice*, 24(2), 135–150. doi:10.1080/13540602.2017.1370420

Mooney Simmie, G. & Moles, J. (2011). Critical thinking, caring and professional agency: an emerging framework for productive mentoring. *Mentoring & Tutoring: Partnership in Learning*, 19(4), 465–482.

Mooney Simmie, G., Moles, J. & O'Grady, E. (2019). Good teaching as a messy narrative of change within a policy ensemble of networks, superstructures and flows. *Critical Studies in Education*, 60(1), 55–72. doi:10.1080/17508487.2016.1219960

Mooney Simmie, G. & Power, S. (2012). Innovations in science education through school university partnership. In K.-H. Hansen, W. Gräber & M. Lang (Eds.) (2012). *Crossing boundaries in science education* (P. 233–254). Münster, New York, München and Berlin: Waxmann Publishers.

Muijs, D. (2015). Improving schools through collaboration: a mixed methods study of school-to-school partnerships in the primary sector. *Oxford Review of Education*, 41(5), 563–586.

Muller, J. K. (2018). *The tyranny of metrics*. Princeton, NJ: Princeton University Press.

Murnane, R. J. & Raizen, P. A. (1988). *Improving the indicators of the quality of science and mathematics education in grades K12*. Washington, DC: National Academy Press.

Murray, J. (2014). *Developing the European agenda for teacher educators*. ILS Mail, 1(14), 3–7.

Murray, J. & Male, T. (2005). Becoming a teacher educator: evidence from the field. *Teaching and Teacher Education*, 21, 125–142.

References 153

Nixon, J. (2004). Learning the language of deliberative democracy. In M. Walker & J. Nixon (Eds.), *Reclaiming universities from a runaway world* (P. 114–127). Maidenhead: Open University Press.

Noddings, N. (2007). *When school reform goes wrong.* New York: Teachers College, Columbia University.

Nunez, I. (2009, December). Activity theory and the utilisation of the activity system according to the mathematics education community. *Educate, Special Issue*, 7–20. Available at: www.educatejournal.org

Nussbaum, M. C. (2010). *Not for profit why democracy needs the humanities.* Princeton, NJ: Princeton University Press.

OECD (2004). *Teachers matter: attracting, developing and retaining effective teachers.* Paris: OECD. Available at: www.oecd.org/education/school/34990905.pdf

OECD (2009). *TALIS: teaching and learning international study.* Paris: OECD.

OECD (2012). *Programme for international student achievement (PISA).* Available at: www.pisa.oecd.org

OECD (2013). *TALIS: teaching and learning international study.* Paris: OECD.

Olson, J. (2002). Systemic change/teacher tradition: legends of reform continue. *Journal of Curriculum Studies*, OP-ED, 34(2), 129–137.

Olson, J. (2007). School reform and the role of the teacher workshops as places of discourse. In M. Lang, D. Couso, D. Elster, U. Klinger, G. Mooney Simmie & P. Szybek (Eds.), *Professional development and school improvement: science teachers' voices in school-based reform* (P. 192–209). Innsbruck: Studienverlag.

Olson, J. & Hansen, K.-H. (2012). New directions in science education and the culture of the school – the CROSSNET project as a transnational framework for research. In K.-H. Hansen, W. Gräber & M. Lang (Eds.), *Crossing boundaries in science teacher education* (P. 9–31). Münster: Waxmann.

Olson, J., James, E. and Lang, M. (1999). Changing the subject: the challenge to teacher professionalism of innovation in OECD countries. *Journal of Curriculum Studies*, 31(1), 69–82.

Olson, J. & Lang, M. (2004). Science and technology and the didactics of citizenship. *Journal of Curriculum Studies*, 36, OP-ED, 543–553.

Opfer, V. D. & Pedder, D. (2011). Conceptualising teacher professional learning. *Review of Educational Research*, 83(3), 376–407. doi:10.3102/0034654311413609

Oser, F. (1992). Morality in professional action: a discourse approach for teaching. In F. Oser, A. Dick & J.-L. Patry (Eds.), *Effective and responsible teaching* (P. 109–125). San Francisco, CA: Jossey-Bass.

Oser, F. K., Achtenhagen, F. & Renold, U. (Eds.) (2006). *Competence oriented teacher training: old research demands and new pathways.* Rotterdam: Sense Publishers.

O'Buachalla, S. (1988). *Education Policy in Twentieth Century Ireland.* Dublin: Wolfhound Press.

O'Neill, O. (2013). Intelligent accountability in education. *Oxford Review of Education*, 39(1), 4–16.

Page, R. (2003). *Invitation to curriculum.* Vice-Presidential address Division B. Chicago, IL: AERA.

Papagiannis, G. J., Easton, P. A. & Owens, J. T. (1992). *The school restructuring movement in the USA: an analysis of major issues and policy implications.* IIEP research and studies programme, Monograph No. 6. Paris: UNESCO.

Pereira, P. (1992). An introduction to curriculum deliberation. Available at: https://condor.depaul.edu/ppereira/pers/intro.htm (13. 09. 2019).

154 References

Pepper, S. K., Hartman, K. J., Blackwell, S. E. & Monroe, A. E. (2016). Creating an environment of educational excellence: the University of Mississippi-PDS Partnership – the evolution continues. *School-University Partnerships*, 5(1), 74–88.

Picht, G. (1964). *Die Deutsche Bildungskatastrophe: Analyse und Dokumentation*. Ölten: dtv.

Pillow, W. (2003). Confession, catharsis or cure? Rethinking the uses of reflexivity as methodological power in qualitative research. *International Journal of Qualitative Studies in Education*, 16(2), 175–196. doi:10.1080/0951839032000060635

Pinar, W. F., Reynolds, W. M., Slattery, P. & Taubman, P. M. (2008). Understanding curriculum as political text. In W. Pinar, W. M. Reynolds, P. Slattery & P. M. Taubman (Eds.), *Understanding curriculum: an introduction to the study of historical and contemporary curriculum discourses* (P. 243–314). New York: Peter Lang.

Polanyi, M. (1958). *Personal knowledge: towards a post-critical philosophy*. Chicago, IL: The University of Chicago Press.

Posch, P. (1993). Research issues in environmental education. *Studies in Science Education*, 21, 21–48.

Postholm, M. B. (2015). Methodologies in cultural-historical activity theory: the example of school-based development. *Educational Research*, 57(1), 43–58.

Postholm, M. B. (2016). Collaboration between teacher educators and schools to enhance development. *European Journal of Teacher Education*, 39(4), 452–470.

Power, S. A. (2012). *Educational innovation and change in the teaching and learning of science in the contemporary Irish school and classroom*. Unpublished PhD study. Limerick: University of Limerick.

Randi, J. & Corno, L. (1997). Teachers as innovators. In B. J. Biddle, T. L. Good & I. Goodson (Eds.), *International handbook of teachers and teaching* (P. 1163–1221). Dordrecht: Kluwer.

Reith, K.-H. (2017). Methoden-Stunk um PISA-Punkte. *Erziehung & Wissenschaft*, 1, 20–22.

Riquarts, K. & Hansen, K.-H. (1998). Collaboration among teachers, researchers and in-service trainers to develop an integrated science curriculum. *Journal of Curriculum Studies*, 30(6), 661–676.

Roth, W.-M. (2003). Scientific literacy as an emergent feature of collective human praxis. *Journal of Curriculum Studies*, 35(1), 9–23.

Roth, W.-M. & LeeY.-J. (2007). "Vigotsky's Neglected Legacy": cultural-historical activity theory. *Review of Educational Research*, 77(2), 168–232.

Rönnberg, L. (2017). From national policy-making to global edubusiness: Swedish edupreneurs on the move. *Journal of Education Policy*, 32(2), 234–249. doi:10.1080/02680939.2016.1268725

Ruitenberg, C. W. (2009). Educating political adversaries: Chantal Mouffe and radical democratic citizenship education. *Studies in Philosophy of Education*, 28, 269–281.

Santoro, D. A. (2017). Cassandra in the classroom: teaching and moral madness. *Studies in Philosophy of Education*, 36, 49–60.

Sawyer, L. B. E. & Rimms-Kaufman, S. E. (2007). Teacher collaboration in the context of the Responsive Classroom approach. *Teachers and Teaching: Theory and Practice*, 13(3), 211–245.

Scantlebury, K. & Baker, D. (2007). Gender issues in science education research: remembering where the difference lies. In S. K. Abell & N. G. Lederman (Eds.), *Handbook of research on science education* (P. 257–286). London: Lawrence Erlbaum Associates.

Schenke, W., van Driel, J. H., Geijsel, F. R., Sligte, H. W. & Volman, M. L. L. (2016). Characterizing cross-professional collaboration in research and development projects in secondary education. *Teachers and Teaching: Theory and practice*, 22(5),553–569.

References 155

Schmeichel, M., Sharma, A. & Pittard, E. (2017). Contours of neoliberalism in US empirical educational research. *Curriculum Inquiry*, 47(2), 195–216.

Schön, D. (1983). *The reflective practitioner: how professionals think in action.* New York: Basic Books.

Schön, D. (1990). *Educating the reflective practitioner.* San Francisco, CA: Jossey-Bass.

Schwab, J. J. (1970). *The practical: a language for curriculum.* Washington, DC: National Education Association, Centre for Study of Instruction, 1–39.

Schwab, J. J. (1983). The practical 4: something for curriculum professors to do. *Curriculum Inquiry*, 13(3), 239–265.

Schwab, J. (2013, reprint). The practical: a language for curriculum. *Journal of Curriculum Studies*, 45(5), 591–621. (Original published 1969).

Sellar, S. & Lingard, B. (2013). The OECD and global governance in education. *Journal of Education Policy*, 28(5), 710–725. doi:10.1080/02680939.2013.779791

Shields, C. M. (2016). *Transformative leadership in education: equitable change in an uncertain and complex world.* New York: Routledge.

Shirley, D. (2010) Community organization and educational change. In A. Hargreaves, A. Liebermann, M. Fullan & D. Hopkins (Eds.), *Second international handbook of educational change* (P. 169–184). New York: Springer.

Sjöberg, S. (2012). PISA: politics, fundamental problems and intriguing. *La Revue, Recherches en Education*, 14, 1–21.

Sjöberg, S. (2015). PISA and global educational governance: a critique of the project, its uses and implications. *Eurasia Journal of Mathematics, Science & Technology Education*, 11(1), 111–127.

Skerritt, C. (2019). Discourse and teacher-identity in business-like education. *Policy Futures in Education*, 17(2), 153–171. doi:10.1177/1478210318774682

Smith, E. R. (2007). Negotiating power and pedagogy in student teaching: expanding and shifting roles in expert-novice discourse. *Mentoring & Tutoring*, 15(1), 87–106.

Smith, M. K. (2000). Curriculum theory and practice. *The encyclopaedia of informal education.* Available at: www.infed.org/biblio/b-curric.htm (26. 05. 2016).

Solomon, J. & Aikenhead, G. (Eds.) (1994). *STS education: international perspectives on reform.* Ways of Knowing Science Series. New York: Teachers College Press.

Solomon, J. & Thomas, J. (1999). Science education for the public understanding of science. *Studies in Science Education*, 33, 61–90.

Spillane, J. P. (2015). Leadership and learning: conceptualizing relations between school administrative practice and instructional practice. *Societies*, 5(2), 277–294. doi:10.3390/soc5020277

Stadler, H. & Newmann, S. (2012). Austria: video analysis for educational innovation, mentoring and inclusion. In G. Mooney Simmie & M. Lang (Eds.), *What's worth aiming for in educational innovation and change?* (P. 80–88). Münster: Waxmann.

Star, S. M. (1989). The structure of ill-structured solutions: boundary objects and heterogeneous distributed problem solving. In L. Gasser & M. N. Huhns (Eds.), *Distributed artificial intelligence.* Amsterdam: Elsevier.

Steel, S. (2018). Revisioning philosophy instruction in competency-based B.Ed. programs. *Interchange*, 49, 417–431.

Steinert, B., Klieme, E., Merki, K. M., Döbrich, R., Halbheer, U. & Kunz, A. (2006). Lehrerkooperation in der Schule: Konzeption, Erfassung, Ergebnisse. *Zeitschrift für Pädagogik*, 52(2), 185–204.

156 References

Stenhouse, L. (1975). *An introduction to curriculum research and development*. London: Heinemann.

Sterling, S. (2014). Separate tracks or real synergy? Achieving a closer relationship between education and SD, post-2015. *Journal of Education for Sustainable Development*, 8(2), 89–112.

Strike, K. A. (1994). Discourse ethics and restructuring. In M. Katz (Ed.), *Philosophy of Education* (P. 1–14). Urbana, IL: Philosophy of Education Society.

Tan, E. (2014). Human capital theory: a holistic criticism. *Review of Educational Research*, 84(3), 411–445.

Tatto, T. (Ed.) (2007). *Reforming teaching globally*. Oxford: Symposium Book.

Teaching Council (2011). *Initial teacher education: criteria and guidelines for programme providers*. Maynooth: Teaching Council.

Terhart, E. (1999). Developing a professional culture. In M. Lang, J. Olson, K.-H. Hansen & W. Bünder (Eds.), *Changing schools changing practices: perspectives on educational reform and teacher professionalism* (P. 27–40). Leuven: Garant.

Terhart, E. (2000). *Perspektiven der Lehrerbildung in Deutschland. Abschlussbericht der von der Kultusministerkonferenz eingesetzten Kommission*. Weinheim und Basel: Beltz.

Terhart, E. (2013). *Erziehungswissenschaften und Lehrerbildung*. Münster: Waxmann.

Terhart, E. & Klieme, E. (2006). Kooperation im Lehrerberuf – Forschungsproblem und Gestaltungsaufgabe. Zur Einführung in den Thementeil. *Zeitschrift für Pädagogik*, 52(2), 163–167.

Thomas, G. (2013). A review of thinking and research about inclusive education policy, with suggestions for a new kind of inclusive thinking. *British Educational Research Journal*, 39(3), 473–490.

Timperley, H., Wilson, A., Barrar, H. & Fung, I. (2007). *Teacher professional learning and development: Best evidence synthesis iteration (BES)*. New Zealand: New Zealand Ministry of Education.

Toulmin, S. (1958). *The use of arguments*. Cambridge: Cambridge University Press.

Tröhler, D. (2014). Change management in the governance of schooling: the rise of experts, planner and statistics in the early OECD. *Teachers College Record*, 11, 1–26.

Tyack, D. & Cuban, L. (1995). *Tinkering toward utopia: a century of public school reform*. Cambridge, MA: Harvard University Press.

Tyler, R. (1950). *Basic principles of curriculum and instruction*. Chicago, IL: University of Chicago Press.

University of Limerick (2013a). *School placement handbook*. Limerick: University of Limerick.

University of Limerick (2013b). *School placement documentation*. Limerick: University of Limerick.

University of Massachusetts Boston (2014). *Advancing community engaged scholarship and community engagement*. Boston: University of Massachusetts.

Valli, L. & Rennert-Ariev, P. (2002). New standards and assessment? Curriculum transformation in teacher education. *Journal of Curriculum Studies*, 3(42), 201–225.

Vygotsky, L. (1978) *Mind and society*. Cambridge, MA: Harvard University Press, 79–91.

Wagner, I. (2013). Gemeinwesenarbeit in der Sozialen Arbeit. *Magazin Erwachsenenbildung.at, Community Education*, 19. Available at www.erwachsenen-bildung.at/magazin/13-19/meb13-19.pdf

Waitoller, F. R. & Artiles, A. J. (2013). A decade of professional development research in inclusive education: a critical review and notes for a research program. *Review of Educational Research*, 83(3), 319–356.

Warren, M. R., Park, S. O. & Tieken, M. C. (2016). The formation of community-engaged scholars: a collaborative approach to doctoral training in education research. *Harvard Education Review*, 86(2), 233–260.

Watson, C. (2014). Effective professional learning communities? The possibilities for teachers as agents of change in schools. *British Educational Research Journal*, 40(1), 18–29.

Wenger, E. (1998). *Communities of practice: learning, meaning and identity*. Cambridge: Cambridge University Press.

White, S., Blomfield, D. & Le Cornu, R. (2010). Professional experience in new times: issues and responses to a changing education landscape. *Asia-Pacific Journal of Teacher Education*, 38(3), 181–193.

Wijers, M., de Lange, L., Shafer, M. & Burrill, G. (1998). Insight into data. In National Center for Research in Mathematics Science Education & Freudenthal Institute (Ed.), *Mathematics in context: a connected curriculum for grades 5–8* (P. 53–71). Chicago, IL: Encyclopedia Britannica Educational Corporation.

Xing, W. & Marcinkowski, M. (2015). Collaborative assessment tools: a data-centric approach. Presentation at the Advanced Technology for Learning SIG Paper Session. Chicago, IL: AERA annual meeting, April 16–20, 2015.

Xing, W., Wadholm, B. & Goggins, S. (2014). Learning analytics in CSCL with a focus on assessment: an exploratory study of activity theory-informed cluster analysis (P. 59–67) *Proceedings of the Fourth International Conference on Learning Analytics and Knowledge*. doi:10.1145/2567574.2567587.

Yamazumi, K. (2007). Human agency and educational research: a new problem in activity theory. *An International Journal of Human Activity Theory*, 1, 19–39.

Youdell, D. (2011). *School trouble: identity, power and politics in education (foundations and futures of education)*. London: Routledge.

Youdell, D. & McGimpsey, I. (2015). Assembling, disassembling and reassembling "youth services" in Austerity Britain. *Critical Studies in Education*, 56(1), 116–130. doi:10.1080/17508487.2015.975734

Young, A. M., O'Neill, A. & Mooney Simmie, G. (2015). Partnership in learning between university and school: evidence from a researcher-in-residence. *Irish Educational Studies*, 34(1), 25–42. doi:10.1080/03323315.2014.1001203

Young, M.(2007). *Bringing knowledge back in: from social constructivism to social realism in the sociology of education*. Abingdon, Oxon:Routledge.

Zeichner, K. (1994). Research on teacher thinking and different views of reflective practice in teaching and teacher education. In I. Carlgren, G. Handal & S. Vaage (Eds.), *Research on teacher thinking and practice* (P. 9–27). London: Routledge.

Zeichner, K. (2010). Rethinking the connections between campus course and field experiences in college- and university-based teacher education. *Journal of Teacher Education*, 61, 89–99. Available at: www.ctc.ca.gov/educator-prep/TAP/Zeichner.pdf

Zell, P. W. & Malacinski, G. M. (1994). Impediments to developing collaborative learning strategies: the input vs. output conflict. *Journal of Science Education and Technology*, 3(2), 107–114.

Zimmer, J. & Niggemeyer, E. (1992). *Macht die Schule auf, lasst das Leben rein: Von der Schule zur Nachbarschaftsschule*. Weinheim: Beltz.

Zipin, L. & Brennan, M. (2003). The suppression of ethical dispositions through managerial governmentality: a habitus crisis in Australian higher education. *International Journal of Leadership in Education*, 6(4), 351–370. doi:10.1080/1360312032000150742

Index

Locators in *italics* refer to figures and those in **bold** to tables.

accountability: VII, X, XIII, 2–3, 7–15, 25, 29, 31, 42, 67, 95, 119, 134–135, 138, 141; innovative partnership approach 23–24; performance metrics 4–6; systems for 44–52

activity theory 11–12; concepts and structure 19–20, *20*; curriculum innovation 85–87; education system structures 42; GIMMS 124; interacting activity systems as units of the analysis *20*; models for innovative planning based on partnership 90–93, 106–108, **107**; practice turn 38; prospects for higher-order curriculum innovation 138–139; *see also* Cultural-Historical Activity Theory

argumentation 24, 41, 93, 98, 101–102

assessment: data-driven improvement 10–11; 'datafication' 50; international comparisons 4–5, 45, 46; reform 57, 58–59; reform processes 62; teacher education 5–6, 45–46; 'teaching-to-the-test' 52, 120; test fatigue 6

Australia: educational change 2–3; partnership approach 15

Austria: Curriculum Workshop 104; GIMMS **123**, 125, 126

authentic learning 52

autonomy: boundary crossing 32, 121; national standards 57, 58, 94–95; partnership-based curricular innovation 82; professionalism 33; school curricula 95; school-university partnerships 24–25; situational factors 51, 53

Bildung 34, 44

boundaries: curricular processes 30–31; different communities 77; education system structures 40–41, 43–44; meaning-making 84; neoliberalism 142; origin of 137; overcoming 85, 122,

boundary crossing: Boundary Crossing Laboratory 87, 90–91; collaboration 52–53; CROSSNET 109–114, 133; Cultural-Historical Activity Theory 65–66, 74, 84; curricular processes 30–31; Curriculum Workshop 106–108, 133–134; deliberative 64, 85–86, 119, 128, 142; education system structures 42, 43–44; epistemic justice 99; GIMMS 116–129; meaning-making 72, 107, 134; multiple communities 15–16; Partnership in Learning between University and School 129–130, 131; partnership-based curricular innovation 85, 87; policy 26; prospects for higher-order curriculum innovation 133, 136–137; structure of this book 25–28; teachers 63

Boundary Crossing Laboratory 87, 90–91

boundary objects 18, 20, 91, **107**, 128, 137

brokering 77, 79–80, 103, 117, 124

CHAT *see* Cultural-Historical Activity Theory

civil society: deliberative democracy 75; neoliberalism 50–51

Index 159

collaboration: among teachers 64; boundary crossing 52–53, 133–134; in the context of school practice 68–72; CROSSNET 113–114; curriculum theory 13–14; Curriculum Workshop 104–106; GIMMS *118*; partnership-based curricular innovation 83–84, *86*, 86–87

collaborative structures: community and partnership 14–16; curricular presuppositions and concepts for collaboration in partnership 21–25; curriculum innovation 80–81; school-university 1

common good 139

communication: boundary crossing 63, 65; competence in pedagogical matters 60, 64–65, 96–97; higher-order teacher deliberation 64–66; public 76–77; responsible communicative action 75–76

community: activity theory *20, 86,* 21, 106, **107**, 107, 124; boundaries between 77; boundary crossing 15–16; Cultural-Historical Activity Theory 15–17; a deliberative turn for teacher education 17–21; GIMMS 128; partnership-based curricular innovation in 84–88; prospects for higher-order curriculum innovation 138–139; *see also* professional learning communities

community development 138, 140–141

Community-Engaged Scholars 83–84

competency: curricular processes 30–33; Curriculum Workshop *95,* 95–97, *96,* 104; reform 57; 'teaching-to-the-test' 52; *see also* performance metrics

consensus 82, 84

context-specific curricular processes 72–74

contradictions XII, 16, 18, 21, 26–27, 81, 85–87, 128, 132–133, 135–137, 139

control systems 44–49

cooperation 43, 65, 97, 120; *see also* higher-order cooperation

Crossing Boundaries in Science Teacher Education (CROSSNET) 27, 95, 109–114, 133, 135

Cross-Professional Collaboration 83

cultural context 7, 24, 31, 72, 74, 130; *see also* sociocultural context

cultural differences 112–113

cultural identity of learners 73–74

Cultural-Historical Activity Theory (CHAT) 13; boundary crossing 18–19, 65–66, 74; Boundary Crossing Laboratory 90–91; community and partnership 15–17; curricular innovations 88; for deliberative democracy 142; education system structures 41; GIMMS 119, 127; models for innovative planning based on partnership 89–90, 106–108, *107*; partnership-based curricular innovation 81; professionalization of teachers 54; prospects for higher-order curriculum innovation 133–142; structure of this book 26–27

boundary crossing 18; 26–27 CROSSNET 112–113; Cultural-Historical Activity Theory 19; deliberative partnership-based schooling 59–63; meaning of curriculum 22; school-based activity 24, 27–28; teacher education 25; teachers' role 55–56

curricular presuppositions for collaboration in partnership 21–25

curricular processes of school improvement 29–33; changing role of school subjects and educational policy 33–40; neoliberalism 49–54; structural conditions of an educational system 40–44; systems for control and accountability of schools 44–49; teachers' role 30–32, 68–70, **70–71**

curricular structures 1; boundary crossing 18; partnership approach 16–17

curriculum: meaning of 22, 29; as a social and context-based process 73; teacher-proof curricula 56

Curriculum Conference 98

curriculum documents 103–104, 106

curriculum innovation: collaboration in partnership 22; collaboration in the context of school practice 68–72; context-specific curricular processes 72–74; Curriculum Workshop approach 89–90, 93–104; processes 67–68; public role 74–78; reform *56,* 58; *see also* deliberative partnership-based curricular innovation

curriculum theory: collaboration 13–14; deliberation 60–62; innovation 22

Curriculum Workshop 78; boundary crossing 106–108, 133–134; elements

of *100*, 100–104; in GIMMS framework 117; as a process approach for deliberative curricular innovation 89–90, 93–104; in school innovation 104–106; in teacher education projects 93–94, 104
Czech Republic, GIMMS **123**, 126–127

data-driven improvement 10–11; *see also* performance metrics
deliberation: curricular processes 38; curriculum theory 60–62; Curriculum Workshop 98; education system structures 41–42; GIMMS 115; Partnership in Learning between University and School 130–131; prospects for higher-order curriculum innovation 137–138, 139, 141–142
deliberative boundary crossing 64, 85–86, 119, 128, 142
deliberative decisions 18
deliberative democracy 35, 63, 67, 75–76, 89, 105, 116, 129, 140, 142
deliberative discourse 30, 61, 75, 98–99, 105, 117
deliberative meaning-making 43, 67
deliberative partnership-based curricular innovation 115–116; GIMMS 116–129, 116–131; in multiple communities 84–88; Partnership in Learning between University and School 116, 129–131; productive collaboration 79–84; prospects for 132–142
deliberative partnership-based schooling 2; higher-order teacher deliberation 64–66; as a new way for reform 55–59; professional development 60; professionalization of teachers 54
deliberative practices: CROSSNET 110; curricular innovation 59–63; democracy 63
democracy: and centralization processes 47; as concept 11–12; cultural context of education 140; curricular processes of school improvement 35; curriculum innovation 74–75; deliberative 35, 63, 67, 75–76, 140, 142; knowledge 52–53; neoliberalism 51, 53, 54; participatory 75; school environment 140
democratic deliberation 61, 65, 130, 136
democratic society 44, 47, 51–54
Denmark, GIMMS 117, **123**
didaktik 33–34

disciplines 35–36; *see also* school subjects
discourse: contradictions 27; deliberative 30, 61, 75, 98–99, 105, 117; diversity 127; of learning 11, 35, 52; performative 13, 48, 116; scientific and humanistic 7; teachers 105
discursive boundary crossing 110
discursive collaboration 85, 89, 113
discursive communication 94
discursive deliberation 55–56, 89–90, 97, 104–105, 115–116, 119
discursive ethics 77, 82, 98–99
discursive justification 39–40, 42, 56, 75, 106, 130–132, 140
discursive leadership 82
discursive spaces 67, 81, 128
diversity, gender awareness 120–129
division of labor: activity theory 20, 21, 86, 89, 107, 108; Boundary Crossing Laboratory 90; Cultural-Historical Activity Theory 15, **107**

eclecticism 60–62, 73
economic context of education 2, 13; market-oriented philosophy 45–46, 48–49; neoliberalism 49–54; online courses 47–48
edu-business 2
education system structures 40–44
educational change 1–3; bigger mechanisms in present trends of reform 3–6, 12, 141; boundaries 17–21; harder mechanisms in present trends of reform 10–17, 141; prospects for higher-order curriculum innovation 132–142; purposes of education 2, 44; tighter mechanisms in present trends of reform 6–10, 12, 141
elementary speech acts 99
environmental education 59, 69
epistemic justice 99
ethics: discursive 77, 82, 98–99; responsible communicative action 75–76
EUDIST 93–94, 95, 104, 105
European projects *see* Crossing Boundaries in Science Teacher Education (CROSSNET); EUDIST; Gender Innovation and Mentoring in Mathematics and Science (GIMMS)
European standardization 48
expansive learning 85, 122

first-order instruction 16
first-order knowledge 65, 84–85

Index 161

flight from the field 14, 69, 134, 60
free markets 49–54

gender awareness 120–129
gender gap 121
Gender Innovation and Mentoring in Mathematics and Science "GIMMS" 27, 95, 116–129, 135
Germany: Curriculum Workshop 104; GIMMS **123**, 125, 126, 127; reform policies 4
GIMMS *see* Gender Innovation and Mentoring in Mathematics and Science
global competition: knowledge society 12–13; PISA 45; reform policies 4–5

hidden curriculum 23, 72, 129
higher-order cooperation 43, 65, 97, 120, 126
higher-order innovation 16, 128, 132–142
higher-order teacher deliberation 64–66
human capital: education system structures 42, 43; neoliberalism 49–54; as policy driver 2; purposes of education 2, 44

inclusion 115, 119–120, 127, 128, 137
information and communications technology (ICT) 35, 81–82
information brochure, Curriculum Workshop 102
Initial Teacher Education (ITE) 31–32, 131
innovation *see* curriculum innovation: collaboration 14; curricular presuppositions for collaboration in partnership 21–25; deliberative partnership-based schooling 59–63; higher-order 16, 128, 132–142; role of teachers vs. scientists 8–10
instruments, activity theory *20, 86 see also* mediating artifacts
integrated curricula 37, 112
integrated science education : PING 1, 97
integration 37, 107, 123, 137
'invisible hand of the powerful' 14
Ireland: Curriculum Workshop 104; GIMMS 117, 120, **123**, 125, 126

justification 42, 44, 51, 55, 56, 130–131, 132–134

Kant, I. 75–76
knowledge, deliberative discourse 98–99, 105
knowledge basis for teaching: collaboration 64; curricular processes 31–32; first and second-order 65, 84–85; neoliberalism 52; from research 47; school subjects 33–34, 35–37; specialisms 38–39, 64; tacit knowledge 7
knowledge society 12–13

language use 24, 76–77, 98–99
leaders 42, 82, 103–104, 108, 133
learning community *see* professional learning communities
Learning Studio 91–93
learning systems 11
local: and centralization processes 46–47; curricular processes 30; educational change 3; personal, dialogic relations 40; reform processes 62
lower-order level 64

market economy 45–46, 48–49, 51
market fundamentalism 50, 51
market-oriented philosophy 45–46, 48–49; *see also* economic context of education
mathematics 36, 119–120, 121, 126, 135–136; *see also* GIMMS
meaning-making 8; boundaries 84; boundary crossing 72, 107, 134; deliberative 43, 67; education system structures 41–42
mediating artifacts 20, *86*, 89, 106–108, **107**, 124
mentoring, GIMMS 116–129
messy narratives: boundary crossing 41, 121, 131; curriculum innovation 16, 115, 122; deliberative discourse 121, 131, 137; in education 91; hybrid space 58; teachers 24, 99, 117, 134; universities 137, policy XI, 75; good teaching 5, 24
metrics *see* performance metrics
models for innovative planning based on partnership 89–90; boundary crossing 106–114; Boundary Crossing Laboratory 90–91; CROSSNET 109–114; Curriculum Workshop 93–104; Curriculum Workshop oundary crossing 106–108; Curriculum

162 Index

Workshop in school innovation 104–106; Curriculum Workshop in teacher education projects 104; Learning Studio 91–93; teacher education projects 104

natural sciences 69, 73, 120, 121, 126; *see also* science
neoliberalism: accountability 132; boundaries 142; curricular processes of school improvement 49–54; education system structures 42; educational change 2–3; New Taylorism 49; partnership approach 15
network 19, 20, 41, 42–45, 69, 76–77, 81–82, 118, 133–135, 141
New Taylorism 48–49
normative argumentation 101–102
normative regulation 40

object, activity theory *20*, 21, *86*, 91–92, 124
OECD: higher-order teacher deliberation 64; national education systems 46; standards 74; *see also* PISA
online courses 47–48, 81–82

partnership approach 14–17; curricular presuppositions for collaboration in partnership 21–25; curricular processes 30; innovation 23–25; *see also* collaborative structures; deliberative partnership-based curricular innovation; models for innovative planning based on partnership
Partnership in Learning between University and School (PLUS) 116, 129–131
partnerships, and reform 58–59
performance metrics: data-driven improvement 10–11; 'datafication' 50; international comparisons 4–5, 45, 46; neoliberalism 50–51; reform 57, 58–59; reform policies 4–6; reform processes 62; scientific theorizing 10; standardization 6–7; teacher education 5–6, 45–46; 'teaching-to-the-test' 52; test fatigue 6; *see also* competence
performative discourse 13, 48, 116
PING "integrated science education" 1, 36, 69, 97
PISA (Programme for International Student Assessment): competence 31;

international comparisons 4, 45; national standards introduction 112; reform 57; test fatigue 6
PISA 4–6, 10, 42, 45, 57, 74, 121
PLUS *see* Partnership in Learning between University and School
policy: boundary crossing 26; changing role of school subjects and educational policy 33–40; Curriculum Workshop 94; prospects for higher-order curriculum innovation 141–142; reform intention 2–3
positivism 7, 83
post-materialism 13
post-positivist 83
practice turn 38
prescribed reform process *56*, 57
privatization 48, 49, 50
productive collaboration 79–84, 134
productive mentoring 25
professional development: competence 31–33; Curriculum Workshop 94–95; deliberative partnership-based schooling 60, 62–63; GIMMS 127, 128; reform processes *56*, 57, 58
Professional Development Schools (PDS) 80
professional learning communities 10, 11, 14–15, 64
professionalization of teachers: deliberative partnership-based schooling 54; neoliberalism 52–53; school-based partnerships 58
public: accountability 132; communication with 76–77; consensus 82; prospects for higher-order curriculum innovation 137–138, 139; role in curriculum innovation 74–78
public space VII, XI, 21, 55, 58, 60, 61, 63, 66, 68, 72, 74–77, 85, 90, 113, 117, 118, 120, 126, 128, 132–133, 137–138, 140, 142; purposes of education 2, 44

qualifications: curricular processes 30–33; 'teaching-to-the-test' 52
quality 30, 31, 48, 50

real-world questions 37–38
reflection 7, 29, 36, 106;
reflexivity 7–8, 115; uncomfortable reflexivity 7–8, 11, 115, 122; critical reflexivity IX, XI, 16, 101, 119

reform: bigger mechanisms in present trends of reform 3–6, 12; boundaries 17–21; collaboration in a curriculum process 68; current trends 2–3; curricular processes of school improvement 35; deliberative partnership-based schooling 55–59; harder mechanisms in present trends of reform 10–17; local and national context 62; processes *56*; recent history 1–2; school-based change 55; school-based vs. prescribed *56*, 57–58; systems for control and accountability of schools 44–49; tighter mechanisms in present trends of reform 6–10, 12

reform policies XIII 4–5, 9, 23, 31

rules: activity theory 20, 21, *86*, **107**, 107, 108; Cultural-Historical Activity Theory 15

school environment: Boundary Crossing Laboratory 90–91; CROSSNET 112–113; curriculum construction 98; Curriculum Workshop 94–104; democracy 140; Learning Studio 91–93; Partnership in Learning between University and School 116, 129–131; professional learning communities 11; prospects for higher-order curriculum innovation 133–142

school improvement 138, 140–141

school structures 44–49

school subjects: changing role of school subjects and educational policy 32–42; collaboration in a curriculum process 69, 109; teaching 14, 38–39, 45, 63, 65, 73, 111, 121

school-based change 55

school-based reform process *56*, 57–58

science: boundary crossing 18; collaboration in a curriculum process 69; CROSSNET teacher education 109–114; data-driven improvement 10–11; disciplinary knowledge 35–37; GIMMS 27, 95, 115, 116–131; PING (integrated science education) 1, 36, 69, 97; practice turn 39; teacher education 8–10; *see also* natural sciences

Science, Mathematics and Technology Education (SMTE) 36–37

second-order knowledge 65, 84–85

sex differences 127; *see also* gender awareness

social co-participation 11, 14–15, 62

social function of schooling 13

sociocultural: boundary crossing 120, 139; context 23, 38, 62, 65, 120, 139; curriculum innovation 62, 74–75, 113; discontinuities 18; gender awareness 121, 126, 136; higher-order teacher deliberation 65; policy 26; practice turn 38; teaching materials 39

Spain: Curriculum Workshop 104; GIMMS **123**, 126, 127

standardization in education: and centralization processes 46–49; current trends 3; deliberative practices 59–60; performance metrics 6–7

structural components, curriculum 23

structural conditions of an educational system 40–44

subjects *see* school subjects

subjects, activity theory 20, *86*, 106, **107**, 108, 124

Sweden: Curriculum Workshop 104; edu-business 2

syllabus 23, 59

system theory, boundaries 18

tacit knowledge XI, 7, 72

teacher education: Boundary Crossing Laboratory 90–91; CROSSNET 109–114; curricular innovation 25; Curriculum Workshop 93–95, 104; a deliberative turn for teacher education as boundary crossing 17–21; knowledge basis for teaching 31–32; performance metrics 5–6, 45–46; prospects for higher-order curriculum innovation 134–135; scientific innovations 8–10

teacher-proof curricula 56

teachers: boundary crossing 63; as collaborators 13–14; context-specific curricular processes 73; curricular innovation 55–56; curricular processes 30–32, 68–70, **70–71**; curriculum construction 98; importance of 62–63; as intellectuals 53; knowledge basis 31–32; partnership approach 14–17; role in innovation 8–10; role in reform 55; *see also* professional development

teachers' voice 16, 72, 99

Teaching and Learning International Survey (TALIS) 31

Index

teaching staff 30; central aspects of teacher collaboration *70*, 70–72; international comparisons 45; quality and professionalism 30, 62–63

'teaching-to-the-test' 52, 120

testing *see* assessment

third space 17–18, 65, 79, 137, 138

TIMSS (Trends in International Mathematics and Science Study) 4, 45, 57

Transatlantic Trade Agreement (TTIP) 47–48

United States: and centralization processes 47–48; Community-Engaged Scholars 83–84; performance metrics 45, 46, 52

universities: Boundary Crossing Laboratory 90–91; collaborative school-university structures 1; CROSSNET 112; Curriculum Conference 98; disciplines 36; partnership approach 15–17, 65, 81; Partnership in Learning between University and School 116, 129–131; partnership-based curricular innovation 83–84, *86*, 86–87